Library of
Davidson College

The Pleasures of the Text

Violette Leduc in 1955. © Fonds Violette Leduc / Archives IMEC

843
L475xL

The Pleasures of the Text

Violette Leduc and Reader Seduction

ELIZABETH LOCEY

ROWMAN & LITTLEFIELD PUBLISHERS, INC.
Lanham • Boulder • New York • Oxford

AHR-6960

Selections from Roland Barthes' *Le Plaisir du texte*, Collection "Points," 1972, reprinted with permission of Éditions du Seuil.

Selections from Roland Barthes' *The Pleasure of the Text*, trans. Richard Howard (New York: Hill and Wang, 1975) reprinted with permission of Farrar, Straus and Giroux.

Passages reprinted and translated from the following texts by Violette Leduc: *La Bâtarde* (Coll. Folio, 1964), *Thérèse et Isabelle* (Coll. Rose, 1966), *La Folie en tête* (Coll. Blanche, 1970), and *Le Taxi* (Coll. Rose, 1971); and from Simone de Beauvoir's preface to *La Bâtarde*, were previously published by Éditions Gallimard.

ROWMAN & LITTLEFIELD PUBLISHERS, INC.

Published in the United States of America
by Rowman & Littlefield Publishers, Inc.
4720 Boston Way, Lanham, Maryland 20706
www.rowmanlittlefield.com

12 Hid's Copse Road
Cumnor Hill, Oxford OX2 9JJ, England

Copyright © 2002 by Rowman & Littlefield Publishers, Inc.

All rights reserved. No part of this publication may be reproduced, stored in a retrieval system, or transmitted in any form or by any means, electronic, mechanical, photocopying, recording, or otherwise, without the prior permission of the publisher.

British Library Cataloguing in Publication Information Available

Library of Congress Cataloging-in-Publication Data

Locey, Elizabeth, 1968–
    The pleasures of the text : Violette Leduc and reader seduction / Elizabeth Locey.
        p. cm.
    Includes bibliographical references and index.
    ISBN 0-7425-1526-5 (alk. paper) — ISBN 0-7425-1527-3 (pbk. : alk. paper)
    1. Leduc, Violette, 1907–1972—Criticism and interpretation. I. Title.

PQ2623.E3657 Z765 2002
843'.914—dc21

                                                    2001048507

Printed in the United States of America

♾™ The paper used in this publication meets the minimum requirements of American National Standard for Information Sciences—Permanence of Paper for Printed Library Materials, ANSI/NISO Z39.48-1992.

To Violette's seducees.

CONTENTS

ACKNOWLEDGMENTS

Many people were instrumental in bringing this project to fruition. My greatest debt of gratitude is to Elaine Marks, whose wisdom, patience, guidance, and high expectations over the years have proven invaluable to me. From the very beginning, "sa lecture m'exhaltait." I am also indebted to Judith Miller and the late and much-missed Yvonne Ozzello for their careful readings and many precious suggestions. I thank William J. Berg for his long-standing friendship and encouragement, and especially Teri Stratton for introducing me to "La Bâtarde."

I am grateful to my parents, Lenita and Michael. They had the foresight to introduce a two-year-old to the beauty and joys of French language and culture and their library piqued my interest in French literature from a very early age. In addition, their willingness to check my translations at the last minute has saved me from committing more than one *maladresse*.

I am particularly indebted to Serena Leigh at Rowman & Littlefield. Her belief in the value of this book and her efforts in bringing it to publication have never flagged, and her patience and assistance have been priceless.

My thanksa also go to Andrea Kaston and Travis Kaplow, who were both willing to share ideas and to look over my text for grammatical and logical inconsistencies. Their enthusiasm for my ideas encouraged me to keep writing. My colleague Deb Gerish was also instrumental in helping me with the technical aspects of putting the manuscript in readable format. I am highly appreciative of her talents and good will.

Finally, my gratitude goes to Ted Toadvine for his love, encouragement, patience, and intransigence.

INTRODUCTION

If you ask the average French person what he or she knows of Violette Leduc, the twentieth-century writer, he or she will likely respond with a sideways look and inquire if you do not mean Viollet-Leduc, the nineteenth-century architect. Except for a flurry of scandal surrounding the 1964 publication of *La Bâtarde*[1]—in which Leduc's text was nominated for the prix Goncourt and the prix Fémina but was ultimately dismissed amid charges of "obscenity"—the writings of Violette Leduc remain largely unknown to the French reading public.[2] It was no different during much of her lifetime: in *La Folie en tête*,[3] recounting the months following the publication of her first book, Leduc writes: "Je pleure la nuit: on n'achète pas mon livre. On ne le voit pas aux vitrines des librairies. On n'en parle pas. Aussitôt imprimé, aussitôt disparu. C'est un naufrage qui passe inaperçu [I cry at night: no one buys my book. It is not to be seen in the bookshop windows. No one mentions it. No sooner printed than forgotten. It's a shipwreck that goes unnoticed]" (*La Folie en tête* 132).

Curiously, this unknown writer is the same Violette Leduc who so seduced the literary and artistic elite of postwar Paris, the same Leduc whose first novel was snapped up by Albert Camus for publication in his "Espoir" collection at Gallimard, whose short stories and prose pieces appeared in *Les Temps Modernes* and were quoted in *Le Deuxième sexe*,[4] who was invited to spend weekends at Jean Cocteau's country home. If her works were virtually unknown to the majority of French readers, Violette Leduc was a recognized literary figure among literary figures of contemporary Paris. Simone de Beauvoir begins her laudatory preface to *La Bâtarde*[5] by pointing out this disparity in responses to Leduc's work:

> Quand au début de 1945, je commençai à lire le manuscrit de Violette Leduc—«Ma mère ne m'a jamais donné la main»—je fus tout de suite saisie: un tempérament, un style. Camus accueillit d'emblée *L'Asphyxie* dans sa collection «Espoir». Genet, Jouhandeau, Sartre saluèrent l'apparition d'un écrivain. Dans les livres qui suivirent, son talent s'affirma. Des critiques exigeants le reconnurent hautement. Le public bouda. Malgré un considérable succès d'estime, Violette Leduc est restée obscure.

> [When, at the beginning of 1945, I began to read Violette Leduc's manuscript—"My mother never took my hand"—I was immediately transfixed: a temperament, a style. Camus was quick to include *L'Asphyxie* in his "Espoir" collection. Genet, Jouhandeau,

1

Sartre, hailed the arrival of a writer. In the books that followed, her talent was affirmed. The public refused to have anything to do with them. Despite considerable praise from the critics, Violette Leduc remained obscure.] (*La Bâtarde* 8)

The polarity of these two modes of reception is striking, yet somehow appropriate to this author whose roller-coaster existence is the subject of her texts. The breathless intensity—even desperation—of the way in which the narrator Violette apprehends life is reflected in the titles of Leduc's major texts: *L'Asphyxie*,[6] *L'Affamée*,[7] *Ravages*,[8] *La Bâtarde, La Folie en tête, La Chasse à l'amour*.[9]

✱✱

I would like to pause momentarily to comment upon the issue of autobiography in the case of Leduc. Simone de Beauvoir insisted in one of her own autobiographies[10] that Violette Leduc, the writer, should never be considered as differing from Violette Leduc, the narrator and protagonist of most of her texts: "dans son cas on ne saurait détacher ses livres de la femme de chair et d'os qui en est l'auteur. Elle a fait de sa vie la matière de son œuvre qui a donné un sens à sa vie [in her case it is impossible to separate her books from the flesh-and-bones woman who is the author. She made her life the material for her writings, which gave meaning to her life]" (*La Bâtarde* 63). Beauvoir ostensibly knew Leduc and her writing better than anyone else during her writing career, and while I agree that Leduc did borrow—*heavily*—from her life to produce her texts, I believe that reading Leduc's texts as a simple recounting of her life offers a limited view of her work.[11] Out of her eleven major texts, Leduc only qualified three as autobiographical: *La Bâtarde, La Folie en tête*, and *La Chasse à l'amour*. Leduc's novels are not retellings, but *dramatizations* of her life experiences, to a greater or lesser degree.[12] Even in her autobiographies, Leduc takes strong liberties with actual events. One of the most memorable scenes of *La Bâtarde* is one in which Violette becomes aphonic and grows a grotesque elephant's trunk on the pont de la Concorde. Furthermore, if Leduc had written only from her life, there would be no accounting for the difference between the Isabelle scenes of *La Bâtarde* and those of *Thérèse et Isabelle*.[13] Thus, Leduc's writing must be seen as crafted, embellished, *imagée*, and not a mere recounting of her life.[14]

Because the story of Leduc's life does shed light on the majority of her texts (despite its limited usefulness in investigating a work such as *Le Taxi*, which fails to conform to Leduc's life at all) I make the distinction between Leduc the writer, Violette the protagonist and Violette the narrator. These last two are separated in time, the protagonist existing in the narrated past and the narrator in the narrating present. When I refer to Leduc, I am referring to the actual woman who held pen to paper in her Paris garret or on the mountainside in Provence. In spite of Barthes' announcement that the author is dead, Leduc as a writer is very much alive in her texts. As I will show, one of the most striking ways in which the author maintains her presence in the text is in the active part she takes in seducing her reader. There was a good reason for this: Beauvoir writes that "Tout de suite [Leduc] a compris que la création littéraire pouvait être pour elle un salut [Right away she understood that literary creation could be a salvation for her]" (*La Bâtarde* 15). In order for her salvation through writing to be complete, Leduc herself must be there, standing behind Violette.

If Leduc seeks salvation in her writing, it is to the reader that she looks for this redemption. Many critics, beginning with Beauvoir, have noted the primacy of the role of the reader in Leduc's writings—most visibly in her autobiographical trilogy. Leduc signals it herself when she has Violette address the reader directly on the first page of her autobiography, reaching out through the text for "Lecteur, mon lecteur [Reader, my reader]" (*La Bâtarde* 25).[15]

This book examines the different narrative and stylistic strategies which Leduc employs in her ongoing attempts to reach and seduce this reader, and, through the reader, to actualize her own salvation. Because of their primary roles in Leduc's literary production, let us briefly examine Leduc's interaction with her first readers, Maurice Sachs and Simone de Beauvoir.

When Violette Leduc began writing the manuscript mentioned in Beauvoir's preface, it was at the request of her friend and mentor, writer Maurice Sachs. This first writing project, as well as all of the subsequent ones, can be read as an attempt on the part of Leduc to seduce her reader. Sachs, the author of *Le Sabbat*, was gay. In spite of—or perhaps because of—Sachs' sexual orientation, Violette was profoundly attracted to him. Suffering under his "petits baisers abstraits [little abstract kisses]" (*La Bâtarde* 543), she refers to this time as "Mon séjour au paradis de l'amour impossible [my stay in the paradise of impossible love]" (*La Bâtarde* 546). To pass the time, and also with an eye to winning his affection, Violette told him stories of her childhood. It is clearly marked in the text as a seduction attempt: "Je parle de mon enfance à Maurice, je lui parle de ma mère sans me lasser de radoter. Je vois que je l'ennuie. Je continue puisque *je lui fais la cour* avec mes malheurs [I speak to Maurice of my childhood, I tell him of my mother without tiring of my rambles. I can see that I am boring him. I continue because *I am courting him* with my misfortunes]" (*La Bâtarde* 545, emphasis added). Knowing that Sachs was not interested in her did not stop Violette from trying to seduce him. Sachs soon tired of the stories, however, and told her that she must write them down. It is at this time that she began her first novel, *L'Asphyxie*:

> —Vos malheurs d'enfance commencent de m'emmerder. Cet après-midi vous prendrez votre cabas, un porte-plume, un cahier, vous vous assoirez sous un pommier, vous écrirez ce que vous me racontez.
> —Oui, Maurice, dis-je, vexée.

> ["Your childhood memories are starting to get on my nerves. This afternoon you will take your bag, a pen, a notebook, you will sit yourself down under an apple tree, and you will write down what you've been telling me."
> "Yes, Maurice," I said, offended.] (*La Bâtarde* 548).

Violette's vexation is of note: although writing was that which eventually gave her life its meaning, at her career's outset she is testy at the notion of having to put her stories into writing for Maurice, instead of telling them straight out. Perhaps worried that she will make a less effective courtship, she nevertheless obeys, noting that at least with Sachs and his young friend Gérard, "[l]a littéra-ture mène à l'amour, l'amour mène à la littérature [literature leads to love, and love leads to literature]" (*La Bâtarde* 548). If we extrapolate this attitude to the rest of Leduc's writing career—and I suggest that we should—then we can see that Leduc can be considered to have written her novels as love letters to her readers; that is, as seductions.

Leduc's relationship with Simone de Beauvoir was longer and much more complicated than the one she had with Maurice Sachs. The professional admira-tion between the two writers was mutual, but on Leduc's end it was supple-mented with obsessive romantic love and sexual desire. In spite of Simone de Beauvoir's obvious distaste for and frustration with Leduc's continuing atten-tions, she nevertheless continued to support Leduc both morally and financially throughout her writing career.[16] Perhaps Beauvoir's most important contribution after recognizing Leduc's worth as a writer was by broadcasting this informa-tion to the reading public in her preface to *La Bâtarde*.

As with most Leduc critics after her, Beauvoir's project was not only to introduce Leduc and her works, but also to convince the reader of the injustice of the public ignorance of Leduc's talents.[17] Significantly, Beauvoir's is also a project of seduction: she intends, with the preface, to seduce new readers into the Leduc fold, just as she herself was seduced when she read the first sentence of *L'Asphyxie*. The final sentences of this preface make that clear: "L'échec du rapport à autrui a abouti à cette forme privilégiée de communication: une œuvre. Je voudrais avoir convaincu le lecteur d'y entrer: il y trouvera beaucoup plus encore que je ne lui ai promis [The failure of her relations with others ended at this privileged form of communication: an œuvre. I would like to convince the reader to enter it: she or he will find there much more even than I have prom-ised]" (*La Bâtarde* 23). An endorsement of this kind from such a prominent literary figure as Beauvoir was of great value to Leduc.

With this preface, Simone de Beauvoir helped to deliver Violette Leduc from obscurity by boosting her from the Parisian literary scene into the public eye in 1964. It was neither the first nor the last time she would use her position to further Leduc's career. Indeed, without her Leduc may never have begun publishing at all. As a member of the editorial board of *Les Temps Modernes*, Beauvoir was influential in getting excerpts of *L'Asphyxie* published in the sec-ond issue of that magazine in 1945, and it was through her that Albert Camus was introduced to this text, which he subsequently published in his "Espoir" collection from the Gallimard house. Beauvoir also cited Leduc in two different chapters of volume II of *Le Deuxième sexe:* twice she mentioned the narrator's experience in *L'Asphyxie* as characteristic of little girls in the chapter "Enfance," and in "L'amoureuse" she quoted a long passage from the then still-unpublished *Ravages*.[18] When Leduc's books failed to sell, Beauvoir arranged a small monthly stipend for Leduc with her publisher Gallimard. Perhaps her most important role in Leduc's life as a writer was that of reader and taskmaster. In *La Folie en tête*, Violette describes how Beauvoir would meet with her every two weeks to read what she had written and make editorial changes. Violette would have done anything not to disappoint her idol. But she did not have to wait for those biweekly meetings to be confronted with Beauvoir's critical gaze: Violette kept a photograph of Beauvoir above her worktable. "Je mis ma blouse de ménagère à carreaux bleus et blancs, je continuais d'écrire avec l'application et la tranquilité d'une employée. Je m'arrêtais, je regardais les yeux de Simone de Beauvoir sur le mur du réduit [I put on my blue and white checked housewife's smock, I would continue to write with the application and calm of an employee. I would stop, I would look at the eyes of Simone de Beauvoir on the wall of my tiny room]" (*La Folie en tête* 130).[19] Beauvoir played this role until after Leduc's untimely death: it was she who posthumously edited and published Leduc's final manuscript, *La Chasse à l'amour*. For these reasons, Beauvoir can be considered to have been Leduc's primary reader, in the dual sense of first and ideal.

In spite of Beauvoir's admiration for Leduc as a writer, she was often frustrated by the demands that Leduc made on her—both for her time and for her affection. Deirdre Bair's biography of Beauvoir, and more recently the publication of Beauvoir's correspondence with her American lover, Nelson Algren,[20] indicate that Beauvoir saw her in a very negative light. In her letters to Algren, Beauvoir consistently referred to Leduc as "the ugly woman" (*Simone de Beauvoir* 314). According to Bair, Beauvoir threatened that any efforts on Leduc's part to see her more often than their bi-weekly meetings would result in their termination (*Simone de Beauvoir* 348). Mireille Brioude[21] qualifies this version of their relationship as "sadomasochiste" ("Simone de Beauvoir et son ombre" 115). Another version appears in Leduc's second novel, *L'Affamée*, a violent and disturbing novel which dramatizes the frustrating relationship between the first person narrator and the mysterious and distant "Madame"—a thinly veiled reference to Simone de Beauvoir. Brioude describes *L'Affamée* in the following terms:

> *L'Affamée* c'est aussi la réécriture fantasmatique des lettres à Simone de Beauvoir, un délire de la souffrance amoureuse, passionnelle et obsessionnelle. Ainsi, pour la première fois, nous, les lecteurs, nous trouvons-nous devant un phénomène de théâtralisation extrême de cette souffrance. Le texte (lu aussi par Beauvoir!) est une mise en scène de son indifférence et surtout une mise en scène d'un "je" qui livre ses transes au lecteur, en donnant lieu sur le papier à d'étonnantes scènes où le corps s'écrit dans le manque, où l'hystérie devient lettre.

> [*L'Affamée* is also the phantasmagoric rewriting of her letters to Simone de Beauvoir, a frenzy of amorous, passionate, obsessive suffering. Thus, for the first time, we the readers find ourselves faced with an extreme thearicalizatio n of this suffering. The text (also read by Beauvoir!) is a *mise en scène* of her indifference, and especially a *mise en scène* of an "I" which delivers up its agonies to the reader, giving rise on paper to surprising

scenes in which the body is written in lack, in which hysteria becomes letter.] ("Simone de Beauvoir et son ombre" 117–18)

For Isabelle de Courtivron,[22] the desire for the other in the Leduc-Beauvoir couple is not as unidirectional as it appears in *L'Affamée*. She suggests that while Beauvoir enjoyed editing others' works, and probably received a good deal of satisfaction from her protégée's eventual literary success, there was likely an even stronger bond. Courtivron suggests that Leduc represented a chaotic figure onto whom Beauvoir could project her own "dark side:"

> It can be argued that just as Leduc projected her "angelic half" onto Madame/Beauvoir, so perhaps Simone de Beauvoir, trapped in her own dutiful image and in her permanent role of "petite conscience morale" for Sartre, disciplined herself not to express her anxiety and rage for fear of shattering her carefully constructed image, or rendering useless the unique role with which she had identified herself. Hence, she may have found relief in splitting herself off to merge with the passionate and chaotic Violette, her other, darker side. ("From Bastard to Pilgrim" 146)

The idea that Beauvoir may have needed Leduc in much the same way as Leduc needed Beauvoir, though expressed in terms of a desire for distance instead of merging, is fascinating. Courtivron's comment about Beauvoir's "fear of shattering her carefully constructed image" is particularly apt in a discussion of *L'Affamée*, precisely where the narrator's constant urge is to shatter all mirrors, mirrors which reflect her image as the radical opposite of Madame/Beauvoir's: that of a woman completely out of control.

No matter what Leduc represented for Beauvoir personally, professionally, or psychologically, it is clear that for Leduc she was of primary importance, particularly in her role as reader. Beginning with *L'Affamée*, Beauvoir was always Leduc's first reader. As such she was her greatest critic and judge. Gagnon[23] seconds this notion: "Evidemment, Simone de Beauvoir est la lectrice idéale, celle dont la lecture est évoquée avec émotion: 'Je relisais ce qu'elle avait lu: une femme de grand talent me suivait à travers mes pages. Sa lecture m'exaltait' [Obviously, Simone de Beauvoir is the ideal reader, whose reading is evoked with emotion: 'I reread what she had read: a woman of great talent was following me across my pages. Her reading exalted me']" (Gagnon 158 citing *La Folie en tête* 71).

**

In her article "The Dream of Love: A Study of Three Autobiographies,"[24] Elaine Marks examines the relationship between autobiographer and reader, a relationship that she calls the "dream of love." The "trinitarian narrator"—the author-narrator-protagonist of autobiography—has a unique effect on the reader: that of seduction.

The trinitarian narrator always designs the same scheme whereby to seduce the reader-confidant. The dream of love is projected repeatedly within the text. The reader, confidant and victim, will eventually fall in love with the trinitarian narrator's dream of love and through the dream with the trinitarian narrator. This, I think, helps to explain the unconscious appeal of autobiographies for the writer and for the reader. ("The Dream of Love" 74)

This assessment of the rapport between reader and writer rings especially true when it comes to Leduc's writing, and *La Bâtarde* in particular.[25] That Leduc seeks to establish a relationship with her reader is clear. In addition to addressing "Lecteur, mon lecteur" at the beginning of *La Bâtarde*, there are at least fifteen other instances throughout this text in which Leduc calls out to her reader.[26] Simone de Beauvoir is the first to point out that for Leduc, "Le lecteur accomplit l'impossible synthèse de l'absence et de la présence [The reader achieves the impossible synthesis of absence and presence]" (*La Bâtarde* 15).

This is crucial to understanding Violette Leduc's relationship with her reader. Violette's personal relationships all failed to make her happy. All of the people to whom she was closest were both too absent and too present. I believe that Violette's mother established this pattern in her life: Berthe—Violette's original love—encouraged Violette's attentions (*L'Asphyxie* shows her modeling outfits for her daughter, and in *La Bâtarde* Violette recounts how they shared a bed during the First World War). However, she eventually betrayed them by marrying.[27]

If Violette could not find the ideal love object in those around her, she did eventually discover the perfect balance of presence and absence in her reader. Writing became a salvation for her because through literature she could have a satisfying relationship for the first time in her life. As Courtivron aptly remarks, "By the time Leduc was writing *La Bâtarde*, each reader had been cast as judge, lover, torturer, witness, confidant and voyeur—roles that had previously been imposed on her real-life lovers and acquaintances" (*Violette Leduc* 64). Again, from the beginning Berthe incarnated all of those roles for Violette, and Violette demanded that her lovers—actual or desired—repeat this incarnation.

In my opinion, the role of lover is the reader's most important one. According to Marks, the dream of love also contains erotic elements: "The reader is seduced not only by the facts of the narrator's life, but by the appeal that is being made to him explicitly to forgive and to accept, implicitly to love. This love, although it does not take the form of physical desire, is nonetheless erotic, a diffuse eroticism directed towards the narrator and his creation" ("The Dream of Love" 87). Leduc's rapport with her reader is perhaps more physical than most. At one point near the end of *La Chasse à l'amour* (and hence the end of Leduc's life), Violette becomes explicit in her erotic invitation to the reader: "Lecteur. Partageons. Comment? Avec ta main. Ta main sur mes genoux. Je me plie dans mon fauteuil de toile. J'écrase mes lèvres tièdes de soleil sur ta peau. Je regarde, j'écoute. Tout est pour nous [Reader. Let us share. How? With your hand. Your hand in my lap. I bend over in my lawn chair. I press my sun-

warmed lips on your skin. I am watching, I am listening. Everything is for us]"
(*La Chasse à l'amour* 355).

It is the purpose of this volume to examine Leduc's "dream of love" for her
reader: the different ways in which she tries to seduce her reader, both emotionally and psychosomatically. Chapter one is dedicated to the question of narrative
seduction. Taking Ross Chambers' work as my starting point, I elaborate a
spectrum of literary seduction and reading pleasure. The extreme ends of this
continuum are illustrated by the reading pleasures taken by "Emma Bovary"
(hers are strictly narrative) and by Roland Barthes (he is seduced by the effects
of language). At the end of this chapter I give examples from Leduc's texts
which could seduce readers on either extreme.

As this text concerns reader seduction, chapter two details Violette's reading history as recounted in *La Bâtarde* and *La Folie en tête*. During her childhood, Violette rejected books until her mother betrayed her love by marrying. In
an attempt to identify with her absent father, Violette took up reading modern
literature. Her seduction by literature was primarily Bovaryan in nature during
the period depicted in *La Bâtarde*: her physical birth through her birth as a
writer at age 37. In *La Folie en tête*, which begins as she is showing her first
manuscript to Simone de Beauvoir, Violette remains an avid reader. As a writer
in her own right, however, she becomes more concerned with the effects of
style, showing that she has added a Barthesian level to her reading pleasures. In
La Folie en tête we also see Violette's attempts to seduce real readers, the
schoolboys Patrice and Flavien. As these readers crossed the line between presence and absence, these affairs were ultimately frustrating for Violette.

Chapter three concerns the realization of Leduc's dream of love. Two of her
readers—René de Ceccatty and Michele Zackheim—were so seduced by her
writings that they were inspired to write books of their own about their seduction. Ceccatty's *Eloge de la Bâtarde* is both a critical treatment of her work and
a more personal recounting of the effect that those writings had on his life.
Zackheim's *Violette's Embrace* is a fictional biography of Leduc, and at the
same time it serves as a vehicle for Zackheim to speak of her own life. The invented character of Lili Jacobs—purportedly Leduc's long-time neighbor—was
a Jewish resistance fighter. This figure allows Zackheim to exorcise demons
concerning anti-Semitism and the Holocaust in particular. In both cases—as in
the case of Violette Leduc, let us recall—reading lead to writing in a cycle of
seduction.

Part II of this volume examines the strategies employed by Leduc to seduce
her readers. Chapter four concerns the erotic touch, in *La Bâtarde* and *La Folie
en tête*. This touch is rendered more physical through the effects of what I call
associative positioning, in which the reader, as narrative seducee, is positioned
with Violette the protagonist as the seducee of a sexual initiation. This effect is
produced as well through the use of "image-sensations," metaphors which help
concretize the association of narrative seducee and sexual seducee. These metaphors are understood physically at the same time as or even before they can be
decoded intellectually and so reinforce the psychosomatic nature of this "touch."

In this chapter I also address the thorny issue of erotica vs. pornography. That *La Bâtarde* is erotic and not obscene is illustrated through a comparison between it and *Histoire d'O*.

Chapter five examines the role of the erotic look in *Thérèse et Isabelle*. Both Thérèse and Isabelle look at each other sexually, but to avoid the kind of dominating, distancing look—the look of the voyeur—that occurs in texts with erotic components such as *Histoire d'O*, Leduc has structured her text so as to bring the reader inside the loving couple. Through what I call "autovoyeurism" the reader is conflated with Thérèse's mirror image, and is in this way sutured into the text. (As I show, an excellent illustration of autovoyeurism is the 1968 film version of *Thérèse et Isabelle*, in which the older, narrating Thérèse visits her former school and there watches as a younger version of herself plays out scenes with Isabelle. She and the younger Thérèse—played by the same actress—are conflated with each other through editing tricks.) When Thérèse makes love to her mirror image, she is also making love to the reader located there, and as such the text can be read not only as the passionate retelling of a lesbian sexual initiation, but also as a declaration of love for the reader.

Chapter six is a reading of the erotic voice in *Le Taxi*, a text which refuses to fit the "pattern" of Leduc's writings. Instead of relating closely to her life, *Le Taxi* concerns an incestuous brother and sister who make love to each other in a taxi as it cruises through Paris. In addition, instead of featuring a strong narrative presence, in this text there is no narrator at all, for it is written entirely in direct discourse. Based on a narratological reading of this text, I suggest that having no narrator at all allows Leduc to place both herself and her reader as actors inside the *histoire*, each alternately taking the voices of the brother and sister. In this way, Leduc comes closest to realizing her dream of love. *Le Taxi* is an outsider text—outside the rest of her corpus, and linked to her other works only through the relationship it establishes with the reader—and because, written as it was so late in her career, it incorporates many of the seductive strategies seen in her other narratives of sexual initiation (image-sensation, conflation, etc.), I suggest a radical reading of this text. I believe that *Le Taxi* should be read as the story of a brother and sister in a taxi but also as a dramatization of and metaphor for the relationship which Leduc desired to have with her reader.

***

In these chapters, I will refer to Leduc's reader in the feminine. As we have seen, Leduc's primary reader was Simone de Beauvoir. Because of this, and because I will contend that Leduc often ensures reader identification by suturing that reader into a feminine couple, Leduc's reader must be able to identify with a feminine figure. This identification with the feminine by no means precludes the seduction of male readers. On the contrary, many of Leduc's most ardent supporters have been men: from Camus, Genet, Cocteau and Jacques Guérin in the past, through René de Ceccatty, Michael Sheringham, and Carlo Jansiti today. Seduction by Leduc's writings should not be considered gender-circumscribed.

I undertook the project of investigating the effects of Leduc's writing on her readers because my own literary seduction was very powerful. This seduction was at the same time textual and narrative, rhetorical and erotic. From my first reading of *La Bâtarde* I was seduced intellectually, emotionally, and physically by Leduc's writing style as well as by her story. There are many possible modes of literary seduction, but those are the ones that I will address in the following chapters. Dear reader, it is my hope that after reading this book, you will be seduced by Leduc's writing as well.

PART I:
OF READER SEDUCTION

"Si je lis avec plaisir cette phrase, cette histoire ou ce mot, c'est qu'ils ont été écrits dans le plaisir (ce plaisir n'est pas en contradiction avec les plaintes de l'écrivain). Mais le contraire? Écrire dans le plaisir m'assure-t-il—moi, écrivain—du plaisir de mon lecteur? Nullement. Ce lecteur, il faut que je le cherche, (que je le «drague»), *sans savoir où il est."*

—Roland Barthes, *Le Plaisir du texte*

CHAPTER ONE

The Seductions of Reading: "Emma Bovary" and Roland Barthes

What was it about Violette Leduc's writing that had so seduced the literary world when she returned to Paris after the war? We have seen Beauvoir admit that she was "struck" after having read the first sentence. Perhaps the only person whose opinion Leduc valued as much as Beauvoir's was that of Jean Genet, whose talent she admired with a devotion which she qualifies as quasi-religious, referring to "la myrrhe et l'encens de Genet [Genet's frankincense and myrrh]:" "Chaque livre de lui est la commémoration de souffrances transfigurées. A sa grande-messe, j'arrive en avance pour être au premier rang [Each of his books is the commemoration of transfigured sufferings. I arrive early at his high mass to find a seat in the first row]" (*La Folie en tête* 114). It could be argued that every one of Leduc's books fits this description as well. Indeed, their writing styles were very similar.[1] Genet himself said so, in a letter to Mario Lewis, Paul Morihien's collaborator: "«Je te fais cadeau d'un des plus beaux livres que j'ai lus depuis longtemps, c'est *L'Affamée*. Distribue ce livre comme tu as fait des miens. Les gens qui m'aiment l'aimeront j'en suis sûr.» ['I am giving you one of the most beautiful books that I have read in a long time, it's *L'Affamée*. Distribute this book as you have my own. Those who like me will like it, I am sure.']"[2] Beauvoir confirmed Genet's high opinion for Leduc's writing in a January 1947 letter to Leduc: "«Il (Genet) dit qu'il vous admire pour votre force» ['He says that he admires you for your force']" ("Genet, Violette Leduc" 38). Like Genet, today's reader cannot help but be drawn into the web of Violette's intensity, as she begs us to join her on the pages of her text:

> Lecteur, suis moi. Lecteur, je tombe à tes pieds pour que tu me suives. Mon itinéraire sera facile. Tu quittes les gouttelettes qui venaient te retrouver, tu t'achemines vers la place de la Concorde, tu montes sur le trottoir de gauche. Te voici, nous voici.

> [Reader, follow me. Reader, I fall at your feet so that you will follow me. My itinerary will be easy. You leave the raindrops that were spraying in your face, you make your way toward the place de la Concorde, you step onto the left-hand sidewalk. Here you are, here we are.] (*La Bâtarde* 294)

This implication of the reader occurs at the beginning of one of the most power-ful passages in Leduc's corpus. It is a scene in which Violette is so wounded by the insult of a passer-by that she metamorphoses from a sophisticated woman of style into a monster with an elephant's trunk for a nose and clay flippers in place of her fancy pumps. In her reduced state, Violette cannot speak but only grunt, and considers suicide. This passage, with its staccato rhythms, its repetitions and its graphic descriptions, is brutal and bruising. Its urgency and poignancy are heightened, however, when the reader is forced to join Violette on the stage of her downfall. Witnessing first-hand the complete disintegration of a character with whom one has forged an identification over the course of 300 pages is dev-astating, and either the bond between reader and narrator is shattered or it is permanently sealed. The readers of Leduc's works fall into two camps: those who are completely repulsed by Violette's narrative brutality, and those who are completely seduced by it.

*
**

What is it that makes a text intriguing to one reader or another? In this chapter we will consider the relationship of seduction and narrative through the optic of two radically different styles of reading, with particular emphasis placed on Leducian narrative. That seduction and literature are related is clear: the French word for plot—"intrigue"—contains the kernel of this idea in its Latin root, *in-tricare*: to entice or entrap. Enticement and seduction are surely linked, at the very least on a metonymical level, enticement being one element of seduction.

The narratives that we encounter can and do entice us: at the end of the twentieth century most homes are equipped with an immense array of techno-logically based entertainment possibilities. These options—ranging from the passive watching of television or movies and listening to digitally-mastered mu-sic, to the more active computer "questing" and arcade-style games—make reading appear old-fashioned, even anachronistic to some.

Upon further reflection, however, it becomes clear that all of these "cutting edge" technologies which are competing with reading still are based on narra-tive. The most popular television shows are not the information programs but dramas and situation comedies; certainly no one would deny that films are nar-rative texts; and although much of today's music is accompanied by lyrics, even instrumental pieces tell a story. Similarly, most computer games on the market are teleologically constructed as is narrative; whether the game is of the questing or arcade type, the player tries to accomplish a predetermined mission—solving the mystery or finding the treasure before being killed or losing all one's playing pieces.

Thus, in spite of the ever-expanding leisure-time activity choices, engaging in narrative as a pastime seems to have lost none of its centuries-old appeal. And reading is still flourishing: middle America has embraced bookstore chic (once the domain of urban intellectuals) sparking today's escalating battle between corporate bookstores. All of this points to the fact that the power of narrative is just as strong today as it was centuries ago. Only the medium through which narrative is transmitted is changing.

The theory that seduction can account for our continued attraction to narrative—fictional narrative in particular—is the subject of Ross Chambers' excellent *Story and Situation: Narrative Seduction and the Power of Fiction*.[3] In his study, Chambers moves beyond narratological concerns for structure and discourse in literature to narrative's contextual—situational—factor: "point." Chambers uses the example of the "faggot" joke—told variously among gay people, straight people, and between a gay and a straight person—to illustrate that the point of what is being told, or "the relationships mediated by the act of narration," is often more responsible for the generation of meaning than the actual content of the joke or story itself (*Story and Situation* 3).

It is in this relationship between storyteller and reader/listener that seduction comes into play: in order to gain and maintain the reader/listener's attention, and by extension the authority to narrate, the storyteller must seduce (entice and entrap) the reader/listener. Indeed, in Chambers's model, all narratives are a priori seductive:

> Because there can be no narrative without the authority to narrate, and no authority to narrate without the authorization of another, *whose desire must consequently be inscribed, however spectrally, in the narrative discourse itself*, it is difficult to see the possibility of a narrative act—at least in the present state of Western culture—that is not, at the same time, in small or large measure, an act of seduction. (*Story and Situation* 218, emphasis added)

In Chambers's relational model of the narrative act, the position—and, more importantly, the *desire*—of the reading or listening other must always be taken into consideration by the producer of narrative; in his view the narrative act cannot take place in the absence of that reading or listening other. Thus, the duality inherent in the communicative act necessitates the seduction of the reader/listener by the storyteller. In this way, seduction is posited as the sine qua non of fiction. Chambers suggests that in the context of his book, "'fiction' might be most fruitfully (if radically) defined as the name we give to the narrative moves that, in a given narrative situation, produce authority through seduction" (*Story and Situation* 219). In other words, although the "fact vs. fiction" distinction is murky at best, Chambers suggests using an author's use of seductive narrative tactics—intended to manipulate his or her reader/listener—as the distinguishing characteristic of fiction.

With the understanding that I am taking Chambers's claim of seduction as an integral part of the fictional narrative act as my starting point, let us turn our attention to the different ways in which readers might experience this narrative seduction.[4] I envision narrative seduction as a continuum, and I propose to limit my discussion of the possible effects of narrative seduction to two extreme examples of that continuum: those of "Emma Bovary" and Roland Barthes.[5] In "Emma Bovary,"[6] Flaubert has sketched the "type" of reader who is seduced by

theme and plot, and who uses literature to fulfill herself. In stark contrast to the
model presented by "Emma Bovary," Roland Barthes figures himself in his
writings as the intellectual reader par excellence, seduced by language and the
play of the signifier. After presenting these two "types," I will show how the
writings of Violette Leduc can appeal to both of these kinds of readers.

*
**

Emma Bovary presents us with an interesting case: she is an example of someone whose "life" (were it not for the fact that she is a fictional character herself)
is circumscribed by literature. The influence of literature in Emma's life began
early; during her convent upbringing, she indulged her taste for novels: "Pendant six mois, à quinze ans, Emma se graissa donc les mains à cette poussière de
vieux cabinets de lecture [For six months, then, Emma, at fifteen years of age,
made her hands dirty with books from old lending libraries]" (*Madame Bovary*
96–97/23).[7] It has been argued that this initial 'soiling' via literature is what
ultimately ruined her life, causing her to wish for more—more luxury, more
pleasure, more adventure—than a life with Charles Bovary could ever offer.[8]

Emma's case is certainly an extreme one, but it serves to dramatize the influence of literature and its power to entice and entrap: she dedicated herself to
molding her life to the literary models that held such sway for her, and it finally
cost her that life. The pleasure that Emma took from narrative went beyond the
simple enjoyment of reading that it is for many: it was the framework upon
which she based her potential for happiness. In the end, Charles thought that her
death was attributable to *la fatalité*, but Flaubert suggests that it was *la faute de
la littérature*.

The Freudian notion of incorporation can shed some light on the question
of how Emma came to be so completely influenced by literature. It is defined by
LaPlanche and Pontalis as the "Processus par lequel le sujet, sur un mode plus
ou moins fantasmatique, fait pénétrer et garde un objet à l'intérieur de son corps.
. . . Elle constitue le prototype corporel de l'introjection et de l'identification.
[Process whereby the subject, more or less on the level of phantasy, has an object penetrate his body and keeps it "inside" his body. . . . Incorporation provides the corporeal model for introjection and identification.]"[9] Incorporation, as
its name suggests, consists of bringing an object inside the body (generally but
not necessarily by swallowing it) and keeping it there, merging that object with
the subject from then on. In this case, the subject Emma is an avid consumer of
stories; like the "vieille fille [old maid]" who introduced Emma to romantic
novels and "chansons galantes du siècle passé [love-songs of the last century]"
who "elle-même *avalait* de longs chapitres [herself *swallowed* long chapters]"
(*Madame Bovary* 96/22–23, emphasis added), Emma also devours these narratives.[10] Having incorporated the images of romantic heroes and heroines that she
encountered in story and song during her formative convent years, Emma is
subject to their influence for the remainder of her life. As we will show, it is not

only when she is reading that Emma identifies with literary heroines. Indeed, when a situation similar to those described in her novels—those that she has lived in her fantasy life—presents itself in her "real" life, Emma is compelled, and happily so, to act as though she were in fact one of those novelistic heroines. After her first experience of extramarital sex, Emma looks at herself in the mirror and assesses her newfound identity as an adulterous woman in the following terms:

> Alors elle se rapella les héroïnes des livres qu'elle avait lus, et la légion lyrique de ces femmes adultères se mit à chanter dans sa mémoire avec des voix des sœurs qui la charmaient. Elle devenait elle-même comme une partie véritable de ces imaginations et réalisait la longue rêverie de sa jeunesse, en se considérant dans ce type d'amoureuse qu'elle avait tant envié.

> [Then she recalled the heroines of the books that she had read, and the lyric legion of these adulterous women began to sing in her memory with the voice of sisters that charmed her. She became herself, as it were, an actual part of these imaginings and realized the love-dream of her youth as she saw herself in this type of amorous women whom she had so envied.] (*Madame Bovary* 229–230/101)

In spite of cultural proscriptions (religious, political, and social) against extramarital sexual relations, Emma is not ashamed of what she has just done. On the contrary, she is extremely happy: this is one of the few moments in *Madame Bovary* in which feelings of deception do not immediately follow Emma's fleeting moments of happiness. As the passage shows, this happiness is due to her feelings of identification with "the heroines of the books that she had read." By having made love to Rodolphe, Emma is finally able to realize her dream of joining "lyric legion of these adulterous women" whose image she had incorporated as an adolescent.

This incorporation-identification with (adulterous) romantic heroines virtually requires that she become an (adulterous) romantic heroine herself. In this sense, incorporation might be considered as the highest level of the seduction continuum that extends from enticement to entrapment. "Victims" of seduction (adulterous women shunned by society, for example) are often seen as deserving their fate because much of the seduction continuum suggests a choice: the women in question are tempted, but should be able to resist that temptation. When it comes to incorporation, however, that choice no longer exists: because it operates on an unconscious level, incorporation eliminates the possibility of resistance, entrapping those like Emma.

What, then, is this totalizing image which Emma incorporates? It is one taken from her convent readings of Sir Walter Scott. After reading his novels,

> Elle aurait voulu vivre dans quelque vieux manoir, comme ces châtelaines au long corsage qui, sous le trèfle des ogives, passaient leurs jours, le coude sur la pierre et le menton dans la main, à regarder venir du fond de la campagne quelque cavalier à plume blanche qui gallope sur un cheval noir.

[She would have liked to live in some old manor-house, like those long-waisted châte-
laines who, in the shade of pointed arches, spent their days leaning on the stone, chin in
hand, watching a cavalier with white plume galloping on his black horse from the distant fields.] (*Madame Bovary* 97/23)

This clichéd image of the woman waiting to be swept by her "cavalier" into a
life of passion and adventure, once incorporated, was to become the foundation
upon which Emma constructed her idea(l) of romantic love. Its constitutive elements—the man on horseback and the woman at her window—will return again
and again over the course of the novel. In view of this incorporation, it is not
surprising that it was shortly after her marriage to the decidedly mediocre Charles that she started to feel *déçue*—deceived and disappointed—by her wedded
condition. Although he had first appeared to her on horseback (73), Charles falls
far short of Emma's expectations of her "cavalier." Flaubert once again makes
certain that we know that novels were at the root of her disillusionment: "Emma
cherchait à savoir ce que l'on entendait au juste dans la vie par les mots de *fé-
licité*, de *passion* et d'*ivresse*, qui lui avaient paru si beaux dans les livres
[Emma tried to find out what one meant exactly in life by the words *felicity*,
passion, *rapture* that had seemed to her so beautiful in books" (*Madame Bovary*
94/21). Seduced by what she imagines is the grandeur and excitement of the life
of the literary heroine, she could not be happy in her *petit bourgeois* life with
Charles.

If her husband could not fulfill Emma's longing for a hero of the type that
she has read about in books, someone else could, and does, easily fill that role.
Emma gets her first taste of 'la vie romanesque' at the ball given by the marquis
d'Andervilliers at his château, La Vaubyessard, which represents the closest
approximation of the dreamed-of "old manor-house" in *Madame Bovary*. There,
Emma experiences a vertiginous waltz with "le Vicomte" (*Madame Bovary*
110/33), who becomes her first model "cavalier." It is notable that Emma's previous 'contact' with Viscounts took place during her convent stay and was
equally linked to "la vie romanesque": "Emma fixait ses regards éblouis sur le
nom des auteurs inconnus qui avaient signé, le plus souvent, comtes ou vicom-
tes, au bas de leurs pièces [Emma looked with dazzled eyes at the names of the
unknown authors, who had signed their verses for the most part as counts or
viscounts]" (*Madame Bovary* 97/23). Upon retiring that evening, Emma "*ouvrit
la fenêtre et s'accouda* [*opened the window and leant out*]" (*Madame Bovary*
114/33, emphasis added). Then, on the way home from the ball the following
day, Charles discovers a cigar case that Emma imagines having belonged to the
Vicomte, and even imagines she sees him riding away on horseback (*Madame
Bovary* 115/34). When out traveling, Emma continuously hopes to see the Vicomte and relive their fleeting moment of contact, but she must abandon that
wish when she and Charles move from Tostes to Yonville.

The Vicomte is soon replaced by another model "cavalier," however: Léon
Dupuis. On the night of the Bovarys' arrival at Yonville, they make the ac-
quaintance of the apothecary, Homais, and the young clerk at the auberge.
While Charles and Homais are engaged in conversation, Léon and Emma dis-

cover that they share a passion for literature, and they will spend many an eve-ning reading together. Although Léon lacks the social status—and the horse—Emma does her best to see him as the romantic hero for whom she yearns, even to the point of looking only at his shadow and not at his person as he passes by the house in order to be able to better savor his "image." "Elle était amoureuse de Léon, et elle recherchait la solitude, afin de pouvoir plus à l'aise se délecter de son image. La vue de sa personne troublait la volupté de cette méditation [She was in love with Léon, and sought solitude that she might with the more ease delight in his image. The sight of his form troubled the voluptuousness of this meditation]" (*Madame Bovary* 172/67). In this way, she imparts to him that absence that is characteristic of her novelistic "cavalier." Frustrated by his love for Emma—who returns hers in the form of increased devotion to her family—Léon leaves Yonville to study in Paris. The day following his departure, "Léon réapparaissait plus grand, plus beau, plus suave, plus vague [Léon reappeared, taller, handsomer, more charming, more vague]" (*Madame Bovary* 189/76–77). In fact, Léon is the ideal romantic hero for Emma only insofar as he is consistently absent. It is when her lovers are present that Emma's troubles begiℕ Not long after Léon's departure, Emma experiences her first real seduction at the hands of Rodolphe Boulanger, who appears to Emma for the first time on horseback—dressed very much like the Vicomte—as she is looking lazily out of her window. Given the resonance of this image with her reading of Walter Scott, it is no wonder that she succumbs to its influence, and to him. Emma reacts to the sight of the mounted Rodolphe just as she thinks a Walter Scott heroine would react to the sight of her "cavalier" coming to her rescue. Having identi-fied with that literary heroine, Emma's only choice is to take Rodolphe as her hero and lover. It is after this capitulation (which has occurred in the woods, during the course of an outing on horseback) that Emma considers herself in the mirror and thinks of all of the legions of adulterous women that she admired in books during her adolescence, and whom she now joins, as we have seen above. Her joy fades, however, and the downward cycle of her life begins when Rodol-phe cruelly deceives her just when she thought that they were going to live hap-pily ever after in some far-off place. Even the long-standing affair with Léon ends in disappointment. The fairy tale finally ends, of course, when Emma, overwhelmed by debt and faced with a life without love, swallows arsenic stolen from Homais' shop.

The fact that literature had such charms for Emma indicates that her own life held very few. One of the pleasures she sought from literature was escape: as a reader, she wanted to get away from her own narrative and move into someone else's. Or, more accurately, she wanted that narrative *to be* her own, and accomplished this through incorporation.

For Emma, the desired narrative was the possibility of romance or the ex-citement of adventure, the elements of which were clearly missing from her own life, as Flaubert shows us. Through her reading, she wanted to experience the adrenaline rush of being chased, be it by a wild animal or by a seducer. For in-stance, during her first conversation with Léon, as they are discovering their shared affinity for reading, Léon remarks that he appreciates poets in particular: "—Je trouve les vers plus tendres que la prose, et qu'ils font bien mieux pleurer. ['I think verse more tender than prose, and that it moves far more easily to tears.']" One might anticipate a swoon here, given Léon's obvious sensitivity, in marked contrast with Charles' unromantic character. However, Emma curtly responds that "Cependant ils fatiguent à la longue [Still in the long run it is tiring]," and that "au contraire, *j'adore les histoires qui se suivent tout d'une haleine, où l'on a peur* [I, on the contrary, *adore stories that rush breathlessly along, that frighten one*]" (*Madame Bovary* 148/51, emphasis added). Having incorporated romance narrative—in other words, having turned her life into a romance narrative of her own—Emma is able, during the time that the book is open in front of her (and even when it is not), to erase the difference between herself and the protagonists in the novel. Addicted to diversion and the possibility of love, Emma is a plot reader. The rewards she looks for in novels are strictly narrative.

If "Emma Bovary" is a model of the common-sense, naïve reader—naïve in the sense that she pays very little attention to the workings of language in the text (she finds poetry tiresome and ignores text in favor of the effects of narrative)—then Roland Barthes can be located at the extreme opposite end of this readers' continuum. His reading is the antithesis of naïve insofar as his focus is on the play of language in text and the pleasures which that play might produce in the (body of the) reader. In *Le Plaisir du texte*,[12] Barthes himself offers an explanation of the two types of readers (and readings) that I have outlined here:

> D'où deux régimes de la lecture: l'une va droit aux articulations de l'anecdote, elle considère l'étendue du texte, ignore les jeux du langage (si je lis du Jules Verne, je vais vite: je perds du discours, et cependant ma lecture n'est fascinée par aucune *perte* verbale—au sens que ce mot peut avoir en spéléologie).

> [Whence two systems of reading: one goes straight to the articulations of the anecdote, it considers the extent of the text, ignores the play of language (if I read Jules Verne, I go fast: I lose discourse, and yet my reading is not hampered by any verbal *loss*—in the speleological sense of that word)]. (*Le Plaisir du texte* 22/12)

This is the "system" of reading that we have ascribed to "Emma Bovary" and will subsequently refer to as "Bovaryan," though Barthes himself concedes that he also reads certain less-modern texts in this way. It is a type of reading which heads straight for the plot twists: Emma's comment—that she "adore[s] stories that rush breathlessly along"—is an excellent illustration of this phenomenon: she does not tarry on the descriptions, but rushes breathlessly through the text. This type of reading also "ignores" (in all senses of the word) the play of language. We can further see that Emma falls into this system through her dismissal of poets, the distilled nature of poetry's language being an excellent example of "the play of language": "Still in the long run it is tiring." Finally, this type of reading, in spite of the fact that certain parts are skipped over, produces none of the vertiginous loss produced by *jouissance* that Barthes ascribes to the second manner of reading—one that we will call "Barthesian." He continues:

> l'autre lecture ne passe rien; elle pèse, colle au texte, elle lit, si l'on peut dire, avec application et emportement, saisit en chaque point du texte l'asyndète qui coupe les langages—et non l'anecdote: ce n'est pas l'extension (logique) qui la captive, l'effeuillement des vérités, mais la feuilleté de la signifiance.

> [the other reading skips nothing; it weighs, it sticks to the text, it reads, so to speak, with application and transport, grasps at every point in the text the asyndeton which cuts the various languages—and not the anecdote: it is not (logical) extension that captivates it, the winnowing out of truths, but the layering of significance.] (*Le Plaisir du texte* 22–23/12)

This Barthesian reading, then, can be seen as the contraposition of the Bovaryan variety: where the Bovaryan reading skips over text, the Barthesian reading sticks very close to it. Where "Emma" would be captivated by the chain of events (a text's content), Barthes is focused on the chain of signifiers.

It is substitution that gives rise to the possibility of the pleasure of the text: a "transport" or "verbal loss" that is produced when our reader approaches the text obliquely, from the angle of the signifier and not the signified. Elsewhere, Barthes has said that "ce que [le plaisir] veut, c'est le lieu d'une perte, c'est la faille, la coupure, la déflation, le *fading* qui saisit le sujet au cœur de la jouissance [What pleasure wants is the site of a loss, the seam, the cut, the deflation, the dissolve which seizes the subject in the midst of bliss]" (*Le Plaisir du texte* 15/7). Bliss, or *jouissance*—"la petite mort"—is precisely that place where the subject loses him/herself, where language breaks down: jouissance cannot be spoken.

> Voici d'ailleurs, venu de la psychanalyse, un moyen indirect de fonder l'opposition du texte de plaisir du texte de jouissance: le plaisir est dicible, la jouissance ne l'est pas.

> [Here, moreover, drawn from psychoanalysis, is an indirect way of establishing the opposition between the text of pleasure and the text of bliss: pleasure can be expressed in words, bliss cannot. (*Le Plaisir du texte* 36/21)

The "text of jouissance" (as opposed to the "text of pleasure") is that text in which the reading breaks down. The "coupure," or cutting, that produces this "inter-dit" occurs when one (or more) signifier latches onto another and carries—or cuts—the reader away from the text into that place of jouissance that is beyond language.

The pair "text of jouissance"/ " text of pleasure," then, is very similar to the description that Barthes had previously elaborated in *S/Z*[13] of the "writerly text" versus the "readerly text": the "writerly text" is "ce qui peut être aujourd'hui écrit (ré-écrit) [what can be written (rewritten) today]" (*S/Z* 10/4) and "c'est *nous en train d'écrire [ourselves writing]*" (*S/Z* 11/5). By this, Barthes means that the reader is responsible for producing much of the meaning of the text him or herself. As John Sturrock[14] explains it, these texts "are *scriptible*, or 'writable', because the reader as it were re-writes them as he reads, having been induced to mimic in his own mind the process by which the text came to be written in the first place" (*Structuralism and Since* 71). "En face du texte scriptible [Opposite the writerly text]," Barthes continues, "s'établit donc sa contre-valeur, sa valeur négative, réactive: ce qui peut être lu, mais non écrit: le *lisible* [is its countervalue, its negative,reactive value: what can be read, but not written: the *readerly*]" (*S/Z* 10/4). This "readable" (or readerly) text, of which the vast majority of literary texts are examples, are products for the reader to consume, and although the reader may enjoy them, they are too conventional to allow for the destabilizing, disconcerting experience of textual jouissance.

If Bovaryan readers prefer readerly texts and Barthesian readers prefer writerly ones, these two very different kinds of readers do have their radical seduction by literature in common. The Latin root of the verb "to seduce"—*seducere*—means "to lead away." Certainly these readers are lead in different directions by their preferred texts—"Emma" cares little for text but wants to be a part of the narrative fabric to the point of incorporation, and Barthes underplays narrative fabric in order to concentrate on language, so that he can then be spun away from the text and into jouissance. In spite of this directional difference, however, both of our reader types have arrived at fetishistic attachments to books.

In his discussion of Emma's book fetish, Tony Tanner[15] points out that in the convent, Emma "starts to experience what amounts to an erotic thrill just by handling the books and watching the tissue paper float over the plates" (*Adultery in the Novel* 285).[16] Tanner contends that these sheets of tissue paper will be a "morphological prefiguration" of the many sets of sheets that Emma will encounter in her amorous adventures.[17] The book, for Emma, is intricately bound up with the bed, and Tanner suggests that in a reversal of the usual situation, the bed has become a substitute for the book: "Not exactly that she is trying to love by the book, but rather that she is trying to recapture an experience in the flesh that originated as a sensation caused by paper, and thus to rediscover in 'love' the texture (even more than the text) of the book" (*Adultery in the Novel* 286). Through Emma's association of bedsheets with the sheets of tissue paper in the books that she read at the convent, Emma's identification with her romantic heroines is concretized. The materiality of the book itself allows for a more direct sensation of the romantic stories which she reads: when Emma opens a book , she does not simply follow the story: she slips between the sheets with the hero.

In a contrary action to "Emma's," Barthes (who "outs" his own book fetish in *Le Plaisir du texte*) valorizes text over texture:

> Le texte est un objet fétiche et *ce fétiche me désire*. Le texte me choisit, par toute une
> disposition d'écrans invisibles, de chicanes sélectives: le vocabulaire, les références, la

lisibilité, etc.; et, perdu au milieu du texte (non pas *derrière* lui à la façon d'un dieu de
machinerie) il y a toujours l'autre, l'auteur.

[The text is a fetish object, and *this fetish desires me*. The text chooses me, by a whole
disposition of invisible screens, selective baffles: vocabulary, references, readability,
etc.; and, lost in the midst of a text (not *behind* it, like a *deus ex machina*) there is always the other, the author.] (*Le Plaisir du texte* 45/27).

Again, Barthes is turned on by those textual elements that have sometimes produced jouissance in the past (words and references). However, because not all of
these "invisible screens" are calibrated to excite everyone, Barthes maintains
that the fetish-text chooses *him*. He certainly cannot choose *it*: the same texts
never generate jouissance in the same way twice, if they manage to generate it at
all.

It is interesting to note that Barthes, after tolling the death of the author, is
calling him back again, in the form of the (equally lost) other of textual pleasure. It appears as though Barthes is suggesting that, while it is the text itself that
is desiring, both the author and the reader get caught up in this desire and—
through the mediation of the text—can desire each other: "mais, dans le texte,
d'une certaine façon, *je désire* l'auteur: j'ai besoin de sa figure (qui n'est ni sa
représentation, ni sa projection) comme il a besoin de la mienne [but in the text,
in a way, *I desire* the author: I need his figure (which is neither his representation nor his projection), as he needs mine]" (*Le Plaisir du texte* 45–46/27). Indeed, John Sturrock has pointed out that in the *Plaisir du texte*, "what Barthes
seems to claim is that the relationship between writer, Text [sic], and reader is
an erotic one. Body speaks unto body; the 'body' of the writer, which is the
most real and intimate part of him, is offered to the 'body' of the reader, who
responds equally intimately" (*Structuralism and Since* 72). Here we can assume
that Sturrock uses the term "body" in the sense in which Barthes himself most
often employed it: as the locus (not necessarily physical) of unconscious desires.

Thus we have our second point of contact between the Bovaryan reader and
the Barthesian one, after what I have called their "radical" seduction by literature: they both use their fetish-books as vehicles to meet another desiring figure
located inside the text for some erotic thrills. But is this not the goal of all desiring reading and writing? It is the purpose of this study to show that for Violette Leduc, locating her (desiring) reader inside her (desiring) text has been her
raison d'être as a writer.

If this is so, how, then, would Leduc's writings be received by each one of
our reader types? In spite of the apparent incompatibility of readerly and
writerly texts ("je crois . . . que le plaisir et la jouissance sont des forces paral-
lèles, qu'elles ne peuvent se rencontrer [I believe . . . that pleasure and bliss are
parallel forces, that they cannot meet]"[18]), textual elements abound in the writings of Leduc that could excite "Emma" as well as Barthes. This is true even if
we limit our examples to a single text: *La Bâtarde*.

Excavating Bovaryan pleasures from *La Bâtarde* is a very simple exercise. This text, which ostensibly recounts the events of the first part of the author's life, is full of *peripeteia* for the narrator-protagonist—and for a reader who might identify with her—beginning (as the book does) with Violette's illegitimate birth and ending with her adventures as a trafficker on the black market during the Second World War. In the intervening 600 pages, readers watch from a very close distance as Violette survives the death of her beloved grandmother, two world wars, two lesbian affairs, a marriage and divorce, an abortion, a suicide attempt, her beginnings as a writer, and the perpetual struggle for her mother's affection, to name but a few of the highlights of the plot. The story of Violette's amorous adventures, from clearly incestuous feelings for her mother Berthe, to her frustrated desire for a male homosexual writer, passing through a lesbian sexual initiation at a girls' school and an affair of long standing with another woman—an affair which supports the triangulation of desire via the presence of Violette's future husband but cannot withstand a (paying) voyeur's gaze—should be enough to get the heart of our Bovaryan reader racing. *La Bâtarde* certainly is an example of a text containing "histoires qui se suivent tout d'une haleine;" only the engraved prints which thrilled Emma are missing.

Satisfying Emma's requirements for narrative pleasure, however, would be no great task, even for a writer whose (life-)story was less convoluted than Violette Leduc's. For, as we have seen, the Bovaryan reader takes her pleasure in "readerly texts." The Barthesian reader, on the other hand, is more difficult to please: Barthes prefers "writerly texts," of which there exist very few (Sturrock goes so far as to say that none exist, and that only James Joyce's *Finnegans Wake* comes close [*Structuralism and Since* 69]). And while *La Bâtarde*, from the description that we have just given of it, may appear to be grounded in readability (the episodes do follow chronologically, and the text can be easily digested by the average Bovaryan reader), if we judge it by the criterion of the "text of jouissance"—the writerly text: that text in which the reading breaks down—then *La Bâtarde* shows itself to be just that: a bastardized (hybrid) mix of the readerly and of something approaching the writerly. One example of a passage in which the reading breaks down is the following, written in stream-of-consciousness mode, in which readers are obliged to slow down and read differently, in a more conscious manner:

> ils ne connaîtront jamais ce qui me force à venir ici le samedi j'ai tant de cimetières sur les épaules Fidéline Isabelle Gabriel ça meurt c'est mort fleurissez-nous petite mère entre Havre-Caumartin et Chaussée-d'Antin fleurs de tristesse tant de blancs œillets ébouriffés chez les lingères quand l'incestueuse a perdu son frère la charité monsieur la charité madame si j'osais c'est pour réchauffer mes petits cimetières arrêtons-nous devant ce frais bocage entre les pieds des mannequins d'étalage Hermine je te parle croque la craie mange le tableau rumine notre chambre meublée on ne dit pas un petit peu on dit un peu je ferai attention manman une autre fois

> [they will never know what forces me to come here on Saturdays I have so many cemeteries on my shoulders Fidéline Isabelle Gabriel it's dying it's dead treat us to some

flowers young mother between Havre-Caumartin and Chaussée-d'Antin flowers of sadness so many ruffled white carnations where the washerwomen are when the incestuous
woman has lost her brother charity sir charity madam if only I dared it was to warm my
little cemeteries let's stop here in front of this cool stand of trees between the feet of the
mannequins in the window Hermine I'm talking to you crunch the chalk eat the black-
board chew on our furnished room we don't say a little bit we say a little I'll pay attention manman another time].(*La Bâtarde* 240)

I have cited an extended portion of this passage in order to give my reader an
idea of the movement that takes place there. While this passage does make some
sense to Leduc's reader insofar as there do exist certain textual markers—the
names of known characters, for example—there is a much richer reading to be
made on the level of the signifier. Reading obliquely and listening indirectly,[19]
we can hear the assonance of "Havre-Caumartin" and "Chaussée-d'Antin," "tant
de blancs," and "œillets ébouriffés chez," but more interesting still is when that
assonance produces vertical movement of the signifier, as in the movement from
"frais bocage [cool stand of trees]" to "mannequins d'étalage [mannequins in the
window]." We can also read the horizontal movement of the signifier along the
signifying chain: "mannequins d'étalage" leads to "Hermine" via the association
of the shopping trip to the Schiaparelli boutique, and from there to "la craie
[chalk]" and "le tableau [the blackboard]" because Hermine is a schoolteacher.
The association with school activates the memory of her mother (whom Violette
called "manman" as a child) critiquing her compositions: "on ne dit pas un petit
peu on dit un peu je ferai attention manman," and so on.

There are other passages in *La Bâtarde* which could be called writerly. One
example is an obscure dreamlike passage in which Violette, walking with Hermine on the pont de la Concorde, gets insulted by a passerby. Violette, under
attack by the woman's comment, is reduced to a pre-linguistic state. More
striking still, however, is the morphological transformation that takes place:
Violette's nose grows into a "trompe [elephant's trunk]" (*La Bâtarde* 297) and
her high heeled shoes become "des palmes de boue et de glaise [flippers of mud
and clay]" (*La Bâtarde* 298).

In this passage, which at eight pages is too long to cite, monosyllabic words
containing the phoneme [u], as well as longer words generated by it, are overdetermined. Besides the personal pronoun "nous," which is not unexpected in a
passage that speaks in the first person of a couple on a walk, we find *boue*,
bouche (twice), and *boucherie*; *cou* (three times), *coup/s* (five times), and
coupé; *doux*; *joue/s* (five times) and *jouer*; *mou* and *mouche*. For every one of
these key words but *doux* there exists at least one homonym or lengthening of
the word.

A cursory reading of this passage does very little to produce meaning. The
reader can recognize that it is an important passage by its graphical separation
from the rest of the chapter, the extended hailing of the reader by the narrator
that introduces it, cited above, and by the emotional impact that it produces.
However, beyond a lingering sense of violence and pain (resolved at the end by

the love of Hermine), this passage remains a puzzle—or a rebus, as Freud would have it[20]—for readers approaching it for literal meaning.

Read at the level of the signifier, however, this passage is suggestive of a preoccupation with castration: the images of cutting ("couper") and the butcher ("boucher") are hidden in the shortened form of the words, from which the phoneme [e] has been suppressed. The words themselves have thus undergone the action they describe: that of cutting, amputation, or castrating. With all of this repetition of signifiers and their circular play, this passage provides ample opportunity for Barthesian textual jouissance.

Readers on both ends of this continuum—as well as those situated somewhere in between—will find something to seduce them in Leduc's works. This may be plot, it may be the effects of language, or even certain seductive strategies that allow Leduc to inscribe an erotic touch, look, or voice into the text. Through the deployment of these strategies, Leduc manages to reach through the text to make contact with—and *seduce*—the reader. Seen in this light, Violette Leduc's seductive texts show that reading is not at all old-fashioned, but intensely exciting, both intellectually as well as physically.

CHAPTER TWO

Cycles of Seduction I:
Violette Leduc, Reading, and Writing

In the previous chapter we examined the narrative and textual seduction of the reader as well as the extreme ends of that continuum as exemplified by "Emma Bovary" and Roland Barthes. These two kinds of readers, despite their radically different readerly demands—"Emma" requiring pulse-quickening plot lines of amorous or other adventure and Barthes the linguistic slippage that takes him away from the text and to his own *espace de jouissance*—can find their pleasure in the texts of Violette Leduc. And although the pleasure that the Bovaryan reader takes from the text is often physical, erotic, it must not be confused with the unspeakable nature of Barthesian jouissance, that "petite mort" that involves the temporary loss of self.

In this chapter we will investigate the ways in which Leduc has revealed in her autobiographies that she herself was not immune to textual seduction. I will show how, in *La Bâtarde*, Violette has portrayed herself as a Bovaryan reader, and later, in *La Folie en tête*, how she moved along the continuum towards becoming a Barthesian one. We will see that the impulse for this movement was that she herself had become a writer, and her interest as a reader shifted from the mere vicissitudes of plot to include stylistic techniques and linguistic effects. With an eye to producing what she refers to as "the magic of metaphor" for her readers, Violette began taking different pleasures from the text. This movement along the continuum from preferring readerly texts to writerly ones corresponds to Leduc's shift from being a reader to being a writer. And as we shall see, Leduc is not the only one who goes from being seduced by literature—reading—to seducing through literature—writing.

In *La Bâtarde*, the first volume of what Leduc herself identifies as her autobiography, we see the young Violette appreciating literature in much the same way as Emma Bovary: she is fascinated by narrative early on and reads voraciously, even while neglecting her formal studies. She remains intrigued by novels through her twenties, when she works for the Plon publishing house in Paris, and in her thirties she meets and is befriended by the writer Maurice Sachs, who encourages her to commit to paper her childhood memories, a piece that will later become her first novel, *L'Asphyxie*.

La Folie en tête picks up where *La Bâtarde* leaves off, at the very end of the war. Between the end of *La Bâtarde* and the beginning of *La Folie en tête*, Violette finishes the writing of *L'Asphyxie*. One of the opening scenes of *La Folie en tête* shows her buying a new, orange folder in which to present her writings to Simone de Beauvoir for the first time. *La Folie en tête*, then, is the story of Violette's new life as a writer. Here she is no longer an amateur who writes at a friend's behest. The Violette of *La Folie en tête* is a professional writer with a publisher, an important mentor, and an ever-widening circle of acquaintances who are themselves important literary figures. It is during the course of this novel that Violette's reading pleasure becomes more Barthesian. The pleasure that she takes in reading is no longer limited to the gratifications provided by plot. As a writer in her own right, Violette's interest in style—the way writers manipulate language—comes to the fore. This chapter will trace how the reader becomes the writer by examining Violette's movement along the reader's continuum, from her Bovaryan beginnings in *La Bâtarde* through her Barthesian leanings in *La Folie en tête*. Although her relationship with literature changes over the course of these two novels, the association of literature with seduction remains constant.

For Violette Leduc, literature and seduction are collateral, in the sense of parallel and coordinate: Leduc structures her text so that we rarely see one without the other. This dovetailing of seduction and literature is due in large part to Violette's increasing identification with her absent father, André, an avid reader. Referred to throughout the text as "le séducteur," it is not surprising that Violette's primary understanding of him is in the context of seduction. The idea of seduction was terribly ambiguous for the young Violette, however. She could see that Berthe had clearly remained infatuated with André and his lifestyle, but it was equally obvious that Berthe resented having been left pregnant and penniless, with an unattractive, sickly child to care for. This was particularly true in the period between grandmother Fidéline's death and Berthe's marriage to Violette's stepfather, a period when Violette was obliged to became her mother's confidant. Berthe took pains to warn her daughter daily that "Tous les hommes étaient des salauds [All men were pigs]" (*La Bâtarde* 53), but she cherished the memory of her own "seducer." Violette remarks that "Elle ne pardonnait pas aux autres hommes ce qu'elle avait fait pour un seul [She would not forgive other men for what she had done for just one]" (*La Bâtarde* 54). What goes unsaid is that Berthe did not forgive *Violette* for what she had sacrificed to André. Although she does not articulate it, Violette feels that she has taken her father's place in being blamed for her mother's hardships. Taking the place of "the seducer," however, does signify the possibility of being loved by Berthe, and authorizes Violette's active seduction of her mother.

Before the arrival of the husband, then, Violette and Berthe were romantically linked in Violette's mind. Violette, who had symbolically taken her absent father's place in the family dynamic, also resembled him physically with her big nose and her tendency toward ill health. To seduce her mother, Violette would steal potatoes for her during the war: "Berthe, ma mère, j'étais ton mari avant ton mariage. Je grattais avec mes ongles la terre des jardins, je volais pommes de terre et petits pois [Berthe, my mother, I was your fiancé before you got married. I scratched the ground of gardens with my fingernails, I stole potatoes and peas.]" (*La Bâtarde* 54). Later, she fantasized about going to work in a factory for her: "L'usine, la gamelle. . . . Travailler dans une usine pour elle, lui apporter l'argent de la semaine [The factory, the lunchbox. . . . Working in a factory for her, bringing her that week's pay]"(*La Bâtarde* 60). When Berthe married, however, Violette was confronted by the difficult realization that she was no longer her mother's suitor, and that there would no longer be a place for her in her mother's bed—"notre lit [our bed]" (51). Thus, Violette suffered a fate that "the seducer" had not: whereas André had abandoned Berthe, Berthe abandoned his "reincarnation," Violette. Disillusioned by her mother's betrayal, Violette actively reinforced her association with her father, much to the consternation of her new step-father, who resented the shadow of "le séducteur" that Violette cast: "Je comprenais confusément qu'il aurait voulu m'éffacer. J'étais le poids d'un grand amour, j'étais une mouche sur un linge blanc [I vaguely understood that he would have liked to have erased me. I was the weight of a great love, I was a dark spot on a white cloth]" (*La Bâtarde* 75–76).

André, this shadowy figure who is always present in, yet at the same time painfully absent from, Violette's relationship with her mother, is perceived differently by both women, and even by Violette herself at different times in her life. Early in *La Bâtarde*, the older, narrating Violette gives the following description of her father:

> André. Celui qui te fascine. Grand, mince, élancé, teint clair, yeux rêveurs, cheveux cendrés, long nez. *Pas beau, mais quelle séduction.* Toutes les femmes étaient toquées de lui. *Je te cite.* Quelle race, quels gestes

> [André. The one who fascinates you. Tall, thin, lanky, light complexion, far-away eyes, ash blond hair, long nose. *Not good-looking, but so seductive.* All of the women were crazy about him. *I'm quoting you.* What breeding, what gestures] (*La Bâtarde* 31, emphasis added)

Here, in contrast to her more usual narrative strategy of hailing the reader, Violette addresses her mother in an intimate way. The stress that Leduc places the fact that she is quoting her mother is significant: this is a positive portrait of André, but it is the one seen through Berthe's nostalgic eyes. Having endured the blame that should have been directed at the irresponsible André, the adult Violette, in contrast, has quite a different take on her father, calling him "Lâche, paresseux, [Cowardly, lazy]" and asserting "Non, je ne veux pas de toi, hérédité [No, I want nothing to do with you, heredity]" (*La Bâtarde* 32). Let us remember, however, that this is the voice of the mature, narrating Violette, not the child who lived in her mother's house. At the time being narrated, Violette took refuge in her identification with André.

It was during the summer of 1906 that André Debaralle impregnated Berthe, his mother's beloved companion, while the rest of the family was vacationing in Switzerland. Although he was unmarried and from an extravagantly wealthy family, he was sick with tuberculosis (from which he eventually died) and so was dependent upon his family financially. For this reason, in spite of the fact that there was family precedent for choosing a lower-class spouse,[1] André was afraid to tell his father what he had done. Recently, Leduc biographer Carlo Jansiti has brought to light shocking evidence demonstrating that this branch of the Debaralle family itself came from illegitimate stock,[2] a fact that remained hidden from Leduc, and certainly from her mother Berthe, as well:

> Les Debaralle s'enorgeuillissent d'une tradition quasi millénaire. Ironie du sort, c'est grâce à Violette Leduc, fille d'une domestique, enfant reniée, qu'on les évoque aujourd'hui. *Qui plus est, les Debaralle sont, eux aussi, d'origine bâtarde.* Violette Leduc devait ignorer cette particularité qui n'aurait pas manqué d'enflammer son imagination. Sans doute aurait-elle fait un sort à cette ascendance paternelle en y voyant un signe prémonitoire de son destin.

> [The Debaralle family is extremely proud of their family tradition dating back nearly a thousand years. By an irony of fate, it is thanks to Violette Leduc, the daughter of a servant, a repudiated child, that they are spoken of today. *Even more ironic is the fact that the Debaralles themselves were of bastard origin.* Violette Leduc must have been unaware of this feature, which would surely have stoked her imagination. She most likely would have exploited this paternal ascendance, seeing therein a sort of harbinger of her fate.] (*Violette Leduc* 18–19, emphasis added)

Ironically, André was afraid to bring up the case of the illegitimate daughter to his own father, himself the legitimate son of an illegitimate child. One wonders what Violette Leduc's life would have been like had her grandfather not been so ambivalent about his own bastard origins.

André, perhaps himself ignorant of the family history of illegitimacy, begged Berthe to leave the house, which she did, despite the fact that it was the one place where she had ever been happy in her life. Berthe blamed herself for the pregnancy, and when she resigned her post she was too ashamed to tell André's mother the reason. She went off to live in Arras, away from Valenciennes and the scandal her growing stomach might provoke. If Berthe blamed herself, Violette does not: "Je te jetterai qu'il était mal élevé, ton fils de famille. Il ne devait pas franchir le seuil de ta chambre. Le salon était à tout le monde tandis que ta chambre était ton écrin de subalterne [I would retort that he was poorly brought up, your young man of means. He should not have crossed the threshold of your room. The parlor was for everyone, but your room was your underling's retreat]" (*La Bâtarde* 32). The anger in Violette's narrative voice— "I would retort"—is directed both at her mother as well as her father; as they each abused or neglected her in their own way. However, as we see throughout Leduc's œuvre, she cannot stay angry with her mother for long. And although Violette will never be able to forgive André for his dirty dealings with both of

them, in the context of this healing book, *La Bâtarde*, Violette is able to forgive—though not heal—her mother: "Je veux guérir ta plaie, maman. Impossible. Elle ne se refermera jamais. Ta plaie, c'est lui, et je suis son portrait [I want
to heal your wound, Mother. Impossible. It will never scab over. He is your
wound, and I am the very picture of him]" (*La Bâtarde* 32).

*
**

Despite Leduc's longstanding ill will against the father she repeatedly terms
"cowardly," Simone de Beauvoir is quick to note that Violette's feelings of betrayal by her mother, which subsequently reorient her towards her father, mark
the beginning of her interest in literature. In her preface to *La Bâtarde*, she
writes:

> Tant qu'elle a vécu dans l'ombre de sa mère, Violette Leduc a méprisé les livres; elle
> préférait voler un chou à l'arrière d'une charette, cueillir de l'herbe pour les lapins,
> bavarder, vivre. Du jour où elle s'est tournée vers son père, les livres—qu'il avait
> aimés—l'ont fascinée.

> [As long as she lived in the shadow of her mother, Violette Leduc disdained books; she
> preferred stealing a cabbage off the back of a cart, picking grass for the rabbits, chatting,
> living. From the day when she turned toward her father, books—which he had loved—
> fascinated her.] (*La Bâtarde* 14)

As Beauvoir points out, this is a significant turning point in Violette's life. She
goes from enjoying the rural life of the peasant that was taught to her by her
cherished grandmother, Fidéline, to emulating her well-educated, urbane father.
Much of his lifestyle was beyond her reach financially—"Le séducteur ne vou-
lait que du linge blanchi à Londres [only linen laundered in London would do
for the seducer]" (*La Bâtarde* 77)—but one way that she could afford to culti-
vate this affinity was by sharing his love of literature. Before Berthe's marriage,
reading had been a chore for Violette: "Lire m'assommait [Reading bored me to
death]" (*La Bâtarde* 59). Afterwards, as we shall see, it becomes one of her only
pleasures. The fact that Berthe, although she was an excellent businesswoman,
had no taste for reading or writing—good writing to her was being able to write
an entire letter without making any grammar mistakes—surely reinforced in
Violette's young mind that reading modern fiction represented a distancing from
her mother (and step-father) and a complicity with her father.

The description of the circumstances surrounding a minor operation on her
larynx during a vacation period at the beginning of her mother's marriage illustrates Violette's identification with her father. As she and her mother ride to the
doctor's office in a carriage, the connection with André does not escape her: "je
n'osais pas lui dire: Est-ce la même? Ressemble-t-elle à la calèche qui venait à
Arras? [I didn't dare ask her: Is it the same? Does it look like the carriage which
came to Arras?]" (*La Bâtarde* 79). This is a reference to the time when her fa-

ther would come via carriage to visit Berthe during her pregnancy. On the way home, the ghost of André is even more present as the resemblance between tuberculous father and post-operative daughter is striking:

> Je vomis du sang, après l'intervention, sur les coussins de la calèche. Je supportais la brûlure dans ma gorge mais je ne supportais pas le flot de sang dans la calèche qu'elle avait tant attendue. Je réincarnais André. . . . Je suis sûre aujourd'hui que je voulais cracher le sang comme il le crachait; je voulais me rattacher à lui.

> [After the operation, I vomited blood on the carriage cushions. I could stand the burning in my throat, but I could not stand the stream of blood in the carriage for which she had waited so long. I was André's reincarnation. . . . Today I am sure that I wanted to spit blood as he spit it; I wanted to ally myself with him.] (*La Bâtarde* 79)

Here, Berthe's desire to have André back supports Violette's wanting to be a husband to her. However, this desire comes too late: Berthe has already married. In this passage we also see Violette enjoying the attention that she receives from Berthe as the reincarnation of her father. Interestingly enough, it is not until Berthe has established herself as a middle-class lady with a husband and a business that she begins to appreciate Violette's resemblance to André, instead of resenting it. Ironically, it is precisely this set of conditions that constitutes Berthe's betrayal of Violette and which triggers Violette's turning toward her dead father. As a result, the pleasure of reading is an illicit pleasure, linked to the outlawed figure of her father, the seducer.

Violette's first encounter with a text is at the age of eight, just following the death of her grandmother, Fidéline. She had been entrusted with the mission of transporting a *cahier de chansons* from her neighbor Céline, "la jeune fille sacrifiée qui soignait sa mère et sa grand-mère alitées [the girl who sacrificed her life to tend her bedridden mother and grandmother]" (*La Bâtarde* 60), to another neighbor, Estelle. "Ne l'ouvre pas, surtout ne l'ouvre pas, me dit Céline en me confiant à la nuit tombante un cahier différent des autres [Don't open it, whatever you do don't open it, Céline said in entrusting me with a booklet. Very different from the others at nightfall]" (*La Bâtarde* 49). This *cahier* was different in the sense that it contained erotic material. Violette recounts taking it into the tall weeds of the orchard[3] to read:

> Une femme racontait sa nuit de noces, elle comparait à une anguille le sexe d'un homme dans le sexe d'une femme. Je ne comprenais pas: je refermai l'étrange cahier, je tombai à plat ventre dessus. Je n'imaginais rien ou plutôt j'imaginais trop. Je voyais des anguilles chez les poissonniers: j'imaginais la virilité sinueuse sous le pantalon, depuis le nombril jusqu'à la cheville. Mon poing tapotait ma tempe et, chaque fois que je chuchotais: c'est impossible, la couverture du cahier me répondait: c'est possible. Je sortis des mauvaises herbes, je courus jusqu'à la maison de celle qui attendait le cahier. Nos mains tremblaient également quand je le lui remis.

[A woman was relating her wedding night, she compared a man's penis to an eel in a woman's vagina. I couldn't understand: I re-closed the strange book, I fell flat on my stomach on top of it. I imagined nothing, or rather I imagined too much. I could see the eels at the fish-sellers' stalls: I imagined the writhing masculinity under a man's pant-leg, from the navel all the way down to the ankle. My fist beat against my temple, and each time that I whispered: it's impossible, the book's cover replied: it's possible. I left the weeds, I ran to the house of the one who was expecting the notebook. Our hands were trembling as one when I gave it to her.] (*La Bâtarde* 49–50)

This episode was obviously very troubling for the young Violette. Certainly the image of an eel writhing the full length of a man's pants was vivid and disturbing. She tried to deny or suppress the contents of the cahier by lying on it, and to counter the images in her head by hitting her fist against her temple, by telling herself that they were not possible. In spite of her resistance, the persistent response (also whispered?) of the notebook cover convinces, seduces. Even as Violette hands over the cahier, her trembling hands indicate not so much fear as intrigue.

Immediately following the *cahier* incident, Violette recounts her first sexual experience at the hands of her neighbor Aimé: "Sa main légère monta sous ma jupe. . . . La promenade des doigts me grandissait [His light hand went up under my skirt. . . . The stroking fingers made me bigger]" (*La Bâtarde* 50). Here for the first time we see the cycle of seduction in Violette's story centered on a text: Aimé sings songs to Berthe from the cahier in the orchard, Violette goes to the orchard to read the cahier and then to Aimé for a sexual experience. Violette's excitement at reading the erotic text and the powerful effects she recognizes in erotic literature translate themselves years later into erotic texts of her own.[4]

After this most marking first encounter with texts, Violette's next brush with literature is disappointing. Even though it is again with the complicity of Céline, Violette finds no pleasure at all in reading. Céline resembles Emma Bovary in her reading tastes. In addition to the erotic *cahiers*, she reads books from the Bibliothèque Rose to experience a sense of adventure or romance in her too-mundane life, and lends them to Violette. This latter shuns them, however, refusing even to become a part of the reader's continuum:

Je prenais un livre, je l'ouvrais sur me genoux, je le feuilletais. Les histoires de la comtesse de Ségur m'ennuyaient. Mes malheurs semblaient plus réels que ceux de Sophie quand je perdais une médaille, cent sous, un parapluie

[I would pick up a book, I would open it on my lap, I would flip through it. The stories of the Comtesse de Ségur bored me. My misfortunes seemed more real than Sophie's when I lost a medallion, a penny, an umbrella]" (*La Bâtarde* 60).[5]

She cannot become seduced by this insipid literature, because she sees her own life as more vital.

The next time we see Violette relating to literature, she has returned to school, where she has been sent to live following the wedding. It is in this context that she first becomes seduced. The seduction does not take place immediately, however, demonstrating that seduction by literature was not a simple (if unconscious) gesture of rejection on the part of Violette toward her mother, meant to bolster her association with her father. Instead, Violette's initial resistance to literature at school shows that her seduction was genuine, and that only later did she recognize reading as an act of resistance to her mother.

When Violette arrives at school, then, she can no longer avoid reading, yet is no more seduced than she was earlier. As she reads the plays of Corneille and Racine, with their discourses on adult love, Violette is immune to the power of these classics of French literature. This is not because of any lack inherent in these plays, but because of her continued inability to relate to the situations they describe:

> Comment les enfants de douze à quatorze ans pourraient-elles se mettre dans la peau de créateurs qui ont aimé, fait l'amour avant d'écrire leur drames? Oui, Corneille embellissait le chien dans la chienne pendant nos promenades de jeudi. Voilà le pouvoir de ses tirades.

> [How could twelve- to fourteen-year-old girls put themselves inside the skin of artists who had loved, and made love, before writing their dramas? Sure, Corneille made the dog in the bitch more attractive during our Thursday walks. That was the power of his monologues.] (*La Bâtarde* 78)

This may appear to be an inauspicious beginning for the future writer, but in fact it illuminates the narrator's conception of the power of literature. Her reaction to the romantic turmoil of Rodrigue and Chimène, whose passion she could only equate with animals mating in the streets, is lukewarm. For the young Violette, adult sexual desire is outside the scope of her experience and thus incomprehensible: she can put herself "inside the skin" neither of the writers nor of their characters.

It is not until reading Chateaubriand that literature truly touches our protagonist: "Je frémis enfin pour Chateaubriand, pour Lucile [I quivered finally for Chateaubriand, for Lucile]." This first textual seduction coincides with her identification with incestuous desire. Unlike the incomprehensible adult love of the tragedies of Corneille and Racine, Chateaubriand's story of impossible love between a brother and a sister was something that Violette could relate to: "J'espérais que l'inceste était consommé" [I hoped that the incest was consommated](*La Bâtarde* 79). After Violette's experience with her mother Berthe, whose warm bed and attention Violette lost to her stepfather, the story of intrafamilial love in Chateaubriand's tale made her quiver with recognition. For the first time, she could feel herself *inside the skin* of the writer.

This first experience of the pleasures of reading for Violette Leduc is of interest to us on several counts. Firstly, Violette's pleasure at reading is a physical one: "I quivered."[6] This initial experience of literature that connects with— i.e. *seduces*—the reader on an erotic level will be important to Violette in her future both as a reader and as a writer. It will become the lens through which she sees all literature. In addition, as we shall see in the following chapters, Leduc will endeavor to produce a similar—clearly physical, sexual—reaction in her own readers. In her movement from being a reader to being a writer, Leduc modifies her primary relation to seduction and literature. Once she begins producing literature herself, instead of being merely seduced *by* it, she seduces *with* it.[7]

A second point of interest in Violette's recounting of the first time that she was "touched" by literature is that it foreshadows her future as a writer of autobiographical fiction: "Il décrit admirablement, expliquait notre professeur, mais il affaiblit quand même sa description avec son ombre sur la page. Je soulevais les épaules ['He describes admirably,' our teacher explained, 'but he nevertheless weakens his description with his shadow on the page.' I shrugged my shoulders]" (*La Bâtarde* 79). Here, Violette's teacher tells the students that Chateaubriand lessens his literary impact by telling his own story. Violette cannot understand this reaction, given her own very strong one. Chateaubriand could be said to be Leduc's literary ancestor, with his emphasis on emotional (and for Leduc, physical) impact, poetically accurate description and dramatic stories culled from his own life. For these reasons, this episode was surely a formative one for Violette.

Finally, it is important to note that this first instance of literary seduction directly precedes Violette's bloody carriage ride in which she evokes her father, "the seducer." This association of seduction with literature is critical: as we shall see later, Leduc structures her text in such a way as to suture scenes of seduction to those concerning reading and literature throughout this novel. Disappointed in her relationship with her mother, Violette reads to be seduced. When she eventually becomes a writer herself, she will write in order to seduce others. Given the association of André "the seducer" with literature, one is tempted to speculate that Violette took up literary production to seduce her mother, her original, and lost, love object. Berthe, however, remained unmoved by Leduc's novels her entire life.

*
**

The next time we see Violette in her relation to literature, she is again associated with her father: "Bien habillée, bien chaussée, bien coiffée, je devenais plus indulgente quand j'évoquais le séducteur. Ma mère me détaillait avant que je sorte, elle disait: «Son père, c'est son père» ['Her father, it's her father']" (*La Bâtarde* 85). In addition, Violette reinforces this identification by walking down her father's street, and coughing as he would have done in front of a passer-by.[8]

This seductive performance is followed directly by a scene in which Violette goes to a bookstore, where she is clearly seduced by the books contained within: "J'étais *attirée, intriguée, envoûtée* par les couvertures jaunes des éditions de Mercure de France, par les couvertures blanches des éditions Gallimard [I was *attracted, intrigued, enchanted* by the yellow covers of the Mercure de

France books, by the white covers of the Gallimard books] (*La Bâtarde* 85–86).
This is modern literature, let it be noted; these are her *father's* books, not Céline's boring Bibliothèque Rose. Violette is not just attracted to these volumes,
but describes herself as *enchanted:* "envoûtée." She is also intrigued, and as we
have seen, "intrigue" and its Latin root *intricare* can be used to shed light on the
connection between seduction and literature.

Violette's attraction to books is characterized in terms of seduction
throughout much of *La Bâtarde*: Violette couches her discussion of her relationship with literature in the vocabulary of a sexualized seduction.[9] In this passage,
the white and yellow covers of the modern novels entice Violette from the other
side of the storefront window. Buying and reading one becomes an illicit pleasure for the young protagonist:

> [La vieille demoiselle de magasin] prit *Mort de quelqu'un* de Jules Romains, elle me re-
> garda de travers. J'étais trop jeune pour lire de la littérature moderne. Je lus *Mort de
> quelqu'un*, je fumais une cigarette pour mieux jouir de ma complicité avec un auteur
> moderne

> [(The old crone of a bookseller) took down *Mort de quelqu'un* by Jules Romains, and
> gave me a sideways look. I was too young to be reading modern literature. I read *Mort
> de quelqu'un*, I smoked a cigarette to better enjoy my complicity with a modern writer]"
> (*La Bâtarde* 86).

The oblique look of the bookstore saleswoman is a marker of her disapproval of
Violette's choice of reading material. This look is meant to signify that Violette
is too young for that type of reading, giving the impression that reading modern
literature is an *illicit* pleasure. This impression is confirmed by Violette's assertion that to better enjoy—"mieux *jouir* de"—her complicity with the modern
author—again, there is the sense that she is doing something illicit—she smokes
a cigarette, the post-orgasmic activity *par excellence*. Finally, this "complicity"
always takes place at night, in bed: "Plus tard, *sous mon drap*, lorsque je revins
dans une pension, à la lueur d'une lampe électrique, je retrouvai les granges, les
fruits d'André Gide. . . . [Mon soulier] était le seul confident digne de mes
longues veillées, de mes *transports littéraires* [Later, by flashlight *under the
covers*, when I was back living at school, I rediscovered André Gide's barns, his
fruits. . . . (My shoe) was the only confidant worthy of my *long, sleepless nights*,
my *literary ecstasies*]" (*La Bâtarde* 86–87, emphasis added). Here we can
clearly see how Violette has framed her relation to literature in sexual common-
places. Activities that happen under the sheets and involve ecstasies that last late
into the night and that one confesses only to a confidant cannot help but be
identified with the sexual.

When we see Violette in her relation to literature again, it is once more associated with seduction, but in this case it is a failed one: Violette is lying next
to the sleeping Aline—a girl she met while attending her father's Protestant
church—in a "chambre étincelante de vertu [room sparkling with virtue]" (*La*

Bâtarde 95). Unable to sleep next to the virtuous object of her desire, Violette performs an "examen de conscience," and again it is a question of literature:

> Je ne me disais pas Tolstoï, Dostoïevsky valent des années de collège. Je ne parlais pas d'eux. Ils étaient les confidents de mes nuits blanches. Je vivais dans leur univers, je *me donnais* à leurs personnages, je les engloutissais parce que plus je lisais leurs romans, plus la famine se développait à chaque page.

> [I didn't tell myself 'Tolstoy, Dostoyevsky were worth years of schooling.' I didn't mention them. They were the confidants of my sleepless nights. I lived in their universe, *I gave myself over* to their characters, I devoured them because the more I read their novels, the more the famine grew with every passing page.] (*La Bâtarde* 96, emphasis added)

As Violette lies unsatisfied in Aline's bed, she resorts to thoughts of literature to lessen the disturbing feelings of rejection: she was unable to "give herself" physically to the girl, as she does to the characters of Russian novels. In this case, when Violette's personal seduction was unsuccessful, she turns to literary seduction for satisfaction. It is there that her "famine" can be properly addressed, and where she has no qualms about devouring her imaginary lovers. We can see that here, literature is used by Violette as a substitute for a lover.

Perhaps Violette's reservations about giving herself—and Aline—up to the full force of her desire, "cet arc tendu de l'attente [this bow made taut with waiting]" (*La Bâtarde* 95), are due to the violent expression of sexual desire that she has seen in the past. Some time earlier, Violette had witnessed the tragic love affair between a neighbor boy Cataplame—"un fêlé [a kid who's a bit cracked in the head]"—and Madame Armande, whose "mari se battait au front [husband was fighting at the front]" (*La Bâtarde* 57). For several days Mme Armande had provoked Cataplame sexually with an elaborate ritual involving shaking a dust rag at him from the window. When she finally let him in, nothing was heard from her house for a long time. One day, however, there was a group clustered in front of the house. When Violette inquired as to the reason for the gathering, a girl answered her: "—Cataplame a tranché la gorge de sa maîtresse ['Cataplame slit his mistress's throat']" (*La Bâtarde* 59). The narrative thread is dropped after this sentence and the reader is left to draw her or his own conclusions. This is a common Leducian strategy when dealing with emotionally charged episodes. Leduc silences the narrative voice at such powerful moments, leaving the reader emotionally disoriented. By refusing to provide the reader with a sense of closure or reconciliation, Leduc obliges her reader to fill in the gaps herself, which greatly increases the emotional impact of the story.

This deadly seduction scene immediately precedes the story of Céline's dull books from the Bibliothèque Rose, which hold no interest for Violette. Clearly, these books purporting to contain exciting romances are no match for what has been happening in Violette's own neighborhood. In this case, the scenes of literature and seduction are juxtaposed in order to demonstrate the power of literature *not* to seduce its readers. We see here, as we have seen with the plays of Corneille and Racine, that only with certain kinds of literature is Violette susceptible to seduction. Moreover, it is important to note that literature is not always the seducing force, if it seduces at all. It can be used as an antidote, stand-in, or context for seduction; what must be recalled is that the two are always seen together. By the end of *La Bâtarde*, Leduc's reader has been trained to expect—even create—the connection between literature and seduction.

Later in the novel, Leduc uses reading—at night, under her covers, when she should have been sleeping—as a backdrop to Isabelle's seduction of Violette in the boarding school. Instead of literature substituting for the attention of a lover as with Aline, here a lover will act as a substitute for reading. Later still, Leduc juxtaposes literature and seduction to even greater effect: Violette describes her seduction in the Jardin du Luxembourg by a stranger who converses with her on the topic of modern literature. We will examine this scene in detail as it will be useful to our analysis of seduction techniques in *La Folie en tête*.

The seduction in question takes place during Violette's first visit to the park, prompted by having read "tant de citations sur le Jardin du Luxembourg dans *Comœdia*, dans *Les Nouvelles littéraires* [So many quotations mentioning the Jardin du Luxembourg in *Comœdia*, in *Les Nouvelles littéraires*]" (*La Bâtarde* 165). She had gone to eat her dinner of fresh peaches, and as she sat alone, she was surprised to hear a male voice ask for one. The stranger, an Argentine, chose an unlikely seduction tactic—"Il me disait qu'il aimait la littérature moderne, qu'il lisait Proust [He told me that he loved modern literature, that he read Proust];" unlikely, but how appropriate for a girl of nineteen who has a great susceptibility to being seduced by literature. Violette does not feel threatened by the situation, and even feels protected by the young couples around them—"Qu'est-ce que je risquais? Jeunes filles et jeunes hommes enlacés nous encerclaient sans nous voir [What was the danger? Young men and women in each others' arms surrounded us but paid us no heed]"—but her chaperones, inattentive, leave her vulnerable. Already he has worked his magic on her: "Il changeait mes fruits avec ses doigts effilés, avec son accent chantant. Nous mangions des mangues [He transformed my fruits with his long, slender fingers, his sing-song accent. We were eating mangoes]" (*La Bâtarde* 166).

This seducer, perceived by Violette as a stunning creation,[10] proceeds to eat not one but perhaps all of her peaches, and then suggests—presumably since her dinner was by then gone—that she join him for dinner. The description of him eating the peaches is of interest, as it marks the situation as being sexually charged: "*L'inconnu ouvrit ses jambes*, il se pencha en avant, il mangea une, deux, trois, quatre, cinq pêches. *Le jus mouillait les graviers* [*The stranger spread his legs*, he bent forward, he ate one, two, three, four, five peaches. *The juice dripped on the gravel*]" (*La Bâtarde* 166, emphasis added). Here the counting of the individual peaches increases the tension of the scene, compounding the suggestivity of the peaches themselves and their juice running down between open legs. We know that his seduction is successful because instead of being annoyed at having her dinner unexpectedly devoured, Violette gladly follows him to the restaurant.

At dinner, Violette and the Argentine tried to outdo each other displaying their of knowledge of modern literature. If he was testing her, Violette apparently passed, as he gave her an expensive Pléïade edition of *Du côté de chez Swann* as a memento. Reflecting later on his motives, Violette writes:

> Qu'est-ce qu'il voulait? Initier une Française à la littérature française. Il était si aimable, si correct, si sûr de lui quant à ses connaissances littéraires, qu'il n'existait pas. Il disparut de son hôtel rue Cujas, je l'oubliai. Je ne l'écrivis pas à Hermine, je ne le racontais pas à ma mère.

> [What did he want? To initiate a French girl to French literature. He was so friendly, so proper, so sure of his literary knowledge that he didn't exist. He disappeared from his hotel on the rue Cujas, I forgot him. I didn't write to Hermine about it, I didn't tell my mother.] (*La Bâtarde* 167)

As the readers of Leduc's novel, we cannot be sure of the Argentine's intentions. What is clear, however, is that Violette obfuscates what they were, denying that they were suggestive. We can see that Violette is disingenuous with herself, as she is with her readers, for the following reasons.

Firstly, if Violette decided to keep the encounter with the exotic stranger a secret from both her lover Hermine and her mother—with whom she shared everything—it could not be that "he didn't exist." She chose to pass the matter under silence because it was a betrayal of both women's authority and positions as love object. If she did not feel that what she had done with the Argentine would be seen as objectionable by both women, Violette would not have chosen to hide this incident from both of them. In fact, it was not that he did not exist for Violette—clearly he did—but it was for Hermine and Berthe that he did not exist.

Secondly, it is not true that when he left his hotel in the Latin Quarter, Violette forgot him. In fact, she goes on to say just the opposite:

> *Du côté de chez Swann*. Les deux volumes à portée de la main m'ont suivie pendant plus de trente années. La poussière ne veut pas d'eux. Si je les ouvre, j'entends comme si c'était hier les vocalises de l'accent argentin.

> [*Du côté de chez Swann*. Both volumes have stuck with me m at arm's reach, for thirty years. No dust collects on them. If I open them, I can hear the sounds of the Argentine accent as though it were yesterday.]" (*La Bâtarde* 167)

Far from having forgotten him, Violette experiences a Proustian moment every time she opens the books, which must be often if no dust ever gathers on them. As much as she tries to deny this seduction, Violette was clearly drawn in by the beautiful stranger and his discussion of literature. If we are to believe her report,

LIBRARY OF DAVIDSON COLLEGE

however, in spite of the sexual subtext of their encounter, their intercourse did not lead beyond the discussion of literature.

*
**

In the movement from *La Bâtarde* to *La Folie en tête*, there is traced a parallel movement from being seduced to seducing, from reading to writing. As we have noted, if *La Bâtarde* mainly concerned Violette reading in a Bovaryan manner, in *La Folie en tête* we see her doing more writing than reading, moving Violette towards a Barthesian frame. In fact, one of the opening sections of the book shows her going to Mme Aubijoux's "librairie-papeterie-confiserie-épicerie fine [bookstore-paper stand-candy shop-specialized grocery]" to buy a new folder in which to keep the manuscript for her first book (*La Folie en tête* 12–13). Readers discover later that she is to present her manuscript to Simone de Beauvoir. Violette's enthusiasm for this moment in her life is remarkable. She begins her chapter in the following way:

> Février 1945. Il est le mois le plus extraordinaire de mon existence. Il ne succéda pas à janvier, il ne précéda pas mars-avril-mai. Il est détaché des autres. Il y a vingt ans, il est une feuille de laurier arraché au temps. Je me moquais du mot merveilleux jusqu'à février 1945. Un ballon de foire, un traîne-ruisseau, une pièce de rechange, un pétard lorsque nous sommes à court d'enthousiasme. Février a été merveilleux. Je pleurai pendant trente ans, je brodais février.

> [February 1945. It is the most extraordinary month of my existence, it did not follow January, it didn't precede March-April-May. It's detached from the others. Twenty years ago, it's a laurel leaf torn out from time. I looked down my nose at the word marvelous until February 1945. A circus balloon, a ragamuffin, a spare part, a firecracker when we're short on enthusiasm. I cried for thirty years, I idealized February.] (*La Folie en tête* 12)

As the reader will soon find out, this unfettered enthusiasm for February 1945 is due to the fact that Violette is about to become a published writer. As she points out, this magical moment is a turning point in her life. *La Folie en tête* is the story of this turning point. While both books treat Violette's life, *La Bâtarde* is a book about reading and *La Folie en tête* is a book about writing. Consequently, we can see Violette relocating herself along the continuum of reader seduction.

Throughout *La Folie en tête*, Violette insists upon a difference between how she reads as a writer and how she read as an adolescent; significantly, this is the same difference that we have traced between the Bovaryan and the Barthesian reader.[11] Here, in response to Simone de Beauvoir's query,[12] Violette contemplates reading Samuel Beckett:

> Est-ce que je lis? Récemment j'appuyais *Molloy* de Beckett sur une joue, sur l'autre. . . .
> Un grand écrivain est comme un grand frère, il tombe dans votre existence, c'est un lien plus fort que celui du sang. Il arrive à l'improviste. Il a défriché, vous êtes labouré. . . .

Beckett avec sa spéléologie, ses mots simples . . . et voilà ma prison et ma condition de-
venues un cristal. Rien n'a changé, tout en moi est transparent; j'ai lu *Molloy*.

[Am I reading? Recently I pressed *Molloy* on one cheek, on the other . . . a great writer
is like an older brother, he lands in your existence, it's a bond stronger than blood. He
arrives unexpectedly. He has cleared the ground, you are ploughed under. . . . Beckett
with his speleology, his simple words . . . and suddenly my prison and my condition
have become a crystal. Nothing has changed, everything in my is transparent; I've read
Molloy.] (*La Folie en tête* 311–12)

In this passage we can see Violette using Beckett and his novel for both work
and play. Beckett (and other great modern writers) serves as a role model for
Violette, as a kind of older brother to show her the way in literature. If her
writing had been lying fallow, this figure would change that, making it possible
for her to write again. But this is only a small part of Violette's commentary on
Beckett. What interests us most in this discussion is the way in which her comments evoke a Barthesian reading of *Molloy*. This type of reading, as we have
seen in the previous chapter, is one which occurs obliquely, across the text, and
is very attentive to language as opposed to plot. A writerly text, when read in
this way, can produce jouissance, a verbal loss that transports the reader away
from the writing.

Curiously, this comment about Beckett could have come straight from *Le
Plaisir du texte*. When Violette writes about "Beckett with his speleology, his
simple words" it not only shows that her focus is linguistic, but echoes Barthes'
own words: that a reading should not be hampered by any "*perte* verbale—au
sens que ce mot peut avoir en spéléologie [verbal *loss*—in the speleological
sense of that word]" (*Le Plaisir du texte* 22/12). This loss is vertiginous, taking
the reader away from the text and to an *espace de jouissance* where pleasure
cannot be spoken. There can be no doubt that it is jouissance that she gets from
reading Beckett: her comment that after reading suddenly her body becomes
transparent—transformed into a crystal—is evidence of that; this is a remarkable
description of the post-orgasmic state. Even at the beginning of this passage,
when Violette writes of pressing the book against one cheek and then the other,
it shows that her reading had broken down, that Beckett's "simple words" had
taken her away from the text. Moreover, this is a gesture of tenderness, even
gratitude, which speaks volumes regarding Violette's relation to the book itself.
Here, her seduction appears complete, indeed so complete that it is unspeakable,
and can be expressed only through action, language not being sufficient to the
task.

While Beckett was certainly an influence on our writer,[13] it is the writing of
Jean Genet that looms largest over *La Folie en tête*. In fact, only Violette's
comments about her own writing get more attention than Genet's. Unlike Beckett, who to our knowledge exists only for Violette as the figure behind the writing of the trilogy, Genet is a flesh-and-blood reality for Violette. In *La Folie en
tête*, Genet is an impossible love object for Violette, along with Simone de

Beauvoir and Jacques Guérin. Violette's reading of—and seduction by—his *Miracle de la Rose* predated their first meeting, in the bar at the *Pont-Royal*. When she hears from Beauvoir that the new arrival is Genet, she can only look at his belt buckle; "Son visage, je me le réservais pour plus tard. [I was saving his face for later]" When she manages to gather the courage to look him in the face, she is struck dumb by his piercing look: "Les yeux clairs de Genet m'interloquaient. Ils entraient en moi, ses yeux froids [Genet's light-colored eyes took my voice away. They entered into me, his cold eyes]" (*La Folie en tête* 123). It seems that even if she had not been seduced by his writing, she certainly would not have escaped his cold eyes, so reminiscent of her mother's and Simone de Beauvoir's.

But she *was* seduced by his writing, in both the Bovaryan and Barthesian senses. We can see the Bovaryan aspect of her seduction in her "adolescent" reading:

> Je relis *Miracle de la Rose*. Fièvre, palpitations, frissons comme au temps de ma première lecture, il y a dix-neuf ans. J'étais une adolescente de trente-huit ans, je découvrais le bonheur d'adorer, celui d'admirer. Je suis une adolescente de cinquante-sept ans, je découvre le bonheur d'adorer, celui d'admirer. Pour qui avais-je la fièvre? Pour qui suis-je transie? Pour Harcamone, le condamné à mort. Je relisais Genet, je palpitais.

> [I'm rereading *Miracle de la Rose*. Fever, palpitations, shivers just as when I read it the first time, nineteen years ago. I was a thirty-eight-year-old adolescent, I was discovering the joy of adoration, the joy of admiration. I am a fifty-seven-year old adolescent, I am discovering the joy of adoration, the joy of admiration. For whom did I have this fever? By whom was I transfixed? It was Harcamone, the condemned man. I reread Genet, I was all aquiver.] (*La Folie en tête* 113)

This emotional attachment to the protagonist is typical of the Bovaryan reader, whether it be romantic or an attachment of identification. Here, Violette insists that no matter what her age, she will always feel the emotional tie to Harcamone in her reading that she repeatedly characterizes as adolescent. In this way she shows us that she will always, on some level, be a Bovaryan reader of *Miracle de la Rose*. In addition, when Violette writes, "I was saving his face for later," we find an echo with Emma Bovary's refusal to look directly at Léon but rather only at his shadow, the better to savor his image as her romantic hero. Certainly Genet comes off as Violette's literary hero. Moreover, we are clearly within a sexual context: it is Genet's belt buckle which fixates Violette, and when she does manage to look him in the face, she is *penetrated* by his eyes: "They entered into me, his cold eyes."

However, Violette also manifests a Barthesian relationship with this text. In the same paragraph, referring to Genet and Proust, she writes: "Je suis captive de l'un et de l'autre. *Je lis et je me noie*, ce sont leurs *périodes* [I am the prisoner of the one and the other. *I read and I am drowning*, it's their *intervals*]" (*La Folie en tête* 113, emphasis added). This reference to the intervals or gaps in their writing once again recalls Barthes' elaboration of his theory of the *plaisir du texte*: "c'est la faille, la coupure, la déflation, le *fading* qui saisit le sujet au cœur de la jouissance [the site of a loss, the seam, the cut, the deflation, the *dissolve* which seizes the subject in the midst of bliss]" (*Le Plaisir du texte* 15/7). Once again there is the notion of a "verbal loss." This same notion is present even at her first reading of Genet's text,[14] when she writes that "Je tombe dans la lecture de *Miracle de la Rose* comme on tombe dans l'amour [I fall into the reading of *Miracle de la Rose* as one falls into love]" (*La Folie en tête* 111). Note that she does not use the expression "tomber amoureux," as one might expect. To say "tomber dans l'amour" is to emphasize the act of falling, by focusing the reader's attention on the language.

Finally, we can see the same idea of Barthesian *emportement* in the following passage, in which Violette writes about the experience of recopying a chapter from Genet's novel. She is recopying this paragraph into her own manuscript, while she is sitting in the woods. The act of recopying her favorite text is a labor of love for Violette, and involves the simultaneous act of reading and writing. By recopying Genet's text, Violette can share her appreciation of it with her reader. Moreover, and most importantly for our purposes, the act of recopying obliges her to focus on each word of the text, facilitating the Barthesian, oblique reading, and jouissance. Leduc's description of her recopying is an extended one, but I cite it in its entirety to give the reader a clearer sense of Violette's reaction:

> J'ai arrêté ma lecture à ce paragraphe, j'ai regardé mes mains; mes veines gonflées m'effrayaient. Exceptionnelles, l'atmosphère et la température pendant que je recopiais du Genet. Il ne fait pas chaud, il ne fait pas froid. Tout, tout-tout-tout est pris, retenu dans des tenailles de velours. C'est un spasme, c'est une immobilité à perte de vue. Certitude d'un souvenir imaginaire uni à un événement qui ne se produira pas. Je suis dans un bois et, en même temps, je suis dans Paris avec le même calme, je m'en vais au cinéma, je retrouve un être qui m'aime, je l'aime. Tout vit, tout respire dans le bois, cependant tout semble être mort sans raideur: est-ce cela une atmosphère surnaturelle? Est-ce cette immobilité implacable qui me favorise? Je descends du taxi, mon amant m'attend dans l'entrée du cinéma. Un original tire trois coups de revolver au fond du bois, ensuite les cloches d'un troupeau fleurissent la colline. Je ferme le livre de Genet.

> [I stopped reading at this paragraph, I looked at my hands; my swollen veins frightened me. Very unusual, the atmosphere and temperature while I was recopying Genet. It's not hot, it's not cold. Everything, everything-everything-everything is caught, held in velvet pincers. It's a spasme, it's a stillness as far as the eye can see. Certainty of an imaginary memory attached to an event that will never happen. I am in a woods, and at the same time I am in Paris with the same calm, I'm going to the movies, I'm meeting someone who loves me, whom I love. Everything is alive, everything is breathing in the woods, nevertheless, everything appears dead without stiffness: is this a supernatural atmosphere? Is it this implacable immobility which favors me? I step out of the taxi, my lover awaits at the cinema door. Some joker fires three shots from a revolver deep in the woods, next the bells of a flock cover the hillside with blossoms. I close Genet's book.] (*La Folie en tête* 112)

As she reads and recopies the Genet text, Violette experiences the *emportement* of *jouissance*, for that is clearly what it is a question of in this passage, in spite of the fact that Violette chooses not to call our attention to it as such. It is a time-out-of-time experience, where everything is suspended and in motion simultaneously. Time, in fact, is not only suspended, but looped: the sensation of a memory of something that will not happen in the future indicates that she is on an unreal plane of existence where past and future exist together. This looping-in-suspension furthers the sensation of vertigo that Barthes associates with *jouissance*. There is also a supernatural quality to this moment that characterizes *jouissance*: in this time gap of "la petite mort," everything is alive yet appears dead, but not yet stiffened: only recently—briefly?—expired. Violette's reference to the "velvet pincers" mimics linguistically the expression of sexual ecstasy with Isabelle in *La Bâtarde*: "On me tenaillait, on m'épiçait [There were pincers pulling at me, I was being filled with spices]" (116). The *emportement* does not take place only through time, but also through space: Violette is not only taken away from the book, but also from the woods where she is sitting, to a movie house in Paris. It takes gunshots to awaken Violette from her reverie and bring her back to the woods where she has been sitting with the book. In recopying this passage for her own readers, Violette is shown both seducing and seduced.

✳
✳✳

Thus far we have examined literary seduction in Leduc's works from the perspective of Violette as seducee. However, once she becomes a writer, Violette crosses over to the other side of literary seduction to be the seducer. We see this happen in *La Folie en tête* when Violette has the opportunity to develop personal relationships with two of her readers who are just as prone to literary seduction as she was at their age. Patrice, followed by Flavien—both lonely adolescents who have read and were moved by *L'Asphyxie*—correspond with Violette. This literary seduction harkens back to Violette's encounter with the Argentine, with the older partner seducing with the titles of books and the names of authors. Violette hopes that her correspondence appears to the boys as a literary seduction, but in fact it evolves into a literal, sexual, one.

The moment at which Violette receives Patrice's first letter is consequential, as it is that moment at which she comes to the realization that she might be a writer after all: "Un inconnu, ou une inconnue, m'écrivait aux éditions Gallimard . . . J'avais deux adresses, je n'en revenais pas. Après tout, j'étais peut-être un écrivain [An unknown man or woman was writing to me at the Gallimard press . . . I had two addresses, I couldn't believe it. Maybe I was a writer after all]"(*La Folie en tête* 213). Her hesitation is understandable: as of this time, her first novel had sold but few copies.

This is an important realization for Violette, particularly in the context of our discussion. For the first time, Violette is forced to recognize that she has shifted her position on the continuum of readers. It is unsettling for her, as she recognizes that she is on the other side of the mirror: Violette is no longer the reader who writes fan letters, but the writer who receives them. She points to her past as a writer of such letters twice in this passage. As she signs her reply to Patrice, she writes: "«Avec sympathie attentive.» La «sympathie attentive» me venait d'André Gide à qui j'avais écris à seize ans ['With attentioned interest.' I got the 'attentioned interest' from André Gide to whom I had written when I was sixteen]" (*La Folie en tête* 214). In order to *authorize* the writing of this response to Patrice, Violette borrows Gide's formula. In addition, she remarks that "Je devais refroidir et glacer l'adolescente que j'avais été si je voulais répondre à cet inconnu [I needed to restrain and cool down the adolescent that I had been in order to answer this stranger]" (*La Folie en tête* 213). This suggests that she still feels more akin to Patrice—this "jeune homme fiévreux [feverish young man]" (*La Folie en tête* 214)—than to the writer Gide. But by taking this step, Violette claims the condition of writer for herself, even if she does remain ambivalent. She writes: "Non, je ne suis pas un écrivain. Petite écriture nette, quelconque. L'encre noire, c'est l'écrivain attaché à ce qu'il écrit. Moi, je ferme mon cahier, je l'oublie [No, I'm not a writer. Small, precise, nondescript handwriting. Black ink, now that is the writer attached to what he writes. As for me, I close my notebook and forget about it.]" (*La Folie en tête* 213). Here we can see the tension that surrounds this question for Violette: she very much wants to claim this position, yet is still uncomfortable in it.

As Violette writes back to Patrice, it is clearly a seduction. She demonstrates this as she questions herself upon first reading the letter, "Un lecteur serait-il une proie sur laquelle j'allais me jeter? [Could a reader be a prey upon whom I was about to pounce?]" (*La Folie en tête* 213). She chooses seduction as a narrative tactic, not only for Patrice, but for all of her subsequent readers. The violence of the prey/hunter metaphor that Violette uses is remarkable: the poor student will have no choice but to be seduced. Violette lays her trap ("j'appâtai [I set my bait]") by wondering to Patrice if he is unhappy, knowing full well that he is from his letter. This question guarantees an effusive response from the young reader, who will not be able to resist this writer who seems to understand him so well.

It is plain that Violette understands Patrice instinctively because she had once shared his experience. As an adolescent, she had lived, as he does, "enfermé[e] dans la littérature moderne [shut up inside modern literature]" (*La Folie en tête* 213). This "modern literature" in the context of seduction naturally recalls Violette's experience with the Argentine in the Jardin du Luxembourg, with one major exception: this time it is not she who is being seduced, but she who seduces.

Correspondences between Violette's relationship with Patrice and the one she shared with the Argentine abound. As she writes back to Patrice for the first time, she admits that "C'était ma façon de flirter, de glisser les amabilités dans une zone où tout est possible, où tout est impossible. . . . Je posais mes jalons [It was my way of flirting, of slipping kindness into a zone where everything is possible, where everything is impossible. . . . I was staking my claim]" (*La Folie en tête* 214). Her letter serves the same function as the Argentine's peach-eating performance: she is clearing the path for a relationship with the schoolboy. She, too, can pretend to be well intentioned, but this time, she does not try to hide the seduction attempt from the reader. Indeed, when Violette writes that she would have blushed if Simone de Beauvoir or Jacques Guérin—her current love objects—had seen her letter, it is tantamount to an admission of her earlier seduction, of which she decided not to speak with Berthe or Hermine. She writes: "je les trompais l'un et l'autre. Je décidai de ne pas leur parler de la lettre de Patrice [I was cheating on both of them. I decided not to mention the letter from Patrice]" (*La Folie en tête* 214).

Violette maintains her correspondence with Patrice, and they write each other every other day. Again, as she was seduced by the Argentine, Violette uses her knowledge of literature as her mode of seduction:[15]

> Le perroquet lui parle de Van Gogh, de Jean de la Croix, de la Religieuse Portugaise, de Louise Labé, d'Emily Brontë. *Je fornique avec des titres de livres*, je plastronne avec le peu que je sais, je fricote avec les talents, je tripote les génies. Ma souricière pour Patrice est prête entre les noms de Lorca, Pavese, de Faulkner. *Je cache mes pièges avec les passages d'un livre.*

> [The parrot spoke to him of Van Gogh, of John of the Cross, of the Portuguese Nun, of Louise Labé, of Emily Brontë. *I'm fornicating with book titles*, I'm showing off with the little that I know, I'm messing around with people of talent, I'm trifling with geniuses. My mousetrap for Patrice is set between the names of Lorca, Pavese, Faulkner. *I'm hiding my traps with passages from books.*] (*La Folie en tête* 234, emphasis added)

As Violette lays traps for her young reader, here again we are confronted with the metaphor of the hunter and the hunted. This shows us the dark side of seduction: not just enticement, but entrapment. Violette clearly is not proud of what she does: she calls herself "the parrot," suggesting that she only mimics, and she makes a point of highlighting the disrespectful way in which she treats these favorite writers of hers. She cannot help herself, however, because "Ce jeune homme, c'est une occasion [This young man is an opportunity]" (*La Folie en tête* 234). This need she has to seduce Patrice is not the expression of a need to feel superior—"Quoi de plus salissant que la supériorité? [What is more defiling than superiority]" (*La Folie en tête* 234)—but rather a need to establish a relationship with another person.[16] Indeed, on the following page, after she has mailed another letter, she attempts to feel part of the community of older men and women who buy vegetables in the same tired shop she does. It is in vain, however: "ils le devinent, je n'appartiens à aucune société, même à celle des éjectés [they can guess it, I belong to no society at all, not even that of the cast-offs]" (*La Folie en tête* 235).

In fact what Violette is describing is the classic scenario of the dream of love: as an autobiographer, she wants her reader to fall in love with her protagonist, and by extension, with herself. The difference here is that she manages to get her hands on an "actual" reader. By corresponding with Patrice directly, Violette can use not only her own writings to seduce him, but also those of others. Significantly, these are the writings that earlier had seduced Violette herself as a reader.

More compelling still is the fact that Violette's seduction of Patrice is a sort of *mise en abîme* of Leduc's seduction of her real-life readers, the topic of this text. By showing us Violette's seduction of Patrice through literature, Leduc dramatizes her own literary seduction tactics. The difference, however, is in the result.

In *La Folie en tête*, Patrice comes to visit Violette in Paris. Mad with anticipation, she visits a salon for a permanent[17] and calculates in her head what they will do, where he will sleep.[18] She is disappointed, however, when he does not wish to stay over, but Patrice wins her admiration as he suddenly recites page after page of Breton's *Nadja* for Violette from memory. Calling the recitation "notre prière du soir [our evening prayer]" (*La Folie en tête* 260), Violette is purified by the prose, but most especially touched by the boy's love for the writer. "Un adolescent m'a donné ce qu'il a de plus précieux [An adolescent gave me his most precious gift]" (*La Folie en tête* 261). In this way, the "lesson" that Patrice gives to Violette is not to stray too far from the love of literature. Although their meeting was initially disappointing to Violette, ultimately Patrice's visit was useful to her, insofar as he showed her to appreciate her own writing. In one of the most touching moments in the text, we see Violette embracing her new life as a writer—and, not incidentally, herself—with hope and joy for the first time:

> J'ouvre mon lit, je me glisse dedans. . . . Je suis où je dois être. Deux larmes je suis en paix. Finies les larmes, ce soir. J'ai dans la tête une percée de cri d'alouette, c'est l'espoir à longue portée, c'est la lucidité. Je me lève une heure après et je serre contre mon cœur mon cahier dans lequel j'ai fini d'écrire *L'Affamée*

> [I open my bed, I slip inside it. . . . I am where I should be. Two tears and I am at peace. No more tears tonight. In my head I have a clearing born of a lark's song, it's hope in the long-term, it's lucidity. I get up an hour later and squeeze the notebook in which I have just finished *L'Affamée* against my heart.] (*La Folie en tête* 261)

This passage shows Violette literally embracing herself as a writer, indicating that she has overcome her mixed feeling upon receiving Patrice's first letter. This new hope and lucidity are particularly welcome in a book which recounts the author's paranoia and lack of faith in her writing, due to poor book sales. In this case, one of her readers was able to sweep away that darkness, at least for a night.

In contrast to the relationship with Patrice, Violette's correspondence and subsequent encounter with Patrice's friend Flavien does not end so well. Once again, after a passionate exchange of letters, there was to be a meeting. Violette took the train out to his sad little town in Normandy. After waiting in the hotel

all night for him, she had just decided to read in bed[19] before taking the next
train out when he finally arrived. Violette would have been better off missing
him completely, as the visit degenerates progressively. Flavien is a disappointment on all counts. Not only is he no James Dean (269), but he is riddled with
migraines (which he professes to love) and is controlled by his mother. Violette
wonders "Que me donnera-t-il ce Flavien toujours triste? [What will this eter-
nally sad Flavien give me?]" (*La Folie en tête* 271). Certainly not the physical
love that her "ovaries" clamber for. A completely unsatisfying lover, he does
not allow her to touch him, and only likes to kiss interminably: "Si tu voulais,
tordu, ce serait facile, j'ai l'appétit de te connaître. Embrasser, il fallait encore
[If you wanted to, twit, it would be easy, I have an appetite to know you. We
had to keep on kissing]" (*La Folie en tête* 273). He even insists that she hide her
underwear, because "Les dessous d'une femme, c'est laid [Women's underwear
is ugly]." Finally, after several days of anticipatory vaginal contractions, Violette hemorrhages on the bed. "Il est affolé. Cédera-t-il? Il ne céda pas [He was
horrified. Would he capitulate? No.]" (*La Folie en tête* 276). The next day, the
police arrive, looking for the young man, but Flavien's mother decides not to
press charges. Violette learns that "Je devais aider son fils à percer en littérature.
Percer. Tout cela était grotesque [I was supposed to help her son penetrate the
literary world. Penetrate. It was all too grotesque]" (*La Folie en tête* 277).

Obviously, Violette's visit with Flavien was a monumental disappointment.
In this way theirs was not unlike the majority of Violette's relationships. It does,
however, serve as an excellent illustration of Simone de Beauvoir's comment in
her preface to *La Bâtarde* about the dilemma of presence versus absence in the
life of Violette Leduc. She cites Leduc's *L'Affamée*: "«Mirages identiques de la
présence et de l'absence» ['Identical mirages of presence and absence']"[20] and
comments that for Leduc, "L'absence est un supplice: l'attente angoissée d'une
présence; la présence est l'intermède entre deux absences: un martyre [Absence
is a torture: the anguished wait for a presence; presence is the interlude between
two absences: a martyrdom]" (Beauvoir, *La Bâtarde* 10). In her autobiography,
Leduc chronicles a series of passions that play out these tormenting mirages of
betrayal and disappointment in love. Yet in spite of the seemingly endless series
of anguishes, Violette perseveres in her quest for love. "Pourtant," Beauvoir
continues, "elle a besoin d'aimer. Il lui faut quelqu'un à qui dédier ses élans, ses
tristesses, ses enthousiasmes. L'idéal serait de se vouer à un être qui ne
l'encombre pas de sa présence, à qui elle puisse tout donner sans qu'il lui prenne
rien [Nevertheless, she needs to love. She has to have someone to whom she can
dedicate her impulses, her sadness, her enthusiasms. The ideal would be to de-
vote herself to someone who would not encumber her with a presence, to whom
she could give everything without having anything taken from her]" (*La
Bâtarde* 12). This ideal partner can be none other than Leduc's reader, because
only a "lecteur accomplit l'impossible synthèse de l'absence et de la présence
[reader achieves that impossible synthesis of absence and presence]" (*La
Bâtarde* 15). As we have seen in the cases of Patrice and particularly Flavien,
this reader must always remain a material absence in the writer's life.

*
**

This need for seducing her reader can be traced throughout Leduc's writing history: her writing was always meant as a seduction. As we have seen in *La Bâtarde,* she recounts that her first day of writing was meant as a love letter to Sachs. Later, Simone de Beauvoir takes his place as Leduc's mentor. Knowing that Leduc's second book, *L'Affamée,* is the violent story of the first-person narrator's passion for the thinly-veiled figure of Simone de Beauvoir—variously called "Madame" or "celle qui lit dans un café [she who reads in a café]"—reiterates that Leduc maintains the will to seduce her readers—what we could call a will to seduction.

This is what I find most fascinating about Leduc in relation to her readers. Leduc dramatizes her seduction via literature in her writings, and it is this seduction which compels her to eventually become a writer in her own right. In tracing her seduction—her movement along the continuum from Bovaryan (readerly) texts to Barthesian (writerly) texts, Leduc is at the same time tracing her movement from reader to writer. If Violette Leduc ultimately failed to establish real-life love relationships with her first readers, Sachs and Beauvoir, she nevertheless succeeded in making a profound impact on many other readers whom she seduces into a bond of identification with her narrator-protagonist. This seduction via literature of a new set of readers in its turn inspires numbers of them to become writers of autobiographical material as well. Narrative seduction in this case moves in cycles, repeating itself in one generation after another. This form of reader response to her works was probably not what Leduc was expecting. However, if Leduc as an autobiographer participates in the Dream of Love, as I have proposed, I am certain that she would not have been displeased with it. The act of responding to personal writing with personal writing bespeaks a powerful emotional bond between reader and writer. Indeed, this bond, and the writing that it produces, is proof of the seductions of Violette Leduc and her writings.

CHAPTER THREE

Cycles of Seduction II:
René de Ceccatty and Michele Zackheim

Readers are moved by Leduc's writings—we have seen the effects of Violette's relationships with Patrice and Flavien—but Leduc was especially successful with readers whom she did not know personally. Among these are René de Ceccatty and Michele Zackheim. I will take these two readers as case studies of the success of Leduc's seduction tactics. In both cases, a powerful personal identification with Violette was established after an original reading of *La Bâtarde*.

Ceccatty recounts in his 1994 *Violette Leduc: Éloge de la bâtarde*, the influence that the writings of Leduc had on his life, due to the intense identification he had with her literary persona, summarized here:

> Aucun autre écrivain n'a joué un tel rôle dans ma vie personnelle. Aucun autre n'a suscité en moi un tel besoin immédiat d'identification. C'est ce curieux sentiment que j'ai tenté de décrire, tout en confrontant cette œuvre avec d'autres qui ont compté pour moi. Cette fascination singulière, mes nombreuses rencontres avec d'autres lecteurs passionnés m'ont révélé qu'elle ne m'appartenait pas en propre. Pour une raison ou pour une autre, chacun se retrouvait en elle. Chacun devenait Violette Leduc.

> [No other writer has played such a role in my personal life. No other has provoked in me such an immediate need for identification. It is this strange feeling that I have attempted to describe, all the while comparing (Leduc's) œuvre with others which have been important to me. My many encounters with other impassioned readers have shown me that I am not the only one who has experienced this singular fascination. For one reason or another, everyone found him-or herself in her. Everyone became Violette Leduc.]
> (*Éloge de la bâtarde* jacket description)

Ceccatty lives in a world of books: he has been a literary critic for *Le Monde*, has worked for such publishers as Gallimard and Stock, and has published several of his own novels, as well as novels in translation from Italian and Japanese. For him to assert that no other writer has touched him as deeply as Violette Leduc, then, is very powerful. In Ceccatty's world, Leduc's texts stand above all of the others that he has experienced. They were not only pleasant reading, but

51

played an important role in his personal life, due to his intense personal identification with Violette and certain hazards of circumstance.

The purpose of his book is two-pronged: to describe this "strange feeling" of his identification as well as to discuss Leduc's work alongside the works of others. In this way, Ceccatty's *Éloge* is a unique mix of autobiographical material and literary criticism. I have chosen to cite the jacket blurb here, not only because it represents René de Ceccatty's raison d'être for his book, but also because it is the means by which he will seduce his own potential readers. To do this, he foregrounds his own seduction by literature, and particularly his seduction by Leduc. I think that it is clear, from the dual purpose of his text—his identification and scholarly criticism—that Ceccatty wants to spread the seduction around; he wants to inspire more readers—*his* readers—to read Leduc.

Ceccatty's assertion that no one is immune, that everyone becomes Violette Leduc may seem exaggerated, but it is in part borne out by the publication in 1996 of *Violette's Embrace*, a fictional biography of Leduc with heavy autobiographical overtones by New Mexico artist Michele Zackheim. Again, I cite the reader-enticing jacket description:

> An American woman—a visual artist from the Southwest—acts on unarticulated feelings of kinship with Leduc and retraces the writer's life, traveling through Paris and the French countryside, in an effort to understand Leduc's compulsion to bare herself and, in the process, to come to terms with her own life's journey. . . . *Violette's Embrace* is an artful fusion of fact and fiction: the writer's life an artful reconstruction, the biographer's a vivid creation. The two women's lives, a generation apart, are interwoven with grace, irony, and the brilliant contrast that history provides.

Michele Zackheim, a visual artist with no writing history, here embarks on an ambitious literary undertaking: recreating Leduc's life from her autobiographies, Beauvoir's writings, and letters from and interviews with friends of Leduc. This is not a reporting of Leduc's life, but a re*creation* of it: Zackheim's work is not a reliable biography, and a good part of the creative work has to do with Zackheim weaving her own story into Leduc's. In this way, her writing project is remarkably similar to René de Ceccatty's.[1]

What is striking about these two books is not that two people from such different backgrounds could feel such an affinity for the same author, but that they would express that affinity in such similar ways. Ceccatty's "immediate need for identification" is analogous to Zackheim's "feelings of kinship," and both of these feelings led them to write their own texts. Although Ceccatty's feelings of kinship are perhaps more articulated than Zackheim's, they nevertheless both retrace Leduc's life and their own lives at the same time. In so doing, they and their writings stand in testimony to the seductive powers of Leduc's writings and the feelings of love that those writings solicit. We will examine both of these works in sharper focus to illustrate their radical seduction by literature.

Éloge de le bâtarde is a book that brings together the personal and professional life of Violette Leduc with the personal and professional life of Ceccatty. As with the Zackheim text, Ceccatty's is an "artful fusion" of autobiographical material and literary criticism. It does not deal with his life as a whole, with incidents from his childhood, for example, but focuses on the ways in which reading Leduc influenced his perception of the world, particularly in the realms of literature and love. His first reading of *La Bâtarde* coincided with his beginnings as a writer and with his passion for a young married man—a student like himself—whom he calls Norman. On the final page of his text, Ceccatty gathers in one place a list of the intersections of his life and writings with those of Leduc. It is a seemingly endless inventory, recapping the events he has chronicled throughout the text:

> Je considère ces années passées avec Violette Leduc et loin d'elle avec une sorte de stupéfaction sereine. Voyages à Faucon, thèse, installation dans le XIe arrondissement, nomination fortuite près de Valenciennes, séjour dans cette ville, . . . articles, roman d'attente—si je puis dire—lettres échangées, visites de lecteurs, travaux d'étudiants, recherches, pièces de théâtre, émissions de radio et télévision, débats, traductions suscitées, cours, conversations interrompues et reprises, rencontres, rêveries, amitiés nouées, lectures guidées ou communes, analogies, analyses psychologiques et bien sûr, aussi, engouements littéraires, amours.

> [I look back over these years spent with Violette Leduc and far from her with a kind of serene amazement. Trips to Faucon, dissertation, moving into (Leduc's old Paris neighborhood), fortuitous assignment near Valenciennes, the stay in that city, . . . articles, roman d'attente—if I can call it that—letters exchanged, visits from readers, student papers, research, plays, television and radio programs, debates, translations called for, lectures, discussions interrupted and taken up again, encounters, reveries, friendships formed, guided or shared readings, analogies, psychoanalytic analyses, and also, of course, literary infatuations, loves.] (*Éloge de la bâtarde* 256)

The appearance of this accumulation of intersections at the very end of the book leaves Ceccatty's reader with a rather breathless feeling, and one senses that Ceccatty himself is breathless from his intense association with Violette Leduc. His enthusiasm for her writings, and for these intersections, is contagious, and I imagine that readers previously uninitiated into the pleasures of her texts will not hesitate to pick up a copy of *La Bâtarde* after putting down Ceccatty's *Éloge*. It should be noted that in this list, Ceccatty does not even bother to elaborate on the most important elements: the "literary infatuations" and the "loves." By the end of the book, Ceccatty's reader will be well enough aware of these.

These many intersections, and particularly the coincidental ones early on, encouraged Ceccatty to pay special attention to Leduc and her writings when no one else seemed interested in her work. In a way, however, the accumulation of these intersections seems somehow incidental to the true purpose of Ceccatty's book: to get his readers to read and appreciate Leduc's works. He does this by piquing their personal interest in her by describing his "immediate need": readers may think that Leduc's books will appeal to them on the level of the plot. In order to cement this interest, however, and also to appeal to more scholarly readers—those who have unjustly neglected her in the history of French literature—Ceccatty weaves literary criticism into his discussion of Leduc's effect on his life.

In spite of his pronounced enthusiasm for Leduc, Ceccatty begins his book by telling his readers that he had originally resisted reading any text by Leduc because of what he had heard of her writing in the press. His brother, however (also a writer), had been struck by her character while watching a televised interview and offered Ceccatty a copy of *La Bâtarde*. It was not until a few years later—after Leduc's death in 1972—that Ceccatty actually read the novel. *Éloge* is proof that it was a reading that was to have a profound effect on his life.

This reading, and his seduction by Leduc, coincided with another seduction, which in *Eloge* takes second place only to his seduction by Leduc's writings. In fact, the one explains the other. Ceccatty had just met "Norman"—another student in his Foucault seminar—and his wife "Marcia." Ceccatty's love for the author and for his classmate fed each other. Ceccatty writes: "Je le dis sans crainte du ridicule, il était ma Simone de Beauvoir. Je le savais. Je savourais la lecture de *L'Affamée*, m'y permettant toutes les transpositions personnelles [I say without fear of ridicule that he was my Simone de Beauvoir. I knew it. I savored the reading of *L'Affamée*, allowing myself all of the personal transpositions]" (*Éloge de la bâtarde* 55). Ceccatty uses the explanation of Violette's passion for Beauvoir as a vehicle to explain his feelings vis-à-vis Norman, pushing the analogies of his story with hers. Like Simone de Beauvoir, Norman was the impossible, serene love object, not willing to encourage his passion, but not willing to extinguish it either. Ceccatty, in his turn resembled the narrator of *L'Affamée* with his desperate homoeroticism. Certainly the power of this text was augmented for Ceccatty by the fact that he could read his own tragic story in its pages.

Once he began to recognize a pattern in his life that was similar to Violette's—and some of the similarities were striking[2]—he encouraged it. To write his thesis on Leduc[3] he decided to move into a garret apartment in Leduc's old neighborhood, the XIe arrondissement, that replicated Violette's own writing space—her *réduit*. He readily admits to forcing the issue of identification: "Je désirais pousser plus loin l'identification [I wanted to push the identification even further]" (*Éloge de la bâtarde* 55), and at the end of his text asks himself how much of the identification was naturally occurring and how much cultivated.[4] This suggests that Ceccatty found great pleasure in his association with Leduc. The fact that he would go to lengths to intensify an already-powerful identification speaks to the level of his seduction by Violette Leduc. The effect of forcing this identification is, I believe, to make the case for reading Leduc even stronger: what better way to inspire future generations of readers than to show one's extreme seduction by a writer?

The fact that *Éloge* is a scholarly work mixed with personal impressions and autobiographical elements makes it difficult to classify Ceccatty as a reader. He clearly identifies with Violette on a profound level, indicating a Bovaryan stance. But as he is an established novelist, one might also assume Barthesian characteristics in his reading habits. Indeed, he was influenced by Barthes' fragmented writing style in the composition of his thesis on Leduc.[5] In this text, however, we do not see any of the Barthesian focusing on language that leads to a sense of vertigo and jouissance. This is most probably due to Ceccatty's purpose in writing, which is not to invite his readers to taste the Barthesian pleasures of the text, but to give them insights into the ways in which Leduc's writings fit with each other, her life, and the writings of others.

To this end, Ceccatty discusses a number of other literary figures, among whom are Paolo Pasolini, Marguerite Duras, and Barbara Pym. However, his reading of other writers consistently coincides with a discussion of Leduc's work—her writings serve as a jumping-off point for these discussions—so that the other writers are seen as through a Leducian lens. This is particularly true in the case of Pym. One of Ceccatty's novels, *Babel des mers*, featured an English novelist named Harriet Norman, whose imagined past he had "chargé de nombreux événements de celui de Violette Leduc [filled with numerous events from Violette Leduc's past]" (*Éloge de la bâtarde* 129). Ironically, after finishing the writing of this novel, Ceccatty read the works of Barbara Pym for the first time. It was then that he realized that he had created a character who could have been based on Pym: "J'atteignais donc Barbara Pym à travers un personnage imaginaire. Ce retour de la fiction à la réalité, d'un double à son modèle était une expérence inédite [I thus arrived at Barbara Pym through an imaginary literary character. This return from fiction to reality, a double back into its model, was a novel experience]" (*Éloge de la bâtarde* 141). The coincidence of having created Harriet Norman based on the unknown model of Barbara Pym is perhaps not as "novel" as he suggests. It echoes the hazards of Ceccatty's life as it intersected with the elements from Leduc's own, as when he meets his "Simone de Beauvoir" while reading *L'Affamée*.

Ceccatty points out that in addition to their shared traits—seen in Harriet Norman—Pym represents a stylistic "return" to Violette Leduc: "Tout comme Violette Leduc, Barbara Pym s'en tient à son environnement étroit et en retire des trésors, par l'acuité de son inépuisable force d'observation [Just like Violette Leduc, Barbara Pym confines herself to her immediate surroundings and through the acuity of her inexhaustible strength of observation, draws treasures from it.]" (*Éloge de la bâtarde* 143).[6] For Ceccatty, in the end everything cycles back to Leduc, in a sort of *éternel retour*.

He ends his book on this cyclical note, which is of particular interest to us. When Ceccatty writes that "Sa lecture a influencé ma vie. Ma vie m'a reconduit à elle [Reading her has influenced my life. My life brought me back to her]" (*Éloge de la bâtarde* 256) we can recognize the cyclical nature of reading and writing with Violette Leduc. Violette's reading eventually led to her writing, and Ceccatty's reading of Leduc led him to write as well. We can see that the notion of seducee becoming a seducer is not a rigid dichotomy, however, because the seducers (writers) do not stop being seduced by literature (reading). Thus the cycle of literary seduction repeats itself from generation to generation.

✢✢

This same cycle of seducee turned seducer (all the while remaining seduced) is seen in Michele Zackheim's novel *Violette's Embrace*. The purpose of Zackheim's text, however, is not at all the same as Ceccatty's. Whereas his is an "éloge," one of the first published full-length scholarly treatments of Leduc's work—placing her alongside and even above more well-known writers—Zackheim's is much more concerned with imparting to her reader her love for this writer. While Ceccatty incorporates many personal details, his writing, far more polished than Zackheim's, forms a protective shield around his personal disclosures. Moreover, although his juxtaposing of the scholarly with the personal does expose him to criticism from his peers, the critics who are likely to read his work are just that: his peers. Zackheim, on the other hand, has no such group from which to seek support. Like Ceccatty, Zackheim's most likely readership is this same group of critics, who are apt to pick up on the gaps in her research (as when she mistakenly calls Jacques Guérin by the name of Guérlin—the name of his perfume company—throughout the text) and her often cumbersome writing style. As easy as it would be to critique *Violette's Embrace*, however, her work should not be held up to the same template as a scholarly treatment. Zackheim is an artist, not a scholar, and it is clearly a piece of art that she is attempting to produce.[7] The difference shows in their choice of titles: one speaks the praises of Leduc, the other is an embrace. Ceccatty's scholarly approach to Leduc's writings gives his work an interesting mix of personal *rapprochement* and critical distance. In contrast, Michele Zackheim foregoes the laudatory distancing of critical work to press herself, her life, and her writing up against the figure of Violette Leduc.

As with Ceccatty, we find an intense personal identification with Violette in the narrator-protagonist of this novel. At the outset, Michele[8] states that "The writer, Violette Leduc, wrote on an edge that reminds me of myself" (*Violette's Embrace* 1) and later declares that Leduc's "descriptions of the physical self are hand-drawn maps leading me to my own landscape, familiar" (*Violette's Embrace* 16). Her identification takes place on multiple levels: the creative and the physical, in addition to the shared experiences and emotions that provoke the sense of identification in the case of Ceccatty. Coincidentally, the young Michele shared Leduc's passion for Simone de Beauvoir, having, at the age of nineteen, made a pilgrimage to Nelson Algren's neighborhood in Chicago where Beauvoir had visited. This pilgrimage is analogous to the one recounted by Leduc in *Trésors à prendre*, in which the writer follows Beauvoir's itinerary through the south of France.

In addition to this Bovaryan identification, however, Michele has obviously experienced a Barthesian pleasure in reading Leduc's writings. From the outset, Michele makes it clear that it is not only feelings of personal identification, but also a deep respect for Leduc's creative and evocative use of language that has endeared this writer to her. Indeed, Michele is very focused on the effects of language by Leduc:

> She places letters, th en words, rising and falling like waves in the sea. The *t*'s are a moment's pause—the *c* and *s* carry her toward the shore. Sometimes a *z* confuses the water—carving an undertow. But gracefully they land on the beach. She moved her Blanzy-Poure pen forward to the next tide of language, she created—she was fearless. She wrote. (*Violette's Embrace* 2)

This passage is remarkable in the degree to which it illustrates a Barthesian reading. This demonstration of the capacity of Leduc's works to be appreciated on a purely linguistic level is in contrast to the Bovaryan reading that we have seen both Ceccatty and Zackheim do previously. Here Michele Zackheim abandons the discussion of narrative completely to lose herself in the "tide of language." Not only do we see her attention "floating" above language, catching itself on certain consonants, but this very image of the tide is evocative of Barthes' notion of verbal loss: Michele is carried away from the text—as if out to sea—when her reading is oblique, unattached. This reading invites her unconscious associations to come to the fore, allowing for jouissance. Indeed, the manner in which she has written this passage is sexually suggestive, as she tries to capture the languid roll of the sea in her own language, as well as in her use of the sea and tide metaphor with its rhythmic fluidity so often associated with feminine jouissance. Even in the sentence introducing this paragraph, there is the suggestion of jouissance: "Her sighs slip through her language." Are these sighs, slipping through the very linguistic gaps which allow for loss, Violette's or Michele's? Our reading of Barthes would suggest that they could belong to both, as we have seen him remark that while most texts are written in pleasure (suggesting that the sighs are Violette's) that does not guarantee that they will be read that way. We have also seen, however, that Michele's reading does conform to the Barthesian model of textual jouissance, suggesting that the sighs of pleasure might just as well be interpreted as her own.

Zackheim's attention to Leduc's language, then, is apparent in her use of rhythm and metaphor to describe her textual pleasure. This poetic writing can be read as a stylistic borrowing from Violette. Michele sometimes tries to capture Leduc's style, as when she writes the following: "How and why does this 'ugly woman' transform language into fluttering angels whispering in my ear" (*Violette's Embrace* 71)? While angels did not form part of Violette's metaphorical currency, the remark is different enough from the surrounding text to be marked as an effort, and close enough to Violette's writing to be identifiable as a pastiche. She will more often borrow Violette's words directly, however, which she puts in italics, as in the following example: "When she needed to leave herself, to move away from her earthly and painful existence, she would *sit in my skin, in my kingdom of white clouds, in my armchair of dove's [sic] downs*" (*Violette's Embrace* 119). By suturing Violette's text into her own—sometimes into a single sentence—Michele brings herself closer to total identification: Violette's embrace.

Zackheim's novel serves as a fictional biography of Violette Leduc, whose life is explained by the invented character of Lili Jacobs, the supposed one-time neighbor and long-time friend of Leduc. This central character serves several important functions within Zackheim's text. First of all, she is a mouthpiece for Zackheim, saying the things about Leduc that Zackheim feels, as when Lili notes that "one of the reasons I was attracted to Violette was my own history" (*Violette's Embrace* 23), or when Lili explains why she has furnished the narrator with important Leduc papers when she has withheld them from scholars.[10] For Zackheim, this is both a justification and an explanation of her work: to correct the oversight of scholars who do not focus enough attention on Leduc's use of language. As a Jewish member of the Resistance during World War II, Lili also facilitates Michele's repeated returns to her own Jewish heritage and the Holocaust. It is ironic in a way for this biography of Leduc to be so focused on the "Jewish Question." In *La Bâtarde*, Violette does nothing to save her Jewish acquaintances from the Nazis. First Esther[11]—Violette's across-the-courtyard neighbor in her apartment in Paris—and later, Gérard[12]—Maurice Sach's young lover in the Normandy village before he goes off to join a work camp—get abducted, but with no emotional reaction from Violette, despite the fact that she had been close to both of them. In fact, Violette benefited greatly by the occupation of Paris, both financially and personally: her success as a black marketeer made her wealthy for the first time, in addition to increasing her self-esteem. Perhaps writing Lili (who echoes Esther's position as neighbor) and her late husband Alain as people to whom Violette was very dedicated was a way for Zackheim to reconcile, and perhaps even to make amends for, Violette's lack of sensitivity in this area.

Lili's continual reference to occupied France, along with Violette's position as a social outcast, then, are elements that invite the majority of Zackheim's autobiographical material into the text. The first time a childhood memory is inserted into the text, Michele writes of the time when she was seven and a neighbor girl asked to feel her head, saying "'I want to feel your Jewish horns'" (*Violette's Embrace* 16). This was the first time that Michele had felt separate from her southwestern community, but it would not be the last. When her family bought a television and Michele "could see how the rest of America looked and how the rest of America lived," she was acutely aware that her Semitic looks separated her from that America represented on television. "By the age of thirteen, my alienation was complete" (*Violette's Embrace* 16).

Zackheim, in an effort to better "embrace" Violette, also has Michele intertwine narration of her personal life with that of Violette's. In one instance, a mulberry tree and the wind are used to suture her experience to that of Violette.

Michele writes "Near the arroyo a short distance from our house in New Mexico is a mulberry tree, similar to Violette's in Faucon" (*Violette's Embrace* 181). Interestingly, no mulberry tree in Faucon has yet been mentioned, and this sentence opens a new section. Michele starts with her life in New Mexico, shifts briefly to Faucon, then back to America and then to the Vaucluse once again.[13] This is followed by a few comments on the "desert mistral" of Michele's New Mexico home, but "Unlike the wind of Provence, our mistral is not bitingly cold; it hurls fistfuls of dry, dust-ridden wind" (*Violette's Embrace* 182). The section ends there, having served no other purpose than bringing Michele's experience closer to Violette's.

Another forced way in which Michele connects her life to Violette's is through shared dates. Lili narrates Violette's life in chronological order, and when she gets to 1971, mentions the "Manifesto of the 343," in which 343 women, including Leduc, admit to having had illegal abortions. It was published in the *Nouvel Observateur* on April 5 of that year. Michele then recalls that on that very date she was five weeks pregnant with her second child. The discussion of reproductive choice opens the door to Michele's memories of pregnancy and childbirth. This tendency of forcing connections indicates that Zackheim was emotionally invested in cementing her identification with Leduc. One senses that she would have relished the intersections with Leduc's life that occurred in Ceccatty's.

René de Ceccatty and Michele Zackheim are clearly both seduced by Leduc's writings, but as writers themselves they have readers of their own to seduce. Ceccatty uses his literary knowledge and his critical acumen to this end, rather in the mode of Violette's Argentine and, later, Violette herself. He impresses his reader with all of the different ways in which his life has resembled Violette's, but most especially with his readings of Leduc's writings next to those of others. Zackheim, on the other hand, is not looking for the intellectual seduction of her reader. In fact, as her title suggests, I believe that what she is seeking is a sort of communion, not only with her reader, but especially with Violette Leduc herself. The passionate tone in which much of the novel is written, the attempts at using Leduc's metaphorical language, the lifting of Violette's words to place them in her own text—all of these elements speak to a desire on the part of Zackheim to enter into a state of commonality, if not communion, with Violette Leduc. It could be said that this is done in an effort to seduce her reader. I think, however, that Zackheim's larger purpose was to give the gift of love back to Violette Leduc.

Zackheim and Ceccatty wanted to seduce their readers. Ultimately, however, it is as though they both wanted to give back—to Leduc, to literature in general—what they had been given: the pleasure of reading.

I have also participated in the same Leduc-inspired reader-to-writer cyclical movement. Years ago, upon my first reading of *La Bâtarde,* I tried to write about it academically but was unable to do so. Three years later I reread *La Bâtarde* in the context of a graduate seminar on French autobiography and chose in part to examine why I had experienced—and was continuing to experience—such difficulty in treating her work critically. I realized then that it was an issue of too much identification with Leduc's protagonist: "I am sensitive in the same places as Violette."

In addition to the intense identification with Leduc's literary persona that I shared with Ceccatty and Zackheim, my two writing projects resembled theirs in several ways. In my first essay, I shared Zackheim's desire to feel "Violette's embrace," expressing the wish to "join her on the page," and even borrowing, like Zackheim, Leduc's metaphorical vocabulary. This, as well as the tactic of laying myself bare on the page,[14] were both borrowed from Leduc. This first writing, which followed my first reading, was written as a reaction against a scholarly approach to writing about Leduc. By the time I wrote about Leduc again, I had moved closer to Ceccatty in my writing project. Like his *Eloge,* my piece was a mix of the scholarly and the personal and in it I tried to explain my seduction by and identification with Violette in terms of my own life experiences.

I share the same remarkable feelings of affinity with Violette that Ceccatty and Zackheim express in their work, and like them, could not resist the impulse to move from reading Leduc to writing about Leduc, all the while embedding my personal story in hers. This movement also represented a gesture toward reader seduction. Unlike the texts of Zackheim and Ceccatty, my essays were written to very specific readers. The first, more erotically charged, essay was written in a more poetic vein as a thinly veiled sexual seduction; the second, more subdued, was intended to seduce a different reader intellectually. But like Ceccatty and Zackheim, my essays were also, ultimately, written as tributes to Leduc's power as an author, and should be understood as a return of the gift of love to the writer that inspired them.

*
**

When first considering the question of Leduc and seduction, it is easy to envision a simple treatment of the pleasures provided by reading texts written by Violette Leduc. But upon further investigation, as readers we can arrive at a much richer place in our thinking on reading, Leduc, and textual pleasures. In exploring the politics of reading—reading as seduction—we can come to a new appreciation of Leduc as a reader—the seducee in this relational theory of narrative—and not just a writer, the seducer. Likewise, those who might originally be seen only as seducees—those readers who reveled in the pleasures of Leduc's texts—clearly show themselves to trace the same trajectory as Leduc herself. These readers—René de Ceccatty and Michele Zackheim, and even myself—who were once the seducees, have become, under the influence of Violette o were once the seducees, have become, under the influence of Violette Leduc, the seducers. In the cyclical movement of seduction, the pleasures of the text are holistic, including reading and writing, seducing and being seduced, presence and absence.

PART TWO:
SEDUCING THE READER

"Autobiographers proselytize; the reader is an easy prey."

—Elaine Marks, "The Dream of Love"

CHAPTER FOUR

Jeux Interdits:
Reading Leduc's Erotic Touch

If Violette Leduc is known outside of critical circles focusing on women's writing and autobiography, it is primarily for her erotic writing.[1] Although I would propose (following Beauvoir, below) that all of her work is infused with the erotic—her unique sense of connection to nature-poetry-language that is, paradoxically, at once palpable and ineffable—it is true that she is most well known for her eroticism. While this may seem a dubious distinction, in fact Leduc played an important role in removing erotic literature, and particularly erotica written by women, from the obscurity in which it had lurked for so long. Claudine Brécourt-Villars reports that "Sans obtenir de prix, *La Bâtarde* fut néanmoins un événement marquant [Although it won no prizes, *La Bâtarde* was nevertheless a significant event]" (*Écrire d'amour* 287). According to Brécourt-Villars, it was the first openly erotic book in the history of French publishing to come out of a major publishing house: "Ce fut en tout cas un livre catalyseur, car pour la première fois, en 1964, un éditeur «non spécialisé» comme Gallimard commençait à introduire l'érotisme dans l'édition courante [In any case, this book was a catalyst, since in 1964, for the first time, a 'non-specialized' publishing house like Gallimard began listing erotic works in its catalogue]" (*Écrire d'amour* 287). Even Genet failed to accomplish that. While the acceptance of erotic literature by major publishing houses may have been an inevitability, many of today's writers are indebted to Leduc and her courage to keep writing, even after *Ravages* was massively censored. It is most remarkable and significant—as well as a testimony to Leduc's fortitude and conviction—that it was a woman writer who succeeded where so many others had failed.

⁑

In this chapter we are considering the seduction of the reader via touch. Because of the distance that necessarily arises from published writing, the notion that Leduc "touches" her readers in a familiar and startlingly physical way may strike some as dubious, if not altogether impossible. Hers is a touch that figures an exchange between two people, even as it remains a text. As we shall see, Leduc manages this touch through what I will refer to as "associative position-ing."[2] By this I mean that within the fictional seduction scenes to be examined here, a textual seduction via the conflation of the position of the reader with that of the seducee is created.

To better understand the mechanism by which associative positioning works, the distinction must be drawn between the narrative past—inhabited in *La Bâtarde* by the young protagonist Violette and her lover Isabelle—and the narrating present, in which the narrator Violette (older now) recounts her seduc-tion by Isabelle to the narratee. We have already seen Leduc's will to seduction of actual readers—Maurice Sachs and Simone de Beauvoir first and foremost, but also Patrice and Flavien. Therefore, it is safe to assume that, in the case of Violette Leduc, at least, the figure of the narratee—the receiver of the narration and the narrator's counterpart—is not the stand-in for any implied reader, but the stand-in for an *actual* one: that flesh-and-blood person who holds the book. From now on, when I speak of Leduc's reader, it is to this flesh-and-blood reader that I refer.

In this chapter, we will examine the seductive strategies used by Leduc in her writing of the sexual initiation in *La Bâtarde*. Within the sexual realm, it is the initiator—the seducer—who uses seductive strategies (through the touch, the look, or a passionate discourse) to "entice or entrap" the seducee, or the one who is to be initiated. This seducee is passive by nature: in the case of sexual initiation the seducee is presumed to be naïve in the ways of sexual relating, and thus does not generally take an active role, at least at the beginning. A similar structure emerges in literary seduction. Again we find the seducer in the active role of the narrator, the one who uses strategies—narrative this time—to entice the narratee (or, in the case of Leduc, the reader herself). It is this reader who is the seducee of literature, and even more so than the sexual seducee, the reader's role is a naturally passive one: she cannot respond in kind to the narrator's se-duction. In this way the sexual initiator and the literary narrator are analogous: both are seducers. Likewise, the sexual initiate and the reader are both seducees.

The narrative of sexual initiation, then, is seductive on two levels: on the level of the story as well as on that of the narration. The two structures overlap seamlessly in the case of first-person narratives in which the narrator is also the seducer. But what happens in an autobiographical narration of sexual seduction in which the narrator was the seducee? In this case there is a shifting of posi-tions, with the (sexual) seducee becoming the (narrative) seducer. The lines of seduction are no longer parallel but continuous, except for the chronological break occurring between the sexual initiation itself and its retelling (the narra-tive past and the narrating present).

This may not at first appear to be a significant change, but in fact the effects are far-reaching. In the first scenario, it is only Violette as the sexual initiate who is the addressee of the sexual seduction: the receiver of pleasure. In the second, however, it is her reader who ultimately becomes the receiver of pleas-ure, the ultimate seducee. The line of pleasure passes through the first seducee—Violette—and when she becomes a narrator, she passes it on to her reader.

When this occurs, the reader is assigned a new position relative to the seducee of the sexual initiation, who in this case is also the narrator: they are associated one with the other in the sexual seduction. Violette the protagonist and her reader overlap in their position as seducees.

Let us examine how this associative positioning functions in the chapter on Violette's sexual initiation in *La Bâtarde*. In this scenario, the young Violette experiences intense sexual pleasure for the first time at the hands of Isabelle. In the retelling of this pleasurable experience, however, it is the reader who experiences the pleasure:

> Isabelle flatta ma hanche. Ma chair caressée se faisait caresse, ma hanche que l'on flattait irradiait dans mes jambes droguées, dans mes chevilles molles. On me torturait menu, menu dans mon ventre.

> [Isabelle stroked my hip. My flesh as she caressed it became a caress, the hip that was being stroked irradiated into my drugged legs, into my limp ankles. I was being tortured ever so slightly in my stomach.] (*La Bâtarde* 115–16)

By recounting this scene of sexual initiation in her own voice, Leduc's older narrator assumes the superior position—that of authority, of the seducer—which effectively places the reader in the position of the young protagonist: in the position of the seduced. Here, we can see that she "receives" the pleasure imposed on her by the seducer, never actively reciprocating. That Violette describes submitting to these pleasures as being tortured highlights the sense of passivity in the seducee. Moreover, it is the discourse of seduction that is primarily responsible for the reader's experience of physical pleasure. Just as Violette is bewitched by the caressing hand of Isabelle, so too is the reader seduced by the narration of the arousing effects of that hand on Violette's body. In fact, when Violette says that "My flesh as she caressed it *became a caress*," she notes that while she herself remained passive, her body was actively responding—*becoming* a caress. I would like to propose that *it was this very body-centered reaction that Leduc was hoping for in her readers*. Even if we could never touch her back, nor necessarily even realize that we were being drawn into her web, she could still seduce us by provoking a degree of pleasure in us when evoking Violette's physical pleasure through what I will call "image-sensations."

The reading of Violette's initiation to the pleasures of the body then becomes an initiation of the reader in its own right: an initiation to the pleasures of the text. In order to make the reader more sensitive to these pleasures—to her "touch"—Leduc employs the image-sensation, a metaphor that translates physical sensations into language. As such, its full meaning cannot be apprehended until it is processed and understood physically as well as intellectually. Elaine Marks suggests the notion of image-sensations when she notes: "The events in three volumes of her autobiography are almost exclusively psychosomatic events translated into a language capable of reproducing in the reader a direct apprehension of the experience it conveys" ('I Am My Own Heroine' 4). Examples of image-sensations in the passage that we have been examining include the "drugged legs" and the "limp ankles." Each of these image-sensations represent admirable translations of the paradoxical combination of heightened physical awareness and sense of tingling detachment in the legs that accompanies sexual arousal. The impact of these image-sensations is increased when combined with that of the waves of heat and light spreading from Isabelle's caress on Violette's hip. When the image-sensation is functioning properly, the reader does not perceive these spreading waves of pleasure as being located on Violette's body only, but can feel them on her own as well. It is in this manner that the reader is seductively touched once she is associated through the line of seduction with Violette the protagonist: they are both recipients of pleasure.

The Leducian model of eroticism and its importance in her œuvre is signaled by Simone de Beauvoir in her preface to *La Bâtarde*. She begins by saying of Leduc that "L'érotisme tient une grande place dans ses livres; ni gratuitement, ni par provocation [Eroticism holds a privileged position in her books, though neither gratuitously nor for provocation's sake]" (*La Bâtarde* 19). By this, Beauvoir differentiates (as do I) Leduc's works from those such as Pauline Réage's *Histoire d'O*, which contain what many in this culture would call gratuitous sex and violence. Beauvoir goes so far as to say that for Leduc, eroticism is the lens through which the world is perceived: "c'est la clé privilégiée du monde; c'est à sa lumière qu'elle découvre la ville et les campagnes, l'épaisseur des nuits, la fragilité de l'aube, la cruauté d'un tintement de cloches [it's the one great, unsurpassable key to the world; it is in the light of eroticism that she discovers the city and the countryside, the depths of the night, the fragility of dawn, the cruelty of chiming bells]" (*La Bâtarde* 20). Beauvoir, then, believes that Leduc experienced her surroundings in a profoundly physical, sensuous, manner, and that therefore she wanted to share this perception with her reader. We have already seen how this functions through the image-sensation of the drugged legs, but Beauvoir points out that it is not only within the context of sexual pleasure that we will find sensation paramount in the writings of Leduc:

> Son rapport avec [autrui] est charnel. La présence, c'est le corps; la communication s'opère de corps à corps. Chérir Fidéline, c'est s'enfouir dans sa jupe; être rejetée par Sachs, c'est subir ses baisers «abstraits»; le narcissisme s'achève dans l'onanisme. *Les sensations sont la vérité des sentiments.*

> [Her relations with (others) are of the flesh. Presence is the body; communication is carried out from body to body. To cherish Fidéline is to hide in her skirts; to be rejected by Sachs is to submit to his "abstract" kisses; narcissism ends in masturbation. *Sensations are the truth of feelings.*] (*La Bâtarde* 19, emphasis added)

Here Beauvoir underlines the pure physicality of Leducian relations. All contact with others, she suggests, is for Leduc a contact that is shot through with sensation. Leduc's texts positively vibrate with carnality. This body-to-body communication takes place not only within the text, between Violette and Fidéline or Sachs or Isabelle, as Beauvoir suggests, but also, I think, *through* the text, between the writer and her audience. We must recall that it was Beauvoir herself who already identified the relationship with the reader as the one healthy relationship that Leduc maintained as an adult. The relations she maintains with her readers prove to be just as body-centered as those Violette has with the characters that people her narrative universe. When Leduc writes from her body to the body of her reader, a real connection establishes itself; we find it difficult to disengage ourselves from her seduction without shutting the book.

That this carnal connection takes place is by no means accidental. Beauvoir states that for Leduc sensations represent the truth of emotions. If that is so, Leduc must also discover a way in which to represent the truth of the sensations; she does this by "writing the body."[3] When Leduc writes the body, she employs many of the techniques commonly associated with this writing style, including the privileging of touch over sight as a vehicle to sexual arousal. In addition, heavy use of metaphor in her texts gains easy access to the unconscious, and much sea imagery, suggestive of the rhythms, power, and mystery of feminine sexuality, is employed as well.

I propose that Leduc wanted to write a seduction from her body to that of her reader—effectively "touching" her reader with a sensation that lies outside the scope of analysis—in order to diminish the distance between her own body and that of her reader. Here is how, in *La Folie en tête*, Violette describes the writing of the first scenes from *Thérèse et Isabelle*, which later became the passages of *La Bâtarde* that we have been studying. Once again, the writing of a seduction scene becomes a seduction in itself:

> J'écrivais, j'écrivais sous leur dictée. J'écrivais d'une main et de l'autre . . . je m'aimais pour les aimer, pour les retrouver, pour les traduire, pour ne pas les trahir. Drogue dans mes pieds. Je les informais. C'est toujours le même cercle et la monotonie. Je jetai la porte-plume sur le cahier. C'est un mouvement perpétuel, il vous veut toute entière. Un bras resta libre sur la table, la tête tomba sur le bras. Je leur parlais. Mon enfer se raréfie, Isabelle, mon ciel s'élargit. Je veux être une explosion de cailloux lancés aux astres. Thérèse, ma prison a le vertige. Comment parviendrai-je à le transcrire, la vague m'emporte, le plaisir rôde. Reviens, Isabelle, tu es revenue. Ta chevelure dans mes bras, dans mes genoux, dans mes jambes, je t'ai retrouvée, je te quitte, captivité. Haute tension, je suis survoltée. La vitesse et la communion.

> [I was writing, I was writing under their dictation. I wrote with one hand, and with the other . . . I loved myself to love them, to get back to them, to translate them, to not betray them. Drugs in my feet. I gave them a form. It's always the same circle and monotony. I threw the pen onto the notebook. It's a perpetual movement, demanding one's full attention. One arm was free on the table, my head fell onto that arm. I was speaking to them. My hell is rarefying, Isabelle, my sky is opening up. I want to be an explosion of pebbles thrown at the stars. Thérèse, my prison is dizzy. How will I manage to tran-

scribe it? I'm being swept away by the wave, pleasure is lurking. Come back, Isabelle,
there you are. Your hair in my arms, my lap, my legs, I have found you again, I'm
leaving you, captivity. High voltage, I am overloaded. Speed and communion.] (*La Folie en tête* 321–22)

In this remarkable passage, we see highly-charged eroticism which is not gratuitous, but assimilated into the pursuit of truth and integrity: both personal and
professional. Leduc's narrator expresses concern over her ability to accurately—
truthfully—express the physical sensations experienced by the young Thérèse.
Writing under the "dictation" of the schoolgirls, replicated via the pleasure she
is producing in her own body, Violette endeavors to "translate" and "transcribe"
those sensations, but without betraying the girls. She does this through the use
of the image-sensation.[4] Of particular note here is her use of the verbs to transcribe and to translate. Translation—from the Latin *transferre*, "to carry across,"
an archaic definition of which significantly meant "to enrapture" —is generally
understood as the expression of something in a different language, while re-
taining the same sense. In the case of Leduc's writing of sensation, the translation is not from one language to another, but from a body to language to body,
through image-sensations: "communication is carried out from body to body,"
indeed.[5]

Through her use of these metaphors, which facilitate reaching the body
because of the unconscious slippage that they produce, Leduc achieves the kind
of fluency that effective translation requires. When one is fluent in a language,
one does not have to think of individual words in one language and translate
them discretely into another; instead, expression of the entire idea in the second
language occurs immediately. The translation ("carrying-across") is produced
automatically, and the first step is skipped. When Leduc writes from her body,
the image-sensations she uses are often more easily and immediately understood
physically than intellectually. In this way, the carrying-across occurs through
language; this is required by the nature of text, thus the related notion of tran-
scription, or "writing across." Comprehension of the image-sensation, however,
occurs on the level of the body.

In addition to her seductive use of the image-sensation in this passage, the
writing of pleasure will entice the reader physically through its style: rhythm
and pacing. Following is the rest of the paragraph about writing in pleasure for
Thérèse and Isabelle. By replicating the rhythm of the mounting sexual pleasure,
Violette allows the reader's body to follow along on the vertiginous ascent:

Je rêve, ou bien on a frappé? Je m'épouse où rien n'existe. On frappe. Impossible, mon
doigt se marie. Le grand mariage pour la grande absence. La terrible divagation sans pa-
roles. On frappe, on frappe. Impossible, je m'en vais retrouver Pasiphaé. On crie devant
ma porte. La catastrophe, je l'ai dans le corps, mon ciel a frissonné. Ne m'appelez pas,
je plonge. Quelqu'un en danger devant ma porte, on recommence à m'appeler. Je tuerais
si je devais cesser. J'étais l'été, je suis quelques gouttes de pluie, je me meurs de gratitude. Une fleur ouverte, une fleur émue, une fumée se balade en moi. On se jette sur ma
porte. On a hurlé mon nom. Je vous l'ai dit, impossible. Mes pieds? Des nymphéas.
Pourriture, tu te répands. Le grand envahissement. Ne m'interrompez pas, ne frappez
pas, ne criez pas. Ma main gauche, ma toute-neuve sur la table, mon fragile, tu m'as

sortie des limbes. C'est grave, on insiste sur l'autre côté de ma porte, on a crié au secours sur le palier. Tu me brûles, perce-neige, un soupir, il faut aider son prochain.

[Am I dreaming, or did someone just knock? I am marrying myself where nothing exists. Someone is knocking. Impossible, my finger is being wed. The grand wedding for
the huge absence. The awesome wordless rambling. Someone is knocking, someone is
knocking. Impossible, I'm off to meet Pasiphaë. Someone is yelling outside my door.
What a catastrophe, I have her in my body, my sky has shivered. Don't call me, I'm
diving in. Someone in danger outside my door, they're calling out to me again. I would
kill if I had to stop now. I was the summer, now I am a handful of raindrops, I'm dying
of gratitude. An open flower, a flower overcome, a wisp of smoke, is wandering inside
me. They're pounding on my door. They've shrieked out my name. I've told you, it's
impossible. My feet? Waterlilies. Decay, you're spreading. The great invasion. Don't
interrupt me, don't knock on my door, don't yell. My left hand, my brand-new hand on
the table, my fragile one, you have brought me out of limbo. It's serious, they keep on
banging, there on the other side of my door, they're crying for help on the landing.
You're burning me, snow-drop, a sigh, one must help one's neighbors after all.] (*La Folie en tête* 322)

I have cited an extended portion of this passage in order to give my reader a
better impression of the style of Leduc's writing about her pleasure.[6] In this
scene the erotic tension is heightened by Violette's internal battle: she must decide whether to continue masturbating or to answer the door. Despite the fact
that there is an audibly desperate person on the landing, Violette herself is qui-
etly desperate, subject to the "perpetual movement, demanding one's full attention." Leduc's narrator captures the rhythm and intensity of Violette's dilemma
by alternately addressing the demands of her body and the demands of the
anonymous "someone" behind the door. The rhythm of the alternation varies. At
the beginning of this citation, Leduc's narrator punctuates Violette's resistance
to being interrupted—her refusal to recognize that someone is knocking—with
the insistent "on frappe," which in French, with its two sharp syllables, mimics
the enervating knocking itself. After the question "on frappe?" is posed, it is
dismissed with a single sentence. When the knocking returns, Violette again
dismisses it, this time even more vehemently, with a three-sentence response,
but the knock finally gains recognition when it becomes doubly insistent: "On
frappe, on frappe." Then, as Violette's resistance—and *pleasure*—mounts, so
does the insistence of the knocker: now the person is yelling. This pattern of
equal resistance to equal force (thesis and antithesis) continues until the last
sentence of the passage. "You're burning me, snow-drop," is once again focused
on the body, in orgasmic answer to the cry for help on the landing. "A sigh"
marks the break—is it a sigh of satisfaction or resignation? Finally, "one must
help one's neighbors after all" signals Violette's acquiescence to the knocker:
synthesis.

This moment of synthesis has repercussions on several levels. On the level
of the text, there is the appearance in a single sentence of both the fixation on
approaching orgasm and the insistent knocker. Secondly, within the narrative
frame, we find the coming together of Violette and the knocker, when Violette

opens the door. Finally, and most germane to our discussion, is the question of the reader. Leduc has constructed this passage in such a way that the reader cannot avoid being influenced by the rhythm of the text. Given the context, the vehemence of expression on both sides of the door coupled with the pacing of the passage—alternating one-upsmanship—produce a tension, a speed, and an urgency that can only suggest the greedy anticipation of sexual pleasure: "speed and communion."

But in this case of solitary lovemaking, the question "communion with whom?" poses itself. It is clearly not communion with the knocker; it was she who threatened it. And despite the fact that finding Thérèse and Isabelle again and telling their pleasure accurately was the raison d'être of her masturbation—"I wrote to get back to them"—in this section, Violette has abandoned Thérèse and Isabelle completely. The two schoolgirls are briefly replaced by the mother of the Minotaur: "I'm off to meet Pasiphaë." It seems Violette was correct to have worried about how to transcribe the pleasure, once it arrived. By now she has become fixated on it and can no longer pursue her original project. Or can she?

Violette claimed to be masturbating to locate Thérèse and Isabelle, but ultimately she appears to have wanted to use them as a vehicle by which to reach her reader. Her desire to experience the pleasure of Thérèse and Isabelle in order to transcribe it into writing was finally so that she could then give it as a gift in the form of a loving touch to the reader. It was a gift given thrice: once each at the publications of *La Bâtarde* and *Thérèse et Isabelle*, when the reader was given the erotic narrative itself, and a third time at the publication of *La Folie en tête*, when the reader was made a present of the (erotic) moment of the production of the (erotic) narrative.[7]

This privileged metatexual moment—Leduc writing about writing—presents us with an interesting situation. Here, we find Leduc's narrator putting herself bodily into the text, and asking—or requiring—that her readers do the same. Barthes has this to say about texts written in pleasure, as we are led to believe that this one was:

Écrire dans le plaisir m'assure-t-il—moi, écrivain—du plaisir de mon lecteur? Nullement. Ce lecteur, il faut que je le cherche, (que je le «drague»), *sans savoir où il est*. Un espace de jouissance est alors créé. Ce n'est pas la «personne» de l'autre qui m'est nécessaire, c'est l'espace: la possibilité d'une dialectique du désir, d'une *imprévision* de la jouissance: que les jeux ne soient pas faits, qu'il y ait un jeu

[Does writing in pleasure guarantee—guarantee me, the writer—my reader's pleasure? Not at all. I must seek out this reader, (must "cruise" him) *without knowing where he is*. A site of bliss is then created. It is not the reader's "person" that is necessary to me, it is this site: the possibility of a dialectics of desire, of an *unpredictability* of bliss: the bets are not placed, there can still be a game.] (*Le Plaisir du texte* 11/4)

Clearly, Leduc's narrator, in this piece as in others, is trying to "cruise" her reader, as Barthes says. We have also seen that the possibility of a dialectic of desire is her aim, as evidenced by her willful seduction of her readers. However, unlike Barthes himself, Leduc's narrator *does* seem to require the reading other and that person's body, because she might not otherwise have taken such pains to inscribe it into her text. In her texts there is created an espace de jouissance, a body-to-body communication.

The most successful of seductions oftentimes occurs when the seducee is unaware that any seduction is taking place. Knowing this, Leduc has very carefully constructed her narrative seductions to appear as though they are not constructed at all, but happen quite naturally. What Leduc does not want is for the text, and therefore the constructed nature of the seduction, to be revealed. Leduc is not always *entirely* successful in her endeavor, however. At times, it is the very writerly nature of her text by which Leduc seeks to seduce her reader that is also that element which allows the reader to see through the seduction. Paradoxically, the more crafted her text appears, the less likely it is that her reader will be seduced. A seduction—this form of sexualized literary seduction in particular—must necessarily appear effortless in order to arrive at its goal. In order to examine more closely the functioning of this paradox, we will look at a further example from *La Bâtarde*:

> La caresse est au frisson ce que le crépuscule est à l'éclair. Isabelle entraînait un râteau de lumière de l'épaule jusqu'au poignet, elle passait avec le miroir à cinq doigts dans mon cou, sur ma nuque, sur mes reins.

> [The caress is to the shiver as dusk is to lightning. Isabelle ran a rake of light from my shoulder down to my wrist, she went over the front of my neck, the nape of my neck, the small of my back with her five-fingered mirror.] (113)

In this passage the reader can sense the work behind the text. Located in the same seduction scene as the excerpt examined earlier ("Isabelle flatta ma hanche"), this passage carries little of the physical impact that Leduc wants to have on her reader. Instead of being able to "feel" the text, readers are placed at a distance from the intended sensation by the too evident construction of it. The first sentence with its analogy appeals more to the mind than to the body, and the intended image-sensation "miroir à cinq doigts" simply seems forced. Neither can be apprehended physically without being processed at length intellectually first, and so despite the fact that they pertain to sensation, the possibility for actual sensation on the part of the reader is attenuated, if not altogether negated. In this way, Leduc's rather obvious attempt to seduce serves only to call attention to that attempt, and thus to destroy it. Ross Chambers calls this the "paradoxical law of narrative power:"

> In order to exert their power, as fiction, these texts are obliged to include in their discursive texture elements that, in their turn, not only permit but require the analysis of the communicational situation on which their fictional power depends. Alongside their seductive power, they have necessarily an analytic power that dismantles the elements of their "charms," their "magic." (*Story and Situation* 221)

We can see how Chambers's theory, elaborated through his work with short stories, applies to this passage in Leduc: the analogy clearly demands intellectual analysis and forces the reader to pause momentarily, breaking the "charm" of the seduction. Moreover, unlike the image-sensation "rake of light"—which seems a plausible way to signify the sensation of a hand moving along a body— the five-fingered mirror is devoid of both warmth and tactile signification and, perhaps as a result, carries little or no weight as a metaphor. These elements together help the reader to see through Leduc's attempt at textual magic.

While at first glance it might appear as though Leduc's textual mastery had slipped momentarily, if we read on we can see that in fact Leduc *wanted* the reader to see through the seduction, as Violette is describing a moment when Isabelle's touch was not arousing her, but distancing her pleasure. In order for the reader to be carried along physically as the partner-in-sensation of Violette, the reader must also experience this unpleasant lapse in pleasure: "L'*artifice* était cynique, la sensation singulière. Je me glaçai, je redoutai ce *raffinement* de bestialité [The *artifice* was cynical, the sensation bizarre. I was turned off, I found this *refinement* of bestiality suspect]" (113–14, emphasis added). Here, Violette realizes the constructed—artificial—nature of Isabelle's seduction, and turns cold because of it. The deliberate nature of Isabelle's moves is illustrated by the words "artifice" and "refinement," both of which suggest calculation or premeditation. Thus, Leduc shows us that she is aware that certain constructions reveal seduction. She further demonstrates that the consequence of that revelation is the automatic shutdown of desire. And yet, Leduc's use of this premeditation is strategic. When Leduc's protagonist becomes aware of the calculation involved in Isabelle's lovemaking, this awareness coincides with the reader's perception of the writer's designs, thus cementing the associative positioning of the reader and the young Violette. Paradoxically, by making the text more visible, and consequently by making the reader's pleasure balk, Leduc actually is able to further concretize the position of the reader relative to Violette.

This passage illustrates the ways in which Leduc's writing disrupts Chambers's law of narrative power, turning that law back on itself. If Chambers claims that textual seduction is destroyed by the analysis that its seductive elements demand, Leduc shows that she knows this, and uses it strategically to dramatize the seduction. Moreover, she ultimately uses this technique to buttress her relationship with—and, by extension, seduction of—her reader.

Using the very elements that according to Chambers's theory "require" analysis—metaphor, for example—Leduc manages to proceed with her seduction rather than undermine it. She does this by creating metaphors that are understood physically, in the reader's body, before they can be understood intellectually.[8] In this way, she bypasses the stoppage created by analysis when it acts on the elements of textual seduction. For example, in "La pieuvre dans mes entrailles frémissait [The octopus in my entrails quivered]" (*La Bâtarde* 125), the physical impact of the image-sensation is much stronger than the intellectual one. The image of an octopus's tentacles uncurling in this woman's entrails makes little sense unless the reader *feels* the octopus. Once the reader has felt the octopus—an uncannily accurate description of a body's response to sexual pleasure—Leduc's brand of seduction-by-sensation has already taken place, and no amount of analysis could dismantle it.

My reader will no doubt by now be wondering how Leduc's seduction-by-sensation—an admittedly erotic touch aimed at producing pleasure on the part of the reader—differs from the pornographic writing found in books and magazines that would never be classified as literature. Drawing a line between erotica and pornography—the artistic and the obscene—has always been problematic. This difficulty was expressed well by the American Supreme Court Justice who claimed that he could not define pornography but he knew it when he saw it. Because pleasure itself is highly subjective, and personal taste even more so, it may indeed seem that this Justice's inability to pin down what is and is not pornographic is universal. Several critics of erotic literature have done just that, however.

Alexandrian, in the *avant-propos* to his *Histoire de la littérature érotique*,[9] claims that there is no difference between the erotic and the pornographic, save that the erotic has "something else added" to the sexual discourse he calls pornography.[10] The difference for him lies instead between the erotic and the obscene:

> Il est beaucoup plus important de faire la distinction entre l'érotique et l'obscène. En ce cas, on considère que l'érotisme est tout ce qui rend la chair désirable, la montre en son éclat ou dans sa fleur, éveille une impression de santé, de beauté, de jeu délectable; tandis que l'obscénité ravale la chair, y associe la saleté, les infirmités, les plaisanteries scatalogiques, les mots orduriers.

> [It is much more important to make the distinction between the erotic and the obscene. In this case, we believe that eroticism is everything that makes the flesh desirable, that shows it in its best light or in blossom, gives an impression of health, beauty, delightful play; whereas the obscene degrades the flesh, associates it with filth, infirmities, scatalogical jokes, and dirty words.] (*Histoire de la littérature érotique* 8)

The "something else added" is what grounds the erotic in a social or loving context, whereas the pornographic is a simple description of sexual pleasures, not anchored in a context of personal relationship. The pornographic, however, in Alexandrian's schema, remains a healthy sexual expression. Although this Frenchman claims that his distinction between the erotic and pornographic is not a difference, many Anglo-Americans would disagree, as our culture puts a moral stamp of disapproval on the more nonchalant sex that Alexandrian's definition of pornography suggests; we would be apt to bundle the two in a single category. However, as *La Bâtarde* comes out of this tradition, it is perhaps best to judge it by its own cultural standards. Alexandrian's definition firmly puts *La Bâtarde* in the realm of the erotic. This book contains none of the dirty or debasing elements that he attributes to obscenity, but the passages concerning Violette and Isabelle certainly highlight the "delightful play" of adolescent sexuality. Moreover, the social context which defines the erotic for him is evident on two levels: on the level of the story the girls' pleasure occurs within a love relationship, and on the level of narration there is also a relational issue. Leduc uses these passages as a vehicle with which to seduce her reader; we must remember that she wishes to realize her "dream of love."

Jeanette Winterson, in her forward to Margaret Reynolds' anthology of women's erotic writing,[11] proposes a slightly different reading of what constitutes the erotic than that suggested by Alexandrian. She does believe that there exists a difference between erotica and pornography. This is mostly a lexical difference, however. Her idea of pornography corresponds roughly to his definition of the obscene: she finds it exploitative, degrading, harmful—terms that are much more caustic than his (the relatively mild "unhealthy," "scatalogical," "dirty"). The suggestion of danger in Winterson's definition is an important marker of how the effects of pornography are perceived by different genders.

From the beginning, Winterson is very political in her discussion of gender and sensual writing. At the outset, she boldly suggests that pornography[12] is "male," so that the line between erotica and pornography is drawn at the gender gap. She writes that the salient characteristics of pornography are that "it is utterly man-centered, that it avoids contact with real women, preferring its own fetishised versions, and that it is all the same" (xxii). Erotica by women, on the other hand, "put[s] a woman back at the centre [sic] of her own sexuality" (xxii). Once again, *La Bâtarde* clearly qualifies as an erotic text according to this definition.

Winterson's primary quarrel with pornography is that it makes real women invisible, despite its claim to celebrate them. The commonly held assumption—held by men, that is—is that in pornography, woman "is central, urgent. She has the power, as body or muse" (xix). The reality, she claims, is quite different: that the pornographic image of woman is nothing more than a male fantasy. As such, the real woman is not only ignored, but commodified: "There is no engagement with the woman either at the level of production or consumption. She is the sum of her parts and these parts are discussed, manipulated, and packaged in much the same way as a set of machine tools" (xix).

Margaret Reynolds herself focuses on the consumption end in her elaboration of the difference between erotica and pornography. For her, the difference lies primarily in how it is consumed. She writes that pornography "consists of those depictions of sexuality which are used exploitatively and selfishly. Erotica consists of those portraits which are used honestly and with love" (xxix). This places the onus on the reader, and not on the writer, of erotic literature to produce its meaning and degree of degradation, if any. This definition suggests that each erotic text exists on a continuum of eroticism, and that the producer of the text cannot control the manner in which it will be perceived and used. While I agree that every reader brings his or her own meaning to a text, and that "one woman's pornography is another woman's erotica" (xxix), I think that this assessment does not tell the whole story. Beauvoir herself writes of Leduc's "audace retenue [restrained daring]" that "elle scandalise les puritains [she scandalizes Puritans]" but that "la chiennerie n'y trouve pas son compte [it's too tame for the hard core]" (*La Bâtarde* 20). Despite personal differences in taste and moral codes, I believe that the power relations set into motion in the sexual situation exert a strong influence over whether or not any text will be viewed as erotic or pornographic.

American poet and lesbian theorist Audre Lorde has also weighed in on the question of the erotic versus the pornographic, in her essay entitled *Uses of the Erotic: The Erotic as Power*.[13] In contrast with Reynolds, Winterson, and Alexandrian, Lorde's conception of the erotic is ontological. For Lorde, the erotic is a state of being, a way of life, a power, a resource, the root of all creativity, and a threat to the oppressions of racism, sexism, capitalism, and patriarchy. It is not associated merely with the sexual, and therein lies both its power and its weakness: women in Euro-american societies are wary of it. She writes:

> The erotic has often been misnamed by men and used against women. It has been made into the confused, the trivial, the psychotic, the plasticized sensation. For this reason, we have often turned away from the exploration and consideration of the erotic as a source of power and information, confusing it with its opposite, the pornographic. But pornography is a direct denial of the power of the erotic, for it represents the suppression of true feeling. Pornography emphasizes sensation without feeling.

Lorde's conception of the erotic in its relation to the pornographic—specifically regarding its deployment in today's Western societies—is in line with Winterson's assessments. Lorde's term "plasticized" echoes Winterson's assertion that women are commodified by pornography. For both writers, the erotic is empowering (it roots women in self-knowledge; it puts them back at the center of their texts), and pornography strips power away from women by creating, disseminating, and perpetuating myths of feminine inferiority, and by disconnecting women from their bodies and sources of knowledge and power. Interestingly, these two lesbian theorists—writing over a decade apart—go to pains to identify the erotic with not just the feminine, but exclusively with the *female*: Lorde calls the erotic "a resource that lies in a deeply female and spiritual plane."[14]

Lorde's vision of the erotic is particularly germane to a discussion of Violette Leduc, as they share the sense that the erotic is a mode of being rather than as a literary or artistic genre. Beauvoir's assertion that for Leduc the erotic is "the one great, unsurpassable key to the world; it is in the light of eroticism that she discovers the city and the countryside, the depths of the night, the fragility of dawn, the cruelty of chiming bells" uncannily prefigures Lorde's claim that the erotic "becomes a lens through which we scrutinize all aspects of our existence." Perhaps it is the poet's eye in each of them that facilitated their entry into the erotic.

⁎
⁎⁎

At this point, in order to clarify Leduc's position as a writer of erotica, it will be fruitful to examine her work in the context of other sexualized writings of the time. *Histoire d'O*[15] is an example of more traditional "pornographic" literature of the period of *Ravages*. *Histoire d'O* and its author, Dominique Aury[16] have such a remarkable number of connections with Leduc and *Ravages* that these connections bear exploring. Both *Ravages* and *Histoire d'O* were presented to Gaston Gallimard in 1954, both were judged too explicit by the censors, both were written by women—truly groundbreaking at the time—who were exactly the same age, and both books were written as seductions. *Histoire d'O* appeared in print one year before *Ravages* (in which the passages we have been examining from *La Bâtarde* were originally intended to appear as part of the Thérèse et Isabelle prologue). In fact, the reason for *Histoire d'O*'s earlier publication date was that Aury did not have a contract with Gallimard, and Leduc did. *Histoire d'O*'s author says that "Gaston Gallimard was a libertarian, open to new ideas, but he respected contemporary conventions and did not want to be involved in a sexual scandal" ("The Unmasking of O" 46). This obviously applied to both texts. Leduc sought to be released to Pauvert (*O*'s publisher) at Genet's suggestion, but Gallimard adamantly refused. Had Leduc's *Ravages* not been censored, the title of first French woman writer of an openly sexual novel might have gone to her and not to Aury. These women authors were of the same age—both she and Leduc were born in 1907 ("The Unmasking of O" 44)—and, one might say, of the same experience. Like Violette's Isabelle, *O*'s lover Jacqueline is based on Aury's first lover at the age of fifteen, whom she met at school: "'Jacqueline was a big, blond, and beautiful girl. We were both fifteen and we were in love with each other.' Did they have an affair? 'Of course, why not? It was quite common in France, that sort of thing'" ("The Unmasking of O" 46). The stories of Leduc and Isabelle, Aury and Jacqueline, are remarkably similar, down to the color of the girls' hair. Finally, and most importantly, like Leduc's *Thérèse et Isabelle/La Bâtarde*, *Histoire d'O* was written as a seduction, as a love letter to her reader and real-life lover, Jean Paulhan. According to John de St. Jorre, Aury

> wrote S*tory of O* for an audience of one; she had never written anything like it before. She was in her mid-forties at the time, and Paulhan was almost seventy. It was both a private document of their passion and *une entreprise de séduction*, designed to ensnare—her word—a highly sophisticated man. ("The Unmasking of O" 43).

It is interesting that both Leduc and Aury share this will to seduction. Perhaps this is because seduction of the reader is the sine qua non of "sexy" writing. I think, however that where traditional writing aims at seducing its readers on a purely physical level—one of titillation only—Leduc and Aury also looked to seduce the hearts and minds of their readers, perhaps even more than their bodies. I have tried to show this with Leduc (her dream of love), and this citation suggests that Aury was also looking for the love of her reader. The difference is that she had it (her affair with Paulhan was long-standing), while Leduc did not. Although Aury's seduction of her reader may appear more overt than Leduc's— she comes right out and says so—the latter's writings shed light on how the two women writers' enterprises were similar.

Despite the apparent similarities, however, upon further investigation we can see that there are many differences at work between the sexual expression of *Histoire d'O* and that of *La Bâtarde*. Though groundbreaking in that it was penned by a woman, *Histoire d'O* remains a far more traditional example of "pornographic" writing than *La Bâtarde*. In Aury's text, for example, the reader is not positioned in the same way as she is in Leduc's. In *Histoire d'O* the reader is more naturally conceived of as masculine instead of feminine, and looks in on the action in a voyeuristic manner rather than being implicated textually by participating in the seduction. In Aury's text, the reader is positioned with René, O's lover, who "gives" her to the "société" and likes to watch while other men use her body. It is precisely this voyeuristic stance that propels *Histoire d'O* into the field of traditional erotic literature: the dominating (a priori masculine) gaze is distancing; as Winterson would have it, the woman is not at the center—the subject—of her own sexuality, but is the object of someone else's. Positioned in this way the reader is not threatened by the text but senses mastery over it as well as over the body of O.

On this point alone, Leduc's erotic scenarios distance themselves from mainstream erotic literature: by bringing the reader into the sexual dynamic, there can exist none of the feelings of distanced domination that voyeurism inspires. Here Violette is at the center of her own story of sexual pleasure, completely present, and the reader is there with her, too. The power relations inherent in seduction, though not equal, present risks for both seducer and seducee: while the seducee runs the obvious risk of succumbing, the seducer risks failing to seduce, and thus looking foolish. In fact, Aury's desire to "ensnare" her reader does not translate, in *Histoire d'O*, into a subtle winning over of the reader by her protagonist. It is less of a seduction than a titillation or a display; O is not forced against her will into a life of sexual servitude, but made to desire it for the sake of her lover, and the reader gets to watch with a mixture of horror and sexual excitement.

How, then, does *Histoire d'O* fit on a spectrum of the erotic to the obscene? Reynolds' point about reception is well-taken: as a feminist, I can only read this text as harmful to women—despite Paulhan's claims to the contrary—but we have seen Aury herself speak lovingly of her text. This tension between readings might also exist between Winterson and Alexandrian. Winterson, I am certain, would agree that this text is harmful to women, and thus should be considered obscene. Her point that obscenity deals only with the body, erasing the woman inside, is beautifully illustrated by O's name when she becomes a nothing—a cipher—from the moment at which she arrives at the château.[17] At the end of the novel, O loses not only her name but also her face as identification when she is taken to a party to be used by guests wearing only an owl mask and a dog leash attached to her genitals. That O does not belong to herself anymore is reinforced by the nightly flogging that she receives. In addition, it is announced to the outside world by a series of markers: the iron ring on her finger, the insignia at the end of a long chain hanging from a ring inserted through one of her labia, and Sir Stephen's initials which are branded on her buttocks. While these markers came with time, O was warned on the night of her arrival at the château that she no longer belonged to herself, but to the society.[18] Clearly, then, this text is an excellent example of what Winterson and Lorde caution against in the pornographic. Instead of discovering her true self—the power of the erotic—O finds herself literally made into a male fantasy, complete with period costumes.

It is somewhat more difficult to attempt to locate Alexandrian's reaction to *Histoire d'O* on this spectrum. There is some evidence that he would categorize Aury's text as obscene based on the fact that it is an unhealthy sexual expression: the beatings and body mutilation "degrade the flesh." However, it is not scatological, and does not ever resort to using 'mots orduriers." In fact, *Histoire d'O* seems to go out of its way to speak euphemistically of body parts, consistently using such expressions as "ventre" and "reins [literally: small of the back]" (rendered in English as "belly" and "buttocks") to indicate vagina and anus. This reticence appears out of place in a text that is otherwise so explicit.[19] What further complicates the issue of locating *Histoire d'O* on the spectrum for Alexandrian is that while O has no relationship with the majority of the men who abuse her,[20] she does in fact love René. Indeed, she continues to love him throughout the course of the novel, even though she was surprised and horrified after her first night of rape and torture to hear herself say so: "Tout haut, il lui dit qu'il l'aimait. O, tremblante, s'aperçut avec terreur qu'elle lui répondait «je t'aime» et que c'était vrai [In a loud voice, he told her that he loved her. O, trembling, was terrified to notice that she answered 'I love you,' and that it was true]"(18/18). Thus, even though the sex acts in *Histoire d'O* are no "delightful play," it is possible that Alexandrian might characterize this text as erotic.

Personally, I believe that the power dynamics evidenced in *Histoire d'O* clearly mark it as an obscene work. This is a sexual initiation of sorts—O has never before been whipped or beaten, much less gang raped—but unlike the sexual initiation in *La Bâtarde*, the power relations never equalize, and in fact only become progressively more polarized. Conversely, Violette Leduc's *La Bâtarde* fits squarely with all of our theorists' definitions of the erotic text. *La Bâtarde* figures desire and pleasure as seen from the inside—from Violette's point of view—and so the woman has not been made invisible or removed from the center of her own sexuality. The sexual expression of Violette's encounters with Isabelle is joyful, the very definition of Alexandrian's "delightful play."

Why was it that Aury skipped the seduction stage and went straight to the (pornographic) heart of the matter? Perhaps the most plausible reason is that it was written for a single reader, and never meant for publication. I believe that Aury's aim was to seduce the *mind* and heart[21] of this member of the Académie Française; as his lover she had seduced him long ago and could touch his body at any time. For Leduc, the impossibility of physical contact with the reader—if not anonymous, at least one who rebuffed her advances—lent urgency to her project to reach through the text to touch her reader.

The question of audience is also relevant when it comes to assessing the degree of obscenity in these two texts. Aury, we must remember, was writing for a specific reader, so she could have guessed what would have moved him. In Paulhan's introductory essay[22]—which stands just as Beauvoir's does at the head of *La Bâtarde* and serves the same purpose—he shows that he was impressed by the radical display of love by O. He cites the text: "«Aussi longtemps qu'on me frappe, ou qu'on me viole de ta part, je ne suis que pensée de toi, désir de toi, obsession de toi» ['As long as I am beaten and ravished on your behalf, I am naught but the thought of you, the desire of you, the obsession of you']" (xi/xxxi). This suggests that for Aury the elaborate descriptions of gang rape and other sadomasochistic behaviors[23] were not meant as an end in themselves, as they would be in traditional male-centered "pornographic" writing. Rather, they would be a means to an end. If these scenes—in which O is willing to give up her identity, her claim to her own body, and even her life at the end—were meant not only to titillate, but especially to show her love for René, then this certainly puts *Histoire d'O* in a class by itself.

Whether or not one is seduced by Aury's text, it is clear that her ideal reader Paulhan was meant to identify with René. There was certainly no chance that Paulhan would risk identifying with this young woman. However, as we have seen, it is precisely this identification that Leduc wants to inspire in her reader. Instead of lingering on scenes of torture narrated in the third person by a detached and disembodied—though not omniscient—(female?) voice, Leduc's Violette describes the "torturous" excess of pleasure experienced willingly at the hands of her lover: "On me torturait menu, menu dans mon ventre."

In the following chapter we will investigate a further method of Leducian textual seduction, once again with the reader's body being inscribed into the text. This time the inscription will occur through what I will call "autovoyeurism" and the conflation of the reader with the mirror image of the protagonist in *Thérèse et Isabelle*. Leduc's tactics in this short novel can be read as a defense against the invasive, dominating masculine gaze that we have seen operating in *Histoire d'O*.

CHAPTER FIVE

Through the Looking Glass:
Reading Leduc's Erotic Look

The look[1] is a principal instrument of passion, and as such is an essential element of the arts. What would be the emotive force of the theater of Racine, for example, or the painting of Manet or Renoir, without the look? In the twentieth century, with the advent of Freud and his theories, as well as worldwide movements of women's liberation, the role of the look has been subjected to intense examination in both the political and the psychological domains. As a result, it has attained primary importance in the literature of today. Within French literature, we find one example of the look and its more obsessive side—voyeurism—in the writings of Marguerite Duras. This is particularly evident in her text *Le Ravissement de Lol V Stein*[2] in which the narrator Jack follows Lol on her walks and watches her obsessively through the windows while hidden in the bushes behind her house. Another striking example of the obsessive look is Alain Robbe-Grillet's *La Jalousie*, in which it could be said that the look—the intrusive, voyeuristic look par excellence—has nearly attained the status of a character in its own right; or conversely, that the narrator is reduced simply to his look.

These books which center on the power of the look, published in 1964 and 1957 respectively, are predated in the writing (although not in the publication) by Violette Leduc's *Thérèse et Isabelle*, the text that we will be examining here. (Significantly, both Duras and Robbe-Grillet were drawn to participate in cinema during the 1960s, a medium in which the look attains primacy as *the* vehicle through which the spectator apprehends the story. It was at this same time that the filmic version of *Thérèse et Isabelle* appeared.)

It is the lesson of these texts that the look is the signifier of desire. In this chapter we will examine the role of the erotic look in *Thérèse et Isabelle*, the figure of the eye in the text, and the manner in which Leduc manipulates her reader's participation in erotic looking. By incorporating a potentially aggressive, detached, dominating reader's gaze into the lovers' inner circle, Leduc renders that gaze safe, and more important, loving.

Taken in the context of her œuvre, *Thérèse et Isabelle* should be considered an interrogation by Leduc of the role of the reader in her texts, a question that is

84   *Chapter Five*

particularly thorny for the autobiographer.[3] As Michael Sheringham notes in his preface to *French Autobiography: Devices and Desires*:

> The ideological aspect of autobiography reflects the fact that it is a private activity con-
> ducted in the public eye. To write is to presuppose a subsequent act of reading, and the
> imagined reader is another manifestation of the otherness with which the autobiographer
> must reckon. (ix)

The public eye versus the private act of looking is precisely the focus—one could say obsession—of Leduc's text. In it, she answers the question of how to deal with the reader's eye, and the fruit of her investigation is the remarkable bond she forms with the reader. The reader, in Sheringham's paradigm of auto-biography, is an "otherness" to be reckoned with; in other words, the reader poses a certain threat to the privacy of the autobiographer. Elaine Marks has also made this observation. As she has it, "Many ardent readers of autobiogra-phies . . . read also out of a shameless curiosity to peek in when the blinds are lowered" ("The Dream of Love" 73). As we shall see in this investigation, Le-duc's innovation in autobiographical writings situates the reader not as an "other," outside the text looking in, but as a "same," inside the text looking on.

One of the most intriguing aspects of Violette Leduc's works is her un-canny ability to suture the reader into the text in a bond of identification with the narrator-protagonist. The verb "to suture" may seem too strong, as readers fre-quently develop feelings of identification with the narrator over the course of a novel or autobiography. However, when one considers that Leduc's narrator consistently presents herself in the worst light—as an emotionally needy out-cast—it becomes clear that few readers would set out to become (one with) *la bâtarde*. And yet, this is what happens time after time. We have seen recent tes-timony to Leduc's seductive powers in the texts by René de Ceccatty and Mich-ele Zackheim.

Twenty years ago, Elaine Marks tried to "explain the unconscious appeal of autobiographies for the writer and for the reader" ("The Dream of Love" 74) by proposing the notion of "a dream of love in which writer and reader ideally merge" ("The Dream of Love" 76). If we are to believe Ceccatty's assertion that "each one became Violette Leduc,"[4] the merging of reader and writer happens frequently in the case of Violette Leduc, and this merging is a felicitous one. Ceccatty does not appear to resent the bond of identification he has formed with Leduc through her writings; on the contrary, he speaks lovingly of her and refers to other "passionate" readers who have also felt this emotional bond. These re-actions would seem to support Marks's assertion that "The relation between loving, being loved, and writing is fundamental to all autobiographies" ("The Dream of Love" 73). It is this loving relationship between Leduc and her read-ers that this thesis seeks to explore.

"Becoming" Violette Leduc, even if it means identifying with someone whose marginalization is nearly total (but whose appeal remains broad), is per-haps understandable when it occurs over the course of a 600-page novel such as *La Bâtarde*. For, as Marks has suggested, "[t]he titillated if not bewitched reader has, *by the end of the book*, entered into an alliance with the narrator and the text which he is loath to terminate" ("The Dream of Love" 87, emphasis added). With *La Bâtarde*, the reader follows the narrator-protagonist's life from before her conception through her first thirty-seven years. In doing so, readers are party to Violette's litany of anguish and desire, pleasure and pain. It is not remarkable, then, that Violette's intense and "bewitching" narrative style, combined with the reader's close proximity to the narrator throughout the course of the novel, serve to create this reader-narrator bond to which Marks refers. What is remarkable, however, is that this same feeling of strong identification occurs in all of Leduc's texts, both short and long. Perhaps the singular nature of the reader-narrator bond in Leduc's writings can best be examined in a study of one of her shortest texts: *Thérèse et Isabelle* was barely stretched to 100 pages by printing it with wide margins on narrow paper. In this novella the narrator does not have the luxury of letting a bond with her reader mature slowly and in its own time. Instead, it must be established immediately.

Thérèse et Isabelle was originally written in the early 1950s as a long prologue to the autobiographical fiction *Ravages* (1955) in which the narrator, Thérèse, recounts her turbulent love affairs with Cécile and Marc. It also represents Leduc's third foray into fiction writing after *L'Asphyxie* (1946), a series of vignettes based on her childhood, and *L'Affamée* (1948), Leduc's most violent and alienating text, which deals with her ravenous desire for her mentor Simone de Beauvoir. At the time, *Ravages* was considered so shocking that the prestigious Gallimard house removed the beginning chapters and several of the more libidinous passages of the novel itself before allowing it to be published. In the 1990s Ceccatty, then an employee of Gallimard, read and published the *rapport de lecture* of the manuscript of *Ravages* (primitively entitled *Le Vert paradis*) written hastily[5] by Jacques Lemarchand on 10 May, 1954:

> C'est un livre dont un bon tiers est d'une obscénité énorme et précise—et qui attirerait les foudres de la justice. Et les cent cinquante pages de l'avortement sont du mauvais Sartre. C'est aussi un livre qui contient des réussites ponctuelles. L'histoire des collégiennes pourrait, à elle seule, constituer un récit assez envoûtant—si l'auteur consentait à entourer d'un peu d'ombre ses techniques opératoires. . . . Publié tel quel, ce serait un livre à scandale—et les qualités du livre, qui en seraient, en outre étouffées—ne justifient pas ce scandale.

> [A good third of the book consists of a tremendous, detailed obscenity—which would bring the wrath of justice down upon us. And the hundred fifty pages of the abortion are bad Sartre. It also contains intermittant successes. The story of the schoolgirls could, all by itself, be a rather enchanting story—if the author could bring herself to shroud her operating techniques a bit. . . . Published as it is, this book would be scandalous—and the qualities of the book, which would, moreover, be stifled by it—do not justify this scandal.] (*Éloge de la Bâtarde* 17–18)

This *rapport* clearly demonstrates that Lemarchand was not a sympathetic reader. Even though Leduc had been critically acclaimed by many writers of the time (among them Beauvoir, Sartre, and Camus), Lemarchand dismissed as "bad Sartre" what Leduc herself considered to be her best work: "*Ravages serait mon livre préféré de Violette Leduc si j'étais un de ses rares lecteurs. C'est dur, c'est précis, c'est rarifié, c'est complexe. Il n'y a pas une courbette. Voilà ce que j'ose dire de mon livre* [*Ravages* would be my favorite Leduc book if I were one of her rare readers. It's tough, it's precise, it's rarefied, it's complex. There is not a single bow and scrape. That's what I dare to say of my book]" (*La Chasse à l'amour* 89). Unfortunately, Lemarchand's assessment of the book—that published "as is" it would cause a scandal—decided its fate, and still does, though perhaps not for long. Even today, the censored portions of *Ravages* have not been reinstated, and as of today there are no official plans to do so.

The rejection of what was to be known as *Thérèse et Isabelle*[6] had profound effects on the author's life. Although Leduc continued to write under the encouragement of Beauvoir, she did not publish another novel until 1964, nearly a decade later. This novel—*La Bâtarde*—was a popular and critical success, and part of what had made it so was the story of Violette's adolescent love affair with Isabelle. Ironically, Leduc had used the beginning portion of the expurgated opening to *Ravages* to write that chapter. In light of *La Bâtarde*'s popularity, in 1966 Gallimard agreed to publish the remainder of that opening as a separate text, under the name of *Thérèse et Isabelle*. The success of *Thérèse et Isabelle* then occasioned a film by the same name directed by Radley Metzger in 1968.

This short novel recounts the sexual initiation of Thérèse, the narrator-protagonist, by Isabelle, another student, in an all-girls boarding school. It is often overlooked in studies of Leduc's writings, frequently dismissed as a variant of the chapter in *La Bâtarde*, and until very recently has been treated seriously only by critics primarily interested in Leduc as a lesbian author.[7] Isabelle de Courtivron, in her book *Violette Leduc* does not precisely dismiss *Thérèse et Isabelle*, but considers it truly important only in its relation to *Ravages*: "Although this short text *can* be read and appreciated on its own, it must be viewed as part of Leduc's third novel, for *Ravages* is best understood in the context of the narrator's brief but pivotal experience of adolescent love" (*Violette Leduc* 22, emphasis added). Written early in her career, *Thérèse et Isabelle* can be read as much more than (just) a remarkable evocation of feminine sexuality or a context for another novel; *Thérèse et Isabelle* can be read as a key to reading Leduc and her relationship with her reader.

The action of *Thérèse et Isabelle* takes place over the course of three days and two nights in the closed environment of a boarding school. Thérèse had come to the school to escape the mother whom she felt had betrayed her by marrying. Having been born out of wedlock, Thérèse had always considered herself the man of the house: "*Je lui disais que j'étais son fiancé. . . . Je ne serai pas son homme de journée, je ne serai pas l'usinier qui lui apportera de l'argent* [I always told her that I was her fiancé. . . . I wouldn't be her hired hand any more. I would no longer be the factory worker who would bring her money]" (*Thérèse et Isabelle* 20). For Thérèse, being the man of the house was not limited to the financial support of her mother: the woman of the house. It also included sharing her bed—"J'avais chaud dans son lit [I was overheated in her bed]" (*Thérèse et Isabelle* 21). Feeling spurned at having been not only displaced from her mother's bed but replaced by a man, Thérèse no longer feels comfortable at home, and so opts for the more anonymous communal life of the boarding school. It is there that she meets Isabelle. "Sur terre il n'y a que toi, sur terre je n'aime que toi, me dit-elle, mais elle a quelqu'un. J'ai rencontré Isabelle, j'ai quelqu'un. Je suis à Isabelle, je n'appartiens plus à ma mère [In the whole world there is no one but you, in the whole world I love only you, she told me, but she has someone else. I met Isabelle, I have someone else. I'm Isabelle's, I no longer belong to my mother]" (*Thérèse et Isabelle* 21). In response to her mother's betrayal, the narrator turns this betrayal back on itself by replacing her mother with Isabelle as the love object.[8]

As the story opens, Isabelle and Thérèse have already begun their association and Thérèse awaits the arrival of the object of her desire in a toilet stall. This toilet stall can be considered a metonymical representation of the boarding school, and its dormitory in particular (where the majority of the lovers' encounters will take place). This is the case insofar as the stall is a very private environment closed to outside eyes, reserved exclusively for the female sex and whose function it is to separate the girls from each other during unsupervised—and unclothed—moments. Leduc's choice of the toilet stall as the setting for the novel's first reader-supervised[9] encounter between the two girls is unusual to say the least, but it sets the tone—close, hot, and illicit—for the rest of the story.

This "closeness" operates on several levels: proximity, restriction (being shut in), and safety (shutting out). In the dormitory and the toilet stall, Thérèse and Isabelle are both shut in (the boarding school) and shutting out (the eyes of others). Ironically, schools such as the one attended by Thérèse and Isabelle were walled in (enclosed) in order to protect the virginity of their young charges; the girls were not allowed out, and no men were allowed in. In this case, however, it is the close(d)ness of the school that allows for our protagonists' sexual encounters: Thérèse only feels safe in an enclosed space. As we shall see, on the one occasion in which the girls are permitted to leave the school grounds, their efforts at sexual union are stymied. When they leave what Hughes refers to as their "cocooned, all-female world," (*Mothers, Lovers and Language* 96) Thérèse and Isabelle lose the safe environment to which they have grown accustomed. Even the suffocation which this kind of closed environment produces is welcomed. Hughes points out that in this text, "'étouffement' is presented positively, as a privileged state which both partners appreciate, because it permits them to consolidate their erotic union" (*Mothers, Lovers and Language* 91).[10] The novel opens as follows:

Je ne détestais plus l'haleine de la désinfection générale qui nous délabrait les soirs de rentrée. L'odeur était le rideau de fond avant notre rencontre. Les cris des enfants fous reculaient. Du siège en bois clair souvent savonné montait une vapeur: la vapeur de tendresse d'une masse de cheveux de lin. Je me penchai sur la cuvette. L'eau dormante reflétait mon visage antérieur à la création de la terre. Je palpai la poignée, la chaîne, j'enlevai ma main. La chaîne balança à côté de l'eau triste. On m'appela. Je n'osais pas mettre le crochet pour m'enfermer.

[I no longer detested the breath of disinfectant that so impaired us on the evenings we returned to school. The smell was the backdrop to our meeting. The cries of the crazed children receded. From the seat of light-colored, often-washed wood there rose fumes: fumes of tenderness from a mass of linen hair. I bent over the bowl. The still water reflected my face before the creation of the world. I fingered the handle, the pull-chain, I removed my hand. The chain swayed next to the dreary water. Someone called my name. I didn't dare lower the hook to lock myself in.] (*Thérèse et Isabelle* 7)

The opening scene, then, finds the narrator hovering by the stalls; she goes in, and finds that she no longer hates the chemical smell of disinfectant because it serves as a backdrop to "our meeting." Although the reader still does not know whom she will meet, we do know that not only is it important enough to sweeten the disinfectant smell, but that for Thérèse it will be the creation of the world. The undisturbed quality of this first paragraph—the stillness of the water and the chain, the distancing of the shouting children, Thérèse's meditative mood—contrasts sharply with the action that follows, but is hinted at by Thérèse's urge to shut herself in:

—Ouvrez, supplia la voix.
Quelqu'un secouait les portes.
Je voyais l'œil. Il bouchait la découpe dans la porte du cabinet.
—Mon amour.
Isabelle arrivait du pays des météores, des bouleversements, des sinistres, des ravages.

["Open up," pleaded the voice.
Someone was rattling the doors.
I could see the eye. It filled the entire cutout in the stall door.
"My love."
Isabelle appeared from the land of meteors, of upheavals, of disasters, of ravages.]
(*Thérèse et Isabelle* 8)

After the initial calm of the scene, what follows is more than a little unsettling, and is even suggestive of violence: someone shaking the doors and calling out to open up, and then the appearance of the eye which blocks the cutout in the door. The stillness is disturbed, but more importantly, the anonymous, public—*threatening*—eye has invaded the private space. This is the first appearance of the figure of the eye, one that will dominate the text. In this instance, however, as in subsequent ones, readers cannot always trust their first impression of the figure of the eye. Here, what initially appears to be threatening—the invasive, anonymous eye that entirely blocks out the world beyond the toilet stall—in this case turns out to be a loving one—"my love." This shift from threatening look to loving look is precisely that movement that Leduc hopes to generate in the look of her readers.

This scene in the toilet stall in which Thérèse and Isabelle meet secretly—the first scene in the novella—is an extremely important one. In the opening paragraph of the text that we have just cited are contained many elements that will show themselves to be overdetermined in the rest of the text: the figure of the eye, as we have noted, but also the door, Thérèse's contemplation of her own reflection, the notion of performance, a concern for enclosure, and the potential misapprehension of the significance of the look. Later in this same episode, we will see that for Thérèse and Isabelle the look is a signifier of desire: "Isabelle me signifia que nous ne nous regardions pas avec assez d'intensité. L'amour est surmenage [Isabelle made it known that we were not looking at each other intensely enough. Love is overtaxing.]" (*Thérèse et Isabelle* 11). In addition, while the stall may be taken as a metonymical stand-in for the gynaeceum itself, the scene which occurs there can be seen as a metaphor for our narrator-protagonist's life at the boarding school: initially it is still and quiet, but it is eventually, and violently, disrupted by Isabelle's presence and her explosive desire. Finally, I believe that this scene in the school toilets can also be taken as Leduc's commentary on the act of reading.

***

The private space that Thérèse has created for herself in the toilet stall is not unlike the one which most readers create when settling down to read: as with Thérèse, we find that the outside world fades away and we look forward to enjoying the book undisturbed. Generally, as readers of a novel, we occupy dual positions in relation to the text and the protagonists: we can identify strongly with the central character or take up a more distanced position (one of outside observer), or both, depending on which ones give us the most reading pleasure. If the stakes of identification become too high, the reader always has the option of retreating to a more distant point of observation. When reading, one tends to shift from inside to outside and back, thus making the positioning of the reader a slippery affair.

When one reads Leduc, however, the possibility of reader-narrator distance is shattered. In Leduc's writings,

> Style becomes performance, a display of histrionic skill, and the reader is pressed to become the *audience*. It is not enough for Leduc to imagine readers *in the comfort of their own surroundings*, free to take or leave what they read; *they have to be there on the stage, and inveigled to participate more directly.* (*French Autobiography* 150, emphasis added)

In this sense, the readers of Leduc's text occupy the dual position of those attending an interactive theater performance: they serve as spectators and participants at the same time (what Sheringham refers to as "the imaginary reader-participant" [*French Autobiography* 150]). Interactive theatergoers view the action of the performance, just as any audience would, but with one key difference: they also *participate* in that performance. Because of the interactive nature of this kind of performance, the line between actor and spectator is blurred, nearly to the point of erasure. This is illustrated by the fact that the actions/reactions of the actors are dependent in large part on the actions/reactions of the audience-participants, who thus become sutured into the story themselves. The audience-participants, then, in order to fulfill their dual roles, literally "have to be there on the stage."

Although Sheringham does not extend his discussion of Leduc's style-as-performance to interactive theater, this is clearly the formula that fits his description of Leduc's relationship with her reader: the stage-presence imperative. Here we are presented with an alternative form of reading that is, at the same time, an alternative form of performance. Performance, with its emphasis on the specular (it demands an audience to watch it), may appear out of place in a discussion of the role of the reader in literary texts. It should not, however, be considered inappropriate in an investigation of the role of the gaze. In fact, *Thérèse et Isabelle* concerns itself with the issue of performance from the outset. The second sentence of the novel reads: "The smell was the *backdrop* to our meeting." If the disinfectant smell in the toilets is the backdrop to the girls' encounter, then what is played out for the reader of the novel must be a performance.

As readers of Leduc, then, we are not permitted the cavalier attitude toward the protagonists that readers often take for granted, and we must be personally invested in our reading. Instead of being able to sit back and casually enjoy the "show" from the safer position of outside observer, Leduc forces us to confront the fact that we as readers are an audience: in a sense, we are voyeurs. At the same time, however, we are also participants. As with interactive theater, in which the line between actor and spectator is unclear, so, too, is the line between reader and participant in *Thérèse et Isabelle*. The threatening, anonymous eye that invades Thérèse's private space by its sudden appearance in the cutout is a dramatization of the very act of reading in its dominating, detached form. Leduc turns the intrusive eye back on the reader and makes us acutely aware of our position as potential aggressor. Like the anticipated yet dreaded Isabelle crashing into Thérèse's still world ("Je n'osais pas mettre le crochet pour m'enfermer"), Leduc disturbs her reader. Yet, at the same time, she brings us pleasure: the pleasures of anticipation, participation, and identification. Although our reflex, like Thérèse's, is to put the hook in the door to close ourselves in, Leduc's lure—her hook—is too inviting, and the temptation to turn the page is always too great.

In *Thérèse et Isabelle*, traditional notions of inside and outside, private and public are folded inside each other. What actually distinguishes them is not so much a question of space per se, but an issue of safety. The safe look is the private/inside look (what I shall call the *intravoyeuristic*[11] look), while the public/outside look (the *extravoyeuristic* look) is one that is posited as threatening. In Leduc's schema, the intravoyeuristic look is that of the two lovers. At first glance, the extravoyeuristic looks come from everyone else: including dormitory monitors, the headmistress, lecherous men, and, ostensibly, the reader. Upon further reflection, however, it becomes clear that the position of the reader, literally coming from *outside* the text, is situated *inside* the couple by Leduc, sutured to Thérèse. At pivotal moments in the novel, Thérèse is seen performing in her relationship with Isabelle in front of her own reflected image in the mirror, as, for instance, when she performs a sort of striptease to the mirror. The reader, as the other pair of eyes watching this performance, becomes conflated with the mirror image, and thus with Thérèse herself. Leduc's use of the mirror device to make of the reader a participant rather than a voyeur effectively diffuses the potential threat of the reader's gaze.

This fuzziness of the line between inside and outside, between self and other, is largely responsible for making Leduc's text so powerful, particularly in terms of reader identification. This shoring up of difference plays an essential part in bringing the reader inside the text—and inside the feminine couple—to be sutured there. If a reader's natural tendency is to identify with the narrator-protagonist, then this blurring serves to magnify that tendency.

⁎⁎⁎

In a move similar to this blurring of the inside/outside, self/other dichotomies, Leduc's disruption of the heterosexual paradigm of penetrator/penetratee that underwrites our notions of power in *Thérèse et Isabelle* can also be read as a lesbian economy. The pleasure that Thérèse and Isabelle take with each other rejects the traditional gender roles, and the power dynamics that accompany them, to enjoy a pure, unfettered, and unapologetic pleasure. Much less radical is the "homoerotic bond between the 'mannish' Cécile and Thérèse" (*Mothers, Lovers and Language* 83) in *Ravages*, which, according to Hughes, simply replicates heterosexual power relations:

> Since it is based to a considerable degree upon "foreign," heterosexual gender positions, and implicitly involves a master/slave model of interaction too (because Leduc clearly equates heterosexuality with the master/slave dynamic in *Ravages*), it embodies what Cixous chooses to term "Lesbianism." A "Lesbian" bond, according to Cixous, is a relationship which remains firmly within the phallic/patriarchal order, "gives way to the latent 'man-within', a man who is reproduced, who reappears in a power situation," and constitutes a union in which "the phallus is still present." (*Mothers, Lovers, and Language* 83)

In *Ravages*, Thérèse's relationship with Cécile, then, can be seen as reproducing the heterosexual status quo, established and maintained by the patriarchal order under which we live. Thérèse, in her role as "wife" to Cécile, inhabits the slave position in the (heterosexually informed) homoerotic union. In her relationship with Isabelle, however, Thérèse experiences none of the heterosexual gender positioning that we see with Cécile:

In *Thérèse et Isabelle*, Violette Leduc is envisaging the currently unacknowledged, the buried—i.e. the possibility of feminine intersubjectivity and female-to-female love. In so doing, she is undermining the coherence of a sociocultural and discursive order that offers women too few figurations of love of the same in the feminine—and may consequently be considered as anticipating, and responding to, the "call to arms" Irigaray articulates in *Le Corps-à-corps*. For this reason, and despite its apparently "apolitical" colour (compared, say, to Wittig's "aggressive" *Le Corps lesbien*), we can read *Thérèse et Isabelle* as a profoundly disruptive text. (*Mothers, Lovers and Language* 96)

According to Hughes, then, Leduc's description of the feminine couple in *Thérèse et Isabelle* predates what Irigaray calls for in *Le Corps-à-corps avec la mère*[12] by nearly three decades. Leduc's figuration of the feminine couple is disruptive not only because it refuses to participate in heterosexually-informed power dynamics, but because in the one instance where an outsider tries to incorporate Thérèse and Isabelle into the phallocentric paradigm, the girls' lovemaking breaks down. Their form of "love of the same in the feminine" cannot survive in the presence of masculine efforts at domination.

*
**

Traditional gaze theory investigates the dominating, invasive masculine gaze as it is directed toward the feminine object.[13] *Thérèse et Isabelle* does not dismiss the masculine gaze: Thérèse's fear of being watched by a stranger casts its shadow over the entire text. It is this very resistance to the extravoyeuristic look, however, that removes it from the circuit of desire. Every time that Thérèse fears that someone is watching what she does with Isabelle, she stops what she is doing and covers her lover: "— On peut nous voir. Je suis sûre qu'ils nous voient. Je m'allongeai sur elle, je la cachai aux autres ['People can see us. I'm sure they're looking at us.' I lay down on top of her, I hid her from the others]" (*Thérèse et Isabelle* 72). Not only does she hide Isabelle's body, but she interrupts the lovemaking. For Thérèse, the extravoyeuristic look simply shuts down the circuit of desire altogether: in the presence of a nonsanctioned onlooker, desire and its expression are suspended. In light of this evidence, we can see that the presence of the reader (potentially a voyeur like the stranger that she fears) is not threatening to Thérèse. That Thérèse is narrating at all presupposes a reader; that the reader does not prevent Thérèse from telling the story, as the presence of a voyeur would, indicates that the reader is perceived as intra-, not extravoyeuristic. The reader gets folded into the feminine couple of Thérèse and Isabelle, and as part of the loving couple poses no threat to them.

The novel's obsession with performance and the extravoyeuristic look is particularly evident in a passage that describes the girls' only excursion outside the walls of the boarding school. This particular passage, which occurs exactly halfway through the narration and thus by the standards of medieval literature would be considered the key passage of the text, heralds its importance by its change of venue and the ramifications of that change. As in the novel's opening, and in fact, throughout the text, the central issue in this scene is theatrical performance and its generator, the audience. Indeed, it is a performance that propels the scene. With Isabelle provoking her by grabbing her under her apron in front of the other girls and even the teachers, Thérèse finds that the only way to avoid a reaction that will reveal their relationship—and cause their separation—is to feign a fainting spell.[14] Isabelle volunteers, at the headmistress's request, to escort Thérèse into town to the doctor's office, but as Thérèse's dizziness was pure performance, the two girls decide to spend the afternoon in more pleasant pursuits. Thérèse hopes that she and Isabelle can go to a *pâtisserie*, but Isabelle has other things in mind: "J'ai une adresse [I have an address]" (*Thérèse et Isabelle* 64). For Thérèse, "le collège était ma maison de rendez-vous [the school was our lovers' meeting-place]" (*Thérèse et Isabelle* 55), but Isabelle desires the real thing.

Once they arrive at the address, Thérèse hesitates, and cannot decide to ring the bell. At this point a man joins them at the door:

—Tu te décides?
—Je n'ose pas, dis-je.
Nous tournions furieusement autour des arbres amputés. . . .
—Tu n'as pas faim? Il y a des pâtisseries, dis-je avec le faible espoir de la détourner de son chemin. . . .
Je ne me décidais pas.
—Vous permettez, dit un barbu, vous permettez à moins que vous n'ayez sonné.
Dans ce cas . . .
—C'est fait, lui répondit Isabelle.
L'homme souleva son feutre, la porte s'ouvrit toute seule.
—Honneur aux dames, dit le monsieur.

["Have you made up your mind?"
"I don't dare," I said.
We were anxiously hanging around under the amputated trees. . . .
"Aren't you hungry? There are pâtisseries," I said, with the feeble hope of changing her mind. . . .
I couldn't decide.
"May I?," said a man in a beard. "May I, unless you've already rung. In that case...
"We already have," said Isabelle.
The man lifted his fedora, the door opened all by itself.
"Ladies first," said the man.] (*Thérèse et Isabelle* 65–66)

Thérèse's ambivalence about entering the brothel is remarkable. Although she had never been portrayed as being as sexually insatiable as Isabelle, she nevertheless had always greeted with relish each new opportunity for intimate contact. The fact that Thérèse's fear of the house overcomes both her desire for Isabelle and her fear of angering her lover further points to this episode as an important one in the text.

Once on the other side of the door, the stranger's aspect changes: "—Vous connaissez sans doute le chemin, insinua-t-il d'une voix gourmande qui ne ressemblait pas à sa voix de dehors ['You know the way, I'm sure,' he insinuated with a greedy voice that wasn't the same as his outside voice]" (*Thérèse et*

Isabelle 66). Before, the girls had considered the "outside" of their space at the boarding school to be dangerous. Even the normally insouciant Isabelle was wary of linking arms with Thérèse in the street, for example: "Il faut se méfier [We need to be careful]" (*Thérèse et Isabelle* 62). In this instance, however, it is the outside that is safer. The man's "inside voice" and the accompanying insinuation appear threatening to Thérèse. Thus, the spatial underpinnings of the novel are subverted: in terms of privacy and safety, the inside (of the *maison-close*) has become an outside. Instead of the safety and protection the word "close" suggests, and particularly in the context of this work, it becomes a threatening space. The man's remarks are intrusive and very suspect and serve to bolster Thérèse's apprehension. Her own aspect changes right along with his. She wants to protect Isabelle from the probing looks of strangers, including the woman who runs the house: "Isabelle ouvrit sa jaquette mais je me mis devant elle. D'une gorge, Mme Algazine ne verrait que le bouclier [Isabelle opened her jacket, but I stepped in front of her. Of a breast, Mme Algazine would see only its shield]" (*Thérèse et Isabelle* 69). Thérèse's positioning of herself as defensive armor highlights her perception of the menace a look poses.

We will recall that previously in the novel the look was also posited as menacing. This was during the opening scene of the text in the toilet stall. Indeed, that scene bears a remarkable resemblance to the one that we will analyze presently, in which Thérèse and Isabelle rent a room from Mme Algazine. In both cases, Thérèse has shut herself into a small space, feels the urge to lock the door, senses that she is being spied upon from the outside by a malevolent eye, is intrigued by her own reflection, and resorts to performance. Reading the opening scene alongside it will enrich our reading of the passage concerning the rented room.

The structures of the passages are similar, as we will show, and Mme Algazine's brothel itself shares certain characteristics with the toilet stall where Thérèse and Isabelle meet in the initial scene. Both the rented room and the stall are small spaces, ostensibly private yet all-too-public, and therefore not very safe for our young couple. In addition, these are both places where one goes to do one's "dirty work," and thus in which the atmosphere is not only close and hot, but illicit as well. As we have seen with the toilet stall, the unease of that atmosphere and a sense of insecurity prompt Thérèse to want to be locked inside: "I didn't dare lock myself in" (*Thérèse et Isabelle* 8). At the brothel, however, this safety measure is unavailable: "Elle voulut fermer la porte, mais elle n'y parvint pas [She wanted to shut/lock the door, but was unable to]" (*Thérèse et Isabelle* 71). From this description, it is impossible to tell if the door to the room shuts at all, or if the key (which does exist) simply will not turn in the lock. Either way, Thérèse is made very uncomfortable by the situation. Having been denied the protection of a locking (or shutting) door, we discover later that the girls have barricaded themselves in by pushing a table in front of the door. Still, this fails to inspire feelings of security in Thérèse, who has already noted that the stairwell was "sinistre" (*Thérèse et Isabelle* 70). This sense of menace in the brothel reaches its apex for Thérèse when she discovers a window in the room. Significantly, like the toilet stall, the rented room is equipped with an aperture whose function it is to let the person on the inside look out. However, in the case of the stall, as we have seen, the cutout was used for looking *in*: "I could see the eye. It filled the entire cut-out in the stall door." Likewise, the rented room contains a window, and again the figure of the eye is evoked:

> —On remue dans la chambre à côté. Regarde, Isabelle, regarde dans le mur.
> —C'est un œil-de-bœuf, dit-elle.
> —On peut nous voir, je suis sûre qu'ils nous voient.

> ["Someone is moving around in the room next door. Look, Isabelle, look on the wall."
> "It's a bull's-eye window," she said.
> "People can see us. I'm sure they're looking at us."]
> (*Thérèse et Isabelle* 72)

Here the window itself—a "bull's-eye window"—is suggestive of intrusive looking. Both in its shape and in its name the window hints to Thérèse that it is made for looking not out but in. That she can hear someone moving around in the next room simply reinforces her conviction that they are being spied upon. This exchange marks the beginning of the already-troubled Thérèse's obsession with voyeurism in the house. Indeed, near the end of the passage at Mme Algazine's, she asserts that "Chaque atome dans cette maison était voyeur [Every atom of that place was voyeuristic]" (*Thérèse et Isabelle* 82).

The voyeuristic eye remains hidden to Thérèse for some time, however, and it is the voyeur's breath that (she thinks) she sees first: "Je voyais la buée d'une respiration sous la porte [I could see the mist of someone's breath under the door]" (78–79). When the eye does appear to her, however, Thérèse cannot ignore it. While Isabelle is insisting that Thérèse make love to her, Thérèse's mind is obsessively occupied with the eye that she believes to be watching them: "— On nous voit, on nous regarde, me suis-je plainte. . . . —Il y a un œil. Je le vois. . . . —Sur la vitre. . . . L'œil. . . .—J'ai peur de l'œil. . . . —Je l'ai vu, l'œil ['They can see us, they're looking at us,' I complained. . . . 'There's an eye. I see it.' . . . 'On the window. . . . The eye. . . . I'm afraid of the eye. . . . I saw it, the eye.']" (*Thérèse et Isabelle* 80–81). The parallel between this scene and the one in the toilet stall is remarkable. Here, once again, Thérèse is deeply disturbed by the disembodied eye that is looking at her through the aperture. This time, however, it is not the cutout, but its stand-in, the bull's-eye window, that serves as the eye's vehicle.

In this repetition of the original scene of the novel, we have the troubling appearance of the menacing, disembodied eye, a personification of the act of looking. In the original scene, however, Thérèse had misapprehended the look as malevolent. Although she was startled and frightened by the appearance of the anonymous eye, it turned out to be the eye of her lover, Isabelle. The disturbing someone—"someone"—was revealed to be not the expected evil presence, but a loving one: "Mon amour" (*Thérèse et Isabelle* 8). Likewise, this redefinition of the eye is again operative in this replication of that scene. Here, we will see that the troubling voyeuristic eye does not belong to a dirty old man hiding behind doors to watch two girls loving each other, but to the reader—the *sanctioned voyeur*—whose presence in the text is a loving one. The threat of the look that was initially perceived as menacing is thus diffused. And whereas Isabelle came through the door of the toilet stall to meet Thérèse as a lover, the reader comes through the looking glass.

Leduc uses what we shall call the mirror device to suture the reader into this scene. For all of her insistence on being afraid that someone might be looking in on her liaison with her lover, Thérèse resorts to performance (which implies an audience) when making love to Isabelle. In fact, it is only the mediating presence of the mirror that allows her to focus on the task at hand. The mirror in question is on an *armoire à glace*, and it is there that the embodiment of the reader in the text first occurs, as we will show presently. The full-length projection of Thérèse's image facilitates the conflation of the reader and her reflection. Had the mirror been smaller, the impression of the presence of an *other* would be radically diminished. A whole body can participate in lovemaking and be invested in the sexual act. A fragmented body is not lovable, and the detached (both emotionally and from its body) eye is still worse, as it can only be intrusive and threatening.

Even though Isabelle's clothes are already off, Thérèse's description of her actions recalls the sexual performance par excellence, a striptease, but a striptease performed on the other: "Je tombai sur Isabelle, je déshabillai la forme des jambes, du cou-de-pied, je me vis dans la glace [I fell on Isabelle, I undressed the shape of her legs, her instep, I saw myself in the mirror]" (*Thérèse et Isabelle* 75–76). It could be construed that the "tease" in question is for Isabelle's sake, but that is not the case. Even Isabelle, so focused on her own pleasure, senses Thérèse's distance: "—Tu me fuis. . . . Tu me négliges, dit Isabelle ['You're avoiding me. . . . You're neglecting me,' said Isabelle]" (*Thérèse et Isabelle* 76). No, Thérèse does not perform for Isabelle, but has found an audience in the mirror: "La chambre était vieille, la glace me renvoyait les croupes et les caresses des couples [The room was old. The mirror reflected the hindquarters and caresses of couples]" (*Thérèse et Isabelle* 76). Having clearly seen her own reflection in the mirror ("I saw myself in the mirror"), Thérèse superimposes an *other* look onto her own, an audience for whom to perform.

It is most intriguing after all of her protestations against the potential voyeur that Thérèse should rely on what I shall call *autovoyeurism* to excite herself. If she derives pleasure from making love to Isabelle, it comes not from the satisfaction of making her lover happy, but from the image of her performance reflected in the mirror and the erotic (voyeuristic) look that is reflected back from it: "J'embrassais son genou, je me regardais dans le miroir, je m'aimais dans mon regard [I kissed her knee, I watched myself in the mirror, I loved myself in my look]" (*Thérèse et Isabelle* 76). Autovoyeurism, then, can be said to be a form of eroticism that in many ways resembles autoeroticism, but is constituted by the erotic *look* in place of the erotic *touch*.

Ghyslaine Charles-Merrien[15] has also analyzed Leduc's use of the mirror. Saying that Thérèse was "à la recherche d'un autre regard [on the lookout for another look]," she elaborates:

> Elle le trouve tout d'abord dans le miroir de l'armoire à glace. En effet, durant les caresses qu'elle prodigue à Isabelle, Thérèse (Violette) ne peut s'empêcher de faire appel au miroir comme elle le fait lors du plaisir en solitaire.

> [She finds it first of all in the mirror on the wardrobe door. In fact, during the caresses she lavishes on Isabelle, Thérèse (Violette) cannot help appealing to the mirror as she does during masturbation.] ("Violette Leduc, ou le corps morcelé" 112)

What is particularly of interest for us is her suggestion that a third person joins the young girls in the rented room:

> Leduc paraît vouloir prouver à ce témoin impérieux, sa capacité à faire jouir une femme. Ce jeu triangulaire incarné par Thérèse-Isabelle-le reflet, déculpe son plaisir. *Là encore, le miroir équivaut à une tierce personne assistant au rite amoureux des deux amantes.* Mais les choses vont se gâter, car progressivement Thérèse (Violette) sent un autre regard se glisser dans le miroir. Cette personne étrangère, qu'elle reconnaît à "la buée d'une respiration sous la porte," puis "dans le miroir," vient rompre l'harmonie du triangle. Malgré les efforts d'Isabelle pour la tranquilliser, Thérèse est de plus en plus certaine d'être épiée, et l'angoisse va s'installer en elle: "On nous voit, on nous regarde." Ici, deux regards étrangers semblent s'affronter: *un regard que Thérèse recherche et provoque (le miroir), un autre qu'elle redoute: celui de l'œil de bœuf. L'un stimule le désir, le deuxième, au contraire, le bloque.*

> [Leduc seems to want to prove to this imperious witness that she can make a woman come. This triangular game formed by Thérèse–Violette–the reflection, increases her pleasure tenfold. *There again, the mirror is equivalent to a third person in attendance at the amorous rites of the two lovers.* But things will take a turn for the worse, as Thérèse (Violette) progressively senses another look slipping into the mirror. This outsider, whom she recognizes by "the mist of someone's breath under the door," then "in the mirror," ruptures the harmony of the triangle. In spite of Isabelle's efforts to calm her, Thérèse becomes more and more certain of being spied upon, and she is overcome with anguish: "They can see us, they're looking at us." Here, the two foreign looks seem to confront each other: *one look which Thérèse searches out and provokes (the mirror) and another which she fears: the bull's-eye window. The one stimulates desire, the second, on the contrary, blocks it.*] ("Violette Leduc, ou le corps morcelé" 112–13 emphasis added)

Charles-Merrien, then, concurs that there is a third person in the mirror, and that what we have referred to as Thérèse's "striptease" is an attempt to "provoke" the look of the mirror-presence. According to Charles-Merrien, Thérèse's performance is intended to show that she can bring a woman to orgasm. Thérèse excites herself by exciting the desire of the "imperious witness" in the mirror. In other words, she is thrilled by seduction.

This critic makes no attempt to identify the presence in the mirror; in her view it matters not who is looking, but only that someone is (as she proposes that Thérèse requires this to stimulate her desire). If, however, this mirror-presence is the reader, as we have proposed, then Leduc's project clearly becomes one of reader seduction. Moreover, once Thérèse has discovered the mirror, she prefers not to look directly at Isabelle in their most intimate moments, but to look at Isabelle's reflection: "Je regardais dans la glace ses mains jointes sur sa toison [I watched in the mirror her hands clasped over her fleece]" (*Thérèse et Isabelle* 76); "je caressais le sexe que je regardais dans le miroir [I caressed the sex which I was watching in the mirror]" (*Thérèse et Isabelle* 78). It follows that Thérèse is not making love to Isabelle at these moments, but to the reader in the mirror.

If the interaction were only between Thérèse and an abstract image of her reflected self, the circuit of desire would not include the reader. At this moment, however, the narrator is clearly expressing what we have seen Elaine Marks refer to as the dream of love, this merging of narrator and reader:

> Both the fascination with the self and the fascination with the others are constantly directed toward the innocent reader who is asked to be both *mirror* for Narcissus and other. The [narrator] wants simultaneously *to be loved by the reader and to love himself*; the former desideratum is a condition of the latter. ("The Dream of Love" 73–74, emphasis added)

We can use Marks's observation to see that Thérèse's statement that she loved herself in her look further signifies that she loved herself in the look of the reader, a look that is reflected back at her from the other side of the mirror. Thérèse requires an appreciative audience in order to perform, and the reader, embodied in Thérèse's reflected image, becomes that audience.

*

The film version of *Thérèse et Isabelle* ups the ante on the role of the audience and the function of autovoyeurism in the text. Film, by its very nature, demands an audience, just as a novel demands a reader. Therefore, we may say that the role of the spectator of the film mirrors that of the reader of the text: they are sanctioned voyeurs in both cases. But in the case of the film *Thérèse et Isabelle*, the voyeuristic function of the audience is made explicit. Like the eye in the cutout in the door of the toilet stall, we shall see that the presence of an older, narrating Thérèse obliges the viewers of the film to be conscious of their position as voyeurs. We have seen that in our text, the detached, voyeuristic look of the reader was destabilized by Leduc and then reabsorbed as the loving look of a participant. As with the literary text, the visual text also divides the voyeuristic looks into two distinct categories: that of the threatening extravoyeuristic gaze and that of the loving look of the spectator/participant.

How does a spectator become a participant in this case? In the film version of *Thérèse et Isabelle*, there is the addition of a third main character to the Thérèse-Isabelle couple: she is an older Thérèse who is the personification of the narrator's voice. Same yet other, the older Thérèse is played by the same actress—Essy Perrson—but she is clearly distinguishable from the younger Thérèse by the large hat she sports throughout the film. The older Thérèse returns to the boarding school for the first time in twenty years. While she tours the empty school grounds, memories of the time she spent there—in particular those memories pertaining to her relationship with Isabelle—are replayed before her eyes. Thus, the older Thérèse also serves principally as an appreciative audience to the couple. The older Thérèse is a spectator, and as such, the spectator of the film will identify with her, for we, too, are watching the love scenes between Thérèse and Isabelle. Even though the older Thérèse does not engage in dialogue with the young couple, she is, however, inextricably tied to them, and not only because she is watching them, or because their set(ting) is her set(ting). The older and younger Thérèses are conflated by the fact that they are very obviously played by the same actress, and further by a particular editing technique which consists of abruptly replacing one Thérèse with the other. For example, when the older Thérèse—seen from behind and wearing the hat—pushes open a door, it is the younger Thérèse—seen from the front and hatless—who appears on the other side. Because she is so clearly conflated with the younger Thérèse through this technique, the older Thérèse can be considered a participant in their love scenes. In fact, it is as though the older Thérèse goes back to the boarding school not only to "replay" the affair with Isabelle, but also to *relive* it.

This suturing of the sanctioned voyeuristic presence into the filmic text serves to suture the spectator into the film. By increasing the spectator's sense of identification with the older Thérèse, the spectator can be said to become a participant in the love affair as well. It is in this way that the potentially dangerous look of the spectator becomes loving. The joining of the spectator to the characters in the film makes of her/his look a sanctioned, intravoyeuristic one.

As we can see, many parallels exist between the look of the spectator and that of the reader of *Thérèse et Isabelle*, whether in its visual or textual version. Of particular interest, however, is the notion that, through the spectator's association with the older Thérèse, s/he also becomes an appreciative audience for the young couple. Likewise, the reader of the text serves this same function. We have suggested that Thérèse's performance in the rented room was not for Isabelle, but for the audience in the mirror. It is important to note that Thérèse *already has* an appreciative audience in Isabelle, and yet she prefers to court the reader in the mirror instead. Thérèse prefers to elicit a response from the reader and not from her lover, whom she continues to frustrate. Why should that be? Looking to enhance the bond with the reader does help to diffuse further the threat of voyeurism. This alone, however, fails to account for Thérèse's seemingly inexplicable abandonment of her lover. A more compelling argument for

Thérèse's neglect of Isabelle in favor of the reader is not the diffusion of a negative contact, but the establishment of a positive one. The fact that Thérèse risks jeopardizing her relationship with Isabelle in order to focus her attention on the mirror points to a reading of this text not in terms of an homage to the author's relationship with Isabelle, but as a pretext for seducing the reader, making the reader fall in love with the writer-narrator. This theory is borne out by reading *Thérèse et Isabelle* in tandem with Leduc's chapter on the narrator's liaison with Isabelle in the explicitly autobiographical *La Bâtarde* that was treated in the previous chapter: the only two major textual differences between the two texts occur in the dénouement and when Thérèse and Isabelle rent the room in town. The fact that the two versions deviate very little from one another serves to call attention to the few differences that do exist and to demand explanations for those differences. Certainly one way to explain Leduc's insertion of the scene in the brothel in *Thérèse et Isabelle* is to read it as a sign of the author's desire to provoke feelings of love from the reader; this interpretation would likewise explain Thérèse's abandonment of Isabelle in favor of the mirror: she is forsaking one lover for another.

The other instance in which *Thérèse et Isabelle* differs radically from *La Bâtarde* is the ending. In *La Bâtarde* the narrator's relationship with Isabelle continues beyond Isabelle's graduation and ends only when Isabelle comes to visit months later. Isabelle is then seen through the disapproving eyes of the narrator's mother—who, it should be remembered, was the narrator's first love: "Berthe, ma mère, j'étais ton mari avant ton mariage [Berthe, my mother, I was your husband before you got married]" (*La Bâtarde* 54). Isabelle loses the luster she had had at the boarding school and the narrator's desire for her is subsequently extinguished. In *Thérèse et Isabelle*, the mother is again responsible for the dissolution of the relationship between the two lovers, but in this case the separation is much more abrupt and occurs against Thérèse's will. In the following exchange, which marks the end of the novel, Isabelle obtains from Thérèse the promise that she will return every night:

> —Tu viendras tous les soirs?
> —Tous les soirs.
> —Nous ne nous quitterons pas?
> —Nous ne nous quitterons pas.
> Le mois suivant ma mère me reprit. Je ne revis jamais Isabelle.

> ["You'll come every night?"
> "Every night."
> "We'll never leave each other?"
> "We'll never leave each other."
> The next month my mother took me back. I never saw Isabelle again.]
> (*Thérèse et Isabelle* 112)

The rupture of this final paragraph, made all the more abrupt by its short sentences and through its juxtaposition with the lovers' promise to see each other every night, sounds a hollow note at the end of this text, which, until this moment, has been suffocatingly close(d). The sense of hollowness in this passage is heightened by the repetition of the final dialogue, a reassurance on the part of Thérèse that rings false, given the fact that she knew her mother was going to retrieve her soon. Very early in the text, even before the lovers use the familiar "tu" form with each other, she tells Isabelle of the certainty of their separation:

> —Séparées, nous le serons, dis-je.
> Isabelle se jeta sur moi. Elle tordait mes poignets.
> —Séparées, nous? Vous êtes folle. En tout cas pas avant les grandes vacances.
> —Vous verrez. Ma mère, Isabelle, ma mère …
> Je m'étranglai.
> —Quoi, votre mère?
> —Il faut que je sois toujours près d'elle.

> ["We will be separated, I said.
> Isabelle threw herself on me. She was twisting my wrists.
> "Us, separated? You're crazy. In any case, not before summer vacation.
> "You'll see. My mother, Isabelle, my mother…
> I was choked up.
> "What about your mother?"
> "I must always be close to her."] (*Thérèse et Isabelle* 15)

Given the false nature of Thérèse's reassurance coupled with the lack of nostalgia at the end of *La Bâtarde*, the critic of Leduc's writings must call into question the supposed nostalgia for Isabelle at the end of this more fictionalized version. An investigation of this sort calls for a new reading of the ending, one that would implicate the reader, rather than Isabelle, as "addressee" of the narrator's desire. Moreover, this would explain why Thérèse can only make love to Isabelle through the mediation of the mirror, suggesting that it is not Isabelle that she wants to seduce.

The theory that Leduc has written *Thérèse et Isabelle* in order to seduce her reader would also illuminate Leduc's insistence on the erotic in this text. The quality of the narration and Thérèse's frequent descriptions of the effects of sexual pleasure on her body, coupled with the preestablished identificatory bond between herself and the reader, open the possibility (or the *probability*) of the inscription of that pleasure on the reader's own body.

As we have seen in the previous chapter, Leduc has employed the strategy that we have called associative positioning to inscribe pleasure on the body of her reader. The effect is produced in this way: Thérèse the narrator is describing to the reader the physical pleasure that she receives from her lover, Isabelle. However, between the receiving of the pleasure and the telling of it, a shift has taken place. Whereas Thérèse the protagonist was a passive seducee, Thérèse the narrator is active: she is addressing the reader. In describing the caresses given to her by Isabelle, she is, in effect, taking Isabelle's place as seducer and giving caresses—verbal, this time—to her reader. As a result of Thérèse's shift from passive seducee to active seducer, the position of seducee is left open. In the narration of pleasure, the only possible addressee—the one seduced—is the reader.

Because of this effect of associative positioning and the use of the mirror device to make love not to Isabelle but to the reader in the mirror, *Thérèse et Isabelle* should be considered less a nostalgic love-poem from Violette Leduc to the absent and lost Isabelle, but an erotic love-poem to the reader, a reader whose love can be reflected back to the writer even today, decades after her death.

In the following, final chapter, we will see how all of the strategies employed thus far by Leduc to seduce her readers are expanded upon in *Le Taxi*. I will show that *Le Taxi* can be read as a metaphor for the type of relationship that Leduc hoped to establish with her reader.

CHAPTER SIX

Invitation au Voyage: Reading Leduc's Erotic Voice

Thus far in the second part of this volume, we have examined Leduc's erotic touch and her erotic look. In this chapter we will investigate Leduc's erotic voice—the ways in which she seduces her readers by speaking directly to them. I will show that in *Le Taxi* Leduc has surpassed her earlier efforts to reach the reader directly. Indeed, in *Le Taxi*, Leduc takes the idea of speaking directly to her reader to its most radical state, wherein she creates a *conversation* with her reader.

Beginning with *La Bâtarde*, Violette Leduc made heavy use of the direct address in her autobiographies. As we have seen, on the very first page of *La Bâtarde* Violette hails her reader: "Lecteur, mon lecteur" (25). It is as though she wants to enlist her reader as an accomplice to the telling of her story from the very beginning. Gagnon suggests that it is at painful moments in the text that Violette calls upon her reader, as when she needs help re-staging the scene of the pont de la Concorde. I do not dispute this interpretation but find it too reductive: it is not *only* in her times of need that Violette hails her reader. Particularly relevant to this topic of reader seduction is the episode in *La Chasse à l'amour* mentioned in the introduction, wherein Violette not only hails her reader but figures that reader as sitting next to her in the sun, receiving Leduc's kiss: "Lecteur. Partageons. Comment? Avec ta main. Ta main sur mes genoux. Je me plie dans mon fauteuil de toile. J'écrase mes lèvres tièdes de soleil sur ta peau. Je regarde, J'écoute. Tout est pour nous [Reader. Let us share. How? With your hand. Your hand in my lap. I bend over in my lawn chair. I press my sun-warmed lips on your skin. I am watching, I am listening. Everything is for us]" (*La Chasse à l'amour* 355). This is very strong evidence that Violette's frequent interventions regarding her reader may be seductive in nature. Her kiss for the reader is an indelible mark of what I have called Leduc's will to seduction. Significantly, it was at approximately the same time that Violette was kissing her reader that Leduc was writing *Le Taxi*.

⁑

Le Taxi stands out as a unique piece in Leduc's corpus, and because of this has long baffled critics; Courtivron has suggested that Leduc's corpus be read as a single text, but *Le Taxi* does not seem to correspond to any of her other writings. To date, no critic has treated this work more than tangentially. The last of her works to be published during her lifetime, *Le Taxi* is among Leduc's shortest texts,[1] along with *Thérèse et Isabelle* and "La Vieille Fille et le mort." More importantly, however, it differentiates itself from the majority of Leduc's works on the levels of both content and form.

Most critics of Leduc would agree that the vast majority of her writings are based on her own personal experiences, whether it be in the case of the fictional autobiographies of *La Bâtarde, La Folie en tête,* and *La Chasse à l'amour,* the autobiographical fictions of *L'Asphyxie, L'Affamée, Ravages,* and *Thérèse et Isabelle,* or the narrative travelogue of *Trésors à prendre.* The few volumes that are generally considered "outside" Leduc's autobiographically-based major corpus are *La Femme au petit renard, La Vieille Fille et le mort* (containing both the eponymous novella and the longer "Les Boutons dorés"[2]), and *Le Taxi.* But even here, *Le Taxi* stands out as separate and distinct, as the first two volumes form a whole unto themselves, both narratively and stylistically. By looking briefly at these texts we can get a better idea of how very different they are from *Le Taxi.*

Unlike *Le Taxi,* these three stories—Leduc's only works to be written in the third person—are *mises en scènes* of the profound alienation from society experienced by their female protagonists. As such, even though they are not overtly autobiographical—we do not recognize the same cast of characters that people her more well-known works—these stories can be read as dramatizations of Leduc's psychic state. Indeed, in a move that echoes Beckett's trilogy, all three could be about the same female protagonist at different periods of her life. First of all, there is Clothilde, the adolescent of "Les Boutons dorés" who, after having been unloved all her life, finds kinship with another only to be permanently separated from him the following day. Then there is the middle-aged Mlle Clarisse of "La Vieille Fille et le mort" who hopes to find love with the dead man whom she discovers in her café, but who is ultimately disappointed because he can give her nothing in return. Finally we encounter the unnamed (unnamable?) older woman who is completely alienated from Parisian society, but who finds happiness and a sense of community at the end of the novel with her mangy fox fur and other familiar objects. Although these texts do not appear to be autobiographical in nature, further analysis does connect them to Leduc's experience—if only psychological—and as such *Le Taxi* is marked as truly unique among Leduc's pieces.

The knowledgeable reader will see Berthe or perhaps Fidéline in the traits of Clothilde, who is sent out to work in other peoples' homes as a young girl, but Violette is also visible in this figure who is rejected by her mother. The café-épicerie of "La Vieille Fille et le mort" is based on the one Violette knew in Anciens, where she went to live in Normandy with Sachs during the Occupation. In *La Bâtarde*, Violette recounts how the dead man in question was based on Jacques Guérin, whom she reincarnated as a vagabond to make him more accessible to her:

> Lecteur, liras-tu *La Vieille Fille et le mort*? Si tu le lis, tu te diras: encore la plante verte au milieu de la pièce, encore l'épicerie contiguë à la salle de café, encore la pile de galoches. Oui. Je n'ai pas inventé le café, le village. Ils existent. Tu pourrais te dire: Maurice Sachs, c'est donc le mort? Tu te tromperais. Le mort est un autre homosexuel que j'ai aimé, le mort est un homme riche et en bonne santé que j'ai changé en vagabond parce que mes doigts pouvaient fermer les paupières d'un vagabond.

> [Reader, will you read *La Vieille Fille et le mort*? If you do, you will say to yourself: again the plant in the middle of the room, again the grocery contiguous with the café, again the pile of galoches. Yes. I did not invent the café, the village. They exist. You could say to yourself: Maurice Sachs is the dead man, then? You would be mistaken. The dead man is another homosexual whom I have loved, he is rich and in good health, and I have changed him into a vagabond because my fingers could close a vagabond's eyelids.] (*La Bâtarde* 510–11)

This passage is a particularly interesting one for the way in which Violette addresses her reader. In it, she attempts to second-guess this reader, speculating that she may have already made the connection between this café and the one in *La Vieille Fille et le mort*. This is not a particularly painful narrative moment, so Gagnon's contention does not apply here. It appears as though Violette interrupts her narration for the sole purpose of forcing the connection between her experience and Clarisse's story. The café in question is where she and Maurice first stopped upon arriving in town. The idea to create a story about a dead man in the café is perhaps sparked by the people whom she observed there that first day: "Un homme est venu. Son cimetière pendait sur ses épaules [A man arrived. His cemetery hung from his shoulders]" (*La Bâtarde* 510). Violette's claim that *her* fingers could lower the eyelids of the vagabond in the story is evidence that she identifies with the character of Clarisse, supporting the notion that, unlike *Le Taxi*, this text is specifically related to Leduc's life.

The evidence connecting the protagonist of *La Femme au petit renard* with Violette is even more substantial. Although she is older than the Violette of *La Bâtarde* or *La Folie en tête*,[3] this text's protagonist shares many traits with her. She lives in a tiny seventh-floor room that is too close to the elevated métro (like Violette's on the rue Paul-Bert), and is pursued by the same feelings of persecution as *La Folie en tête*'s Violette.[4] In addition, she attempts—unsuccessfully—to sell her fox fur, as Violette does in *La Bâtarde*,[5] and spends much of her time counting things. In fact the first two chapters begin in the same manner: "Vingt-quatre, vingt-cinq, vingt-six, vingt-sept, vingt-huit, vingt-neuf, trente, trente et un, trente-deux, trente-trois, trente-quatre, trente-cinq, trente-six . . . fracas [Twenty-four, twenty-five, twenty-six, twenty-seven, twenty-eight, twenty-nine, thirty, thirty-one, thirty-two, thirty-three, thirty-four, thirty-five, thirty-six . . . crash]" (*La Femme au petit renard* 7, 29). Both times she was counting coffee grounds; throughout the book, counting and reciting multiplication tables will soothe her when her anxious feelings become too strong.[6] In Leduc's autobiographies, we will see Violette use the same strategies. In *La Bâtarde*, Violette writes about Pythagoras, whose face "chante le bonheur de compter [sings the joy of counting]," to console herself for Hermine's departure (*La Bâtarde* 329). Later, Violette will calm herself in a nightclub full of German officers during the Occupation by counting: "Je claquais des dents, je comptais tout ce qui pouvait être compté dans la salle [My teeth were chattering, I counted everything in the room that could be counted]" (*La Bâtarde* 470). It is in this way that she will maintain her mental balance.

We can see that in spite of the fact that these texts, and *La Femme au petit renard* in particular, do not tell Violette's life story, they do include recognizable details from her life and can be read as dramatizations of her feelings of persecution and alienation, from society as well as from herself. This is especially evident in Leduc's singular use of the third person pronoun; these texts represent the only times that it is used consistently in her œuvre and certainly within the context of third-person narration.[7] Perhaps Leduc required the critical distance provided by the pronoun "elle" in order to separate herself from the out-of-control protagonist. (In contrast, much of *La Folie en tête* is written in the second person, with Violette addressing Violette not as narrator to protagonist but as a split subject. This second voice is unrelentingly antagonistic and lends urgency to Violette's mounting feelings of persecution.)

Le Taxi, then, is an outsider text within a group of outsider texts: it does not belong to the group of third-person narratives that can be loosely linked to Leduc's experience. It is the story of two teens—a brother and sister, no less—who are in love. They know that they will only have one chance at physical union and choose to make the most of it. With money from jewels stolen from their aunt, they buy lessons in lovemaking from a prostitute and pimp (Cytise and Dane, who are wary of their resemblance) and then outfit a cab with a mattress, shade, and plenty of provisions. The driver is paid handsomely (one million francs [33]) to ignore the activity in the back of the car, and to drive around Paris all day long. Over a period of twelve short chapters, the brother and sister make love and reminisce about their relationship up to that point, stopping occasionally to check their location within the city.

Try as we might to fit this text into the pattern of the rest of Leduc's work, it is very difficult to accommodate the radical differences of *Le Taxi*, which almost certainly accounts for its having passed under critical silence until now. Even those other "outsider" texts, when read carefully alongside Leduc's autobiographies, can be seen as fitting the experience-based pattern. The most obvious place to look for a connection is in the characters, but here there is no conforming *Le Taxi* to Leduc's life. We know that Violette only had a half brother, much younger than she, who could not have been the inspiration for the brother of *Le Taxi*, who is older than the sister, and who has a very strong personality.

This already marks a major departure from her other works: there is not much evidence to tie this text to her autobiographical project. Only one thing suggests an experienced-based inspiration for this piece, and it involves Leduc's husband, Jacques Mercier, known under the name of Gabriel in *La Bâtarde* and Marc in *Ravages*. Violette recounts that on the night of their wedding, Gabriel made a bizarre proposal: "«Aimons-nous comme frère et sœur» . . . Je refusai ['Let's love each other as brother and sister' . . . I refused]" (*La Bâtarde* 404).[8] It is possible that Leduc wrote this story of brother-sister love as a way to explore his mysterious proposal. More likely, it is a compound fantasy, linked to an episode that Thérèse recounts in *Ravages*. The night of their first meeting, Thérèse and Marc travel in a taxi on the way home. Marc says to the driver "«Faites un long détour» ['Take the long way around']" (*Ravages* 31) and there follows a scene censored by Gallimard, evidently one of fellatio: "Je haïssais sa bouche intacte. J'avais dans la mienne un cheveu dont je ne me débarrassais pas [I hated his unsullied mouth. I had a hair in mine that I couldn't get rid of]" (*Ravages* 32–33). It is unclear whether this scene actually took place, as evidence in *La Bâtarde* contradicts it. One might speculate that she wrote *Le Taxi* in reparation for the censoring of her first taxi scene.

*
**

If there are few clearly autobiographical sources for this text, there do exist some intertextual ones: the brother-sister love of Chateaubriand and Lucile, and the *fiacre* scene of *Madame Bovary*.

One potential intertextual source for the material in *Le Taxi* is the writing of Chateaubriand. My reader will recall that the story of Chateaubriand's passion for his sister was the spark that ignited Violette's passion for literature: "Je frémis enfin pour Chateaubriand, pour Lucile. J'espérais que l'inceste était consommé [I quivered finally for Chateaubriand, for Lucile. I hoped that the incest was consummated]" (*La Bâtarde* 79).[9] Although many of the details of the relationship between the brothers and sisters differ (the brother is two years older than the sister in *Le Taxi*, whereas Lucile was born four years before Chateaubriand, for example), the spirit remains the same. In both cases, the youthful lover-pairs are united against a hostile family, and are determined to go to extremes in the service of their passions. As Violette reminds us, however, in *René*, the incest is not consummated: Amélie joins a convent and is later buried in a tomb overlooking the sea. *Le Taxi* might fruitfully be read as the fulfillment of this wish, with Leduc writing the story of the consummation of the passion of a sister and brother for the one that Chateaubriand left out of his own works.

Another, even stronger case for intertextual inspiration for *Le Taxi* comes from *Madame Bovary*. In earlier chapters, I cited the character of Emma Bovary as a type of reader who might be predisposed to seduction by Leduc's texts. Emma's predilection for narratives of illicit romance and fast-paced adventure mark her as one who would read Leduc's works with enthusiasm; *Le Taxi*, with its story of brother-sister love, would be no exception. Indeed, this text might hold special appeal for Emma by virtue of its resemblance to an episode in Emma's own story: the "scène du fiacre" in which she finally succumbs to her passion for Léon in a hired cab as it drives around Rouen.

Leduc's *Le Taxi* recalls Flaubert's *fiacre* scene on a most basic level: both texts recount the consummation of a love affair inside a closed vehicle for hire as it drives aimlessly around a city. Moreover, both episodes are extended ones—taking up an entire afternoon and ending in the early evening—and each calls attention to the length of this itinerary via the listing of streets and neighborhoods passed through. Finally, both the *fiacre* scene and *Le Taxi* end as the female passenger steps out of the vehicle.

As striking as these similarities are, there remain pronounced differences between the two texts. Perhaps most obvious is the difference in length: Flaubert's scene is exhausted after no more than two pages of text, while the same "scene" is stretched to novella length by Leduc. This difference can be accounted for by the difference in point of view. The reader of Flaubert's text witnesses the scene only from outside the carriage, while Leduc's reader is invited inside the taxi. This difference is critical, as it colors the reader's perception of the action inside the car. In spite of these differences, Leduc's text can be seen as a twentieth-century rewriting of Flaubert's wild carriage ride, and thus warrants a brief pause.

Flaubert's "scène du fiacre" takes place as Emma and Léon leave the Rouen cathedral, where they had arranged a tryst. On the eve of this meeting, Emma had decided to put an end to their relationship and had written Léon a letter to that effect. Léon, frustrated with Emma's vacillation and the cathedral's Swiss guards's attempts to interest them in its treasures, finally drags her out with him and calls for a carriage. When the cab arrives, he pushes Emma inside and tells the driver to go "— Où vous voudrez! ['Where you like!']" (316/153). At each halting of the cab, a voice from the interior cries at the driver to continue, much to the driver's confusion and consternation.[10]

The listing of places visited by the cab in this passage is echoed in Leduc's text. At regular intervals, well spaced at the beginning, but occurring more frequently as the day comes to a close, the sister asks the brother to tell her where they are in the city. In response to her repeated "—Où sommes-nous? ['Where are we?']" he answers: "—Place de l'Alma" (*Le Taxi* 15), "—Rue Vivienne" (24), "—Rue du Quatre-Septembre" (34), "—Nous sommes rue de la Convention" (47), "—Rue de Vaugirard" (67), "—Rue Caumartin" (81), "—Devant la gare Saint-Lazare ['In front of the Saint-Lazare train station']" (86),[11] "—Dans une petite rue près du métro Europe ['In a little street near the Europe metro station']" (90), and finally "—Nous sommes boulevard du Grenelle" (*Le Taxi* 97). In the case of both texts, the listing of place-names highlights both the aimlessness and the length of the car's wandering.

Just as important as the *vagabondage* of the vehicles, it is the action occurring inside the cabs that marks *Le Taxi* as intertextually linked to *Madame Bovary*. Leduc's text explicitly portrays the protagonists making love inside the car. Although Flaubert is much more subtle in his rendering, it is equally clear to the reader that a lovemaking scene is in progress. This is evidenced by the imperative against stopping the cab and the tightly drawn shades that shock the onlookers,[12] but most particularly by the discarded remnants of Emma's letter and her disheveled appearance as she arrives—late—to take the coach back to town.[13] It is perhaps not coincidental that Leduc's *Taxi* also ends with the female protagonist stepping out of the cab, ready to take another taxi home.[14] Thus, in spite of the fact that Flaubert offers us a more distanced view of the lovers—as seen through a telescope, rather than the microscope that Leduc offers her readers—these stories of the fulfillment of an illicit love affair in a moving cab are strikingly similar.

*
**

If *Le Taxi* is remarkable in that it departs from autobiographical material, even more striking is the mode in which it is written. With the above-noted exception of the three third-person narratives, all of Leduc's texts are autodiegetic. In fact their narrators make themselves very visible to the reader by addressing her directly, particularly in *La Bâtarde, La Folie en tête,* and *La Chasse à l'amour.* In contrast, *Le Taxi* has no narrator at all. The text consists entirely of dialogue between the brother and sister, and it is through their recounting of their past together that the reader learns the story. The move from an engaging narrator to none at all is a major one and should be accounted for. As this is the only time in her corpus that Leduc makes such a move, we cannot speculate upon her motives by reading this text in conjunction with another like it. I suggest reader seduction as a likely explanation for her abrupt shift to a narratorless style. As I will show, eliminating the narrator erases some of the distance between actual reader and actual writer.

Narration, according to Chambers, happens only in context: the reader/listener gives the narrator the authority to tell the story *(Story and Situation* 218). In *Le Taxi,* the fact that it is a published text implies that there will be a reader. The text itself, however—missing the writer-to-reader liaison that is a narrator—fails to make any overt gesture toward this reader. Without a narrator, there is apparently nothing to help the reader to enter the text and to cut across textual boundaries. And without a narrator, the dialogue seemingly becomes closed, as there is no one to impart—much less comment upon—the dialogue or the events which it describes. This is a singular narrative stance: the reader appears to be both implied and ignored by the text. One way to reconcile this paradoxical stance is by reading *Le Taxi* on one level as a simple dialogue between brother and sister, but also on another level as a dialogue between Leduc and her reader. Read in this way, *Le Taxi* becomes a metatextual commentary by Leduc on the seductive nature of her work and the kind of relationship she hopes to have with her reader.

It has been argued by Robyn Warhol[15] that the engaging narrator—one who directly addresses the reader, as we have seen Leduc do repeatedly throughout her autobiographies—brings that reader to a closer identification with the text, while the distancing narrator makes the story seem less real.[16] Of the engaging narrator, she writes: "Using narrative interventions that are almost always spoken in earnest, such a narrator addresses a 'you' that is evidently intended to evoke recognition and identification in the person who holds the book and reads" (*Gendered Interventions* 29). Warhol argues that the realist women writers of the Victorian era used the device of the engaging narrator to inspire their readers to respond extra-textually, to take action in their own lives after having been moved by the book.[17] We have seen this happen with certain readers in reaction to Leduc's autobiographies: the level of identification with Violette was so high in Ceccatty and Zackheim that they wrote their own texts in response. Warhol would suggest that their enthusiasm for the text is due to Violette's role as the engaging narrator and the strategy of narrative intervention to which she so often resorts.

If we accept Warhol's assertion as true—and it certainly does seem to apply in the case of Leduc's autobiographies—how might this notion function in relation to a text such as *Le Taxi*, one with no narrator? Warhol goes on to say that texts that call attention to themselves *as texts* are inherently distancing for the reader, that metafiction precludes reader identification by its very nature by exposing itself as an invention. She writes: "in constantly coming forward to confront the narratee, the distancing narrator draws attention to the reality of the novel's textuality, dismissing implications that the story is in any literal sense 'true'" (*Gendered Interventions* 44). The following question poses itself in regard to *Le Taxi*: does the fact of not having a narrator (even a distancing one) make *Le Taxi* more visible as a text, and thus supremely distancing? I would argue that, on the contrary, the lack of a narrator in *Le Taxi* makes it even more engaging to the reader.[18]

Leduc wrote *Le Taxi* as a dialogue, entirely in direct discourse. In it, two voices address each other directly, without the mediating presence of a narrator. This conversation between the two voices in the text—in which each voice addresses the other as "you"—can easily be conflated with a conversation between the reader and the writer. Thus, the effect of not having a narrator is not distancing at all, but rather encourages a bond between reader and writer.

Gérard Genette supports this idea. In his "Discours sur le récit"[19] he elaborates the difference between mimesis and diegesis—representation and narration. Because this text is written entirely as direct discourse, Genette would categorize *Le Taxi* as mimesis, what he calls the "imitation absolue" of reality ("Discours sur le récit" 189). I propose that Leduc aimed at creating this effect of "absolute imitation" on her reader, in order to solidify their relationship. It may seem odd to find a text written after the events of May 1968—a time which revolutionized French women's writing in particular—that aspires to mimesis, but it is just this kind of text that Leduc produced.

In the twentieth century, mimesis is seen as a literary convention that belongs to the nineteenth century and its mentality. Today it is considered naïve by most critics, particularly structuralist and post-structuralist thinkers, to believe that literature reproduces reality mimetically. Indeed, even our ability to correctly apprehend "reality" (it can no longer be taken seriously without the scare quotes) has been seriously called into question by sciences ranging from psychoanalysis to physics. As a result of the shattering of the nineteenth-century concepts of unity and control, the idea that mimesis is even possible has become laughable. Today our literature goes to lengths to sharpen readers' sense of distance from what might be called textual "reality." Moreover, much of our literary criticism focuses its attention not on the ways in which writers *represent*, but on the ways in which they *narrate* and *signify*. Indeed, language itself is no longer seen as a simple vehicle to understanding the text, but the stuff of literary study itself.

In today's literary critical environment, then, Leduc's move toward mimesis might appear to be a step backward. I would suggest, however, that in the context of her career-long project to seduce and establish a relationship with her reader, Leduc's choice of the mimetic mode is a radical one. In the previous chapters, we have seen Leduc's narrators use several strategies to get close to the reader: the image-sensation—whereby the reader "feels" Leduc's erotic "touch" physically before it can be made sense of intellectually—associative positioning, the pacing of the erotic narrative, the trick of suturing the reader into the amorous couple through conflation with the mirror image of Thérèse, and most recently the narrative interventions in which the narrator addresses the reader directly. I do not wish to suggest that the strategies employed by Leduc previous to the writing of *Le Taxi* were ineffective: the fact that many readers have been seduced after their first reading of *La Bâtarde* is proof enough that they worked. Instead, what I do suggest is that these narrative moves never provided *direct* access to the reader, as there were always too many degrees of narrative distance between Leduc and her reader.

In *Le Taxi*, which I consider the culmination of Leduc's efforts to seduce her reader, we see her employ both her new as well as old seductive strategies. Leduc uses not only a new strategy of meeting the reader on the scene of the action[20]—as I will show through a discussion of narratology—but also those tactics that we have seen her use in *La Bâtarde* and *Thérèse et Isabelle*. By combining all of these strategies, Leduc found a most effective way to bridge the gap between reader and writer. In order to fully explore the different levels of narrative distance, it is fruitful to look at the structures and vocabulary with which the study of narratology has provided us. Mieke Bal,[21] drawing heavily on Genettian theories of narratology, proposes the following hierarchical structure of narrative instances that "caractéris[ent] le récit comme écriture [characterize the *récit* as writing]." Outside of the *texte narratif* exists the actual author and actual reader, and between them lie six levels of distance: within the *texte narratif* but outside the récit are located the narrator and the implicit or explicit reader; within the récit but outside the histoire are the *"focalisateur"*[22] and the "*«spectateur» implicite*" and finally within the histoire are the "*acteurs*" who interact with each other via *action* or *discours direct* ("Narration et focalisation" 116). We can see from Bal's elaboration that even in Leduc's autobiographies, when Violette speaks directly to the reader (explicit in this case), the address from actual writer to actual reader is mediated by several layers of narrative distance—those of the narrator and the explicit reader or narratee—before the actual writer can contact the actual reader. Already with direct address, Leduc manages to circumvent several other levels of narrative distance: those of the focalizer, the two actors, and the implicit spectator. She does this by using the willful transgression of narrative boundaries by a writer. A good example of this in *La Bâtarde* is when Violette directly addresses her reader, asking the reader to join her and Hermine on the pont de la Concorde: "Lecteur, suis-moi. . . . Tu quittes les goutelettes qui venaient te retrouver, tu t'achemines vers la place de la Concorde, tu montes sur le trottoir de gauche. Te voici, nous voici" [Reader, follow me. . . . You leave the droplets which were coming after you, you make your way toward the place de la Concorde, you step onto the left-hand sidewalk. Here you are, here we are.](*La Bâtarde* 294). As she addresses her reader, Violette takes that reader out of her proper narrative level. Even if we assume that she is speaking to the narratee located within the text and not the actual flesh-and-blood reader who holds the book, this narratee is asked to cross the boundaries of récit and histoire to join the two actors on the bridge.

By having the narrator address the narratee directly, two thirds of the distance between herself and her reader, which Leduc would like to cut through, is eliminated. In *Le Taxi*, however, Leduc has devised an even more efficient mode of reaching that reader. Instead of relying upon a narrator (this figure who will automatically give her two degrees of separation from her reader), Leduc stages[23] a conversation in direct discourse between two actors. In this way, by eliminating the narrating and focalizing levels, Leduc has the greatest chance of speaking directly to her reader. Let us examine how this works in the following passage:

> —Tu ne veux pas comprendre. Trop d'amour vous emporte. Les chevaux sauvages m'entraînent.
> — . . .
> —Je suis parmi eux, je te renverse et c'est comme si je renversais un temple.
> — . . .
> — Je ne m'arrête pas, je galope avec eux. Tu es gisante sur la poussière, je n'ai que toi au monde.
> — C'est si fort?

> ["You don't understand. Too much love can carry you away. The wild horses are dragging me along behind them."
> " . . ."
> " . . . I am among them. I knock you down, and it's as though I were knocking down a temple."
> " . . ."

"I don't stop myself, I am galloping with them. You are a sarcophagus carving stretched out upon the dust, you are all I have in the world."
"Is it that powerful?"] (*Le Taxi* 61)

Here, each voice speaks directly to the other, with no narrator sandwiched between them. I chose this passage also as it highlights the nature of Leduc's project—winning the love of the reader. Here, the first voice tells the other ("tu") of the violent nature of its love for the second voice. In this case, the only mediation is the necessary physical reality of the written text (the "texte narratif") between the actual writer and the actual reader. In this particular passage, the second voice remains silent—much like the reader might—upon hearing this confession.

By stripping away the narrating and focalizing levels of the text—those levels which remind readers that they are dealing with a *text*—to retain only that of direct discourse between two actors, Leduc has managed in *Le Taxi* to produce what Bal calls a *métarécit:* "On devrait séparer le discours rapporté, discours métanarratif, des deux autres types, et le considérer comme métarécit [One should separate direct discourse, which is metanarrative discourse, from the two other types and consider it metarécit]" ("Narration et focalisation" 112). This text is considered metanarrative because it bypasses the narrator completely. Without a narrator, récit cannot happen, although in this case, both histoire and text certainly do. Moreover, if narration is by definition diegetic, then the pure form of *discours rapporté*[24] must be mimetic: it only *shows* (thus the performance) and does not *tell*. Although metanarrative and mimesis may appear to be mutually exclusive, the one calling attention to itself as text and the other insisting on the "reality" of the story, in *Le Taxi*, this is not the case. While the absence of a narrator does serve to draw attention to the text's style, *Le Taxi* is not a traditional metanarrative in the vein of Thackeray's *Vanity Fair* wherein the narrator constantly focuses the reader's awareness on the story's textuality. Instead, *Le Taxi* is best seen as a metanarrative commentary on the role of the reader in Leduc's texts. Unlike a first-time reader of *Vanity Fair* who cannot escape noticing its metanarrative nature, the metanarrative quality of *Le Taxi* only becomes evident when it is read in the context of Leduc's entire œuvre and as a metaphor for Leduc's desired relationship with her reader. This idea will be examined in more depth later in this chapter.

Mimesis, then, in the form that Leduc produces in *Le Taxi*, is not a regressive form of storytelling, but an aggressively radical one. In it, she takes a step away from the narrator upon whom she has relied for so long, and moved (I would characterize it as forward) into a metanarrative region where she can come closest to "touching" her reader.

The move from an engaging narrator in Leduc's autobiographies to the lack of any narrator at all in *Le Taxi* may appear to be a large one, but I suggest that it was only a small step from repeatedly addressing her reader from inside the text as the narrator to maintaining a fantasy conversation with that same reader. In *La Chasse à l'amour* it is the narrator Violette who kisses the reader. In *Le Taxi*, Leduc carries her seduction one step further: without the mediation of a narrator, she engages her reader in an erotic dialogue. That the reader's lines are scripted for her does not necessarily lessen their impact—she is nevertheless drawn in by the insistent use of the imperative and the addresses to "you." As the dialogue recounts the lovemaking scenes in the present of the writing—and the reading—it is as though Leduc actually manages to make love *to her reader*, with the reader and writer taking the place of the brother and sister in the lovemaking scene, as in the following:

> — Tu me drogues.
> — Je vais être déchiré.
> — Je suis veloutée. . . .
> — Un arbre. . . . La foudre. . . . Bientôt.
> — Ton visage est soucieux.
> — Je lutte.
> — Tu m'illumines.
> — Je survole, je plane, je suis aux galères.
> —   Le soleil des nombreux éclairs à minuit. Éclairée au-dedans. Tu m'éclaires.

> ["You drug me."
> "I'm going to be torn apart."
> "I am velvety. . . .
> "A tree. . . . Thunderbolt. . . . Soon.
> "You look worried."
> "I'm struggling."
> "You illuminate me."
> "I'm flying overhead, I'm gliding, I'm being tortured."
> "The sun of heavy midnight lightning. Lit up on the inside. You illuminate me.]
> (*Le Taxi* 44)

Here, Leduc employs the tactic of the image-sensation that we have seen her use in *La Bâtarde*.[25] The reader, as an actor in this scene, gets "touched" by Leduc in both the writing and the reading present. This tactic furthers the reader's implication in the text, a move that began with the elimination of the narrator.

*_**

In *Le Taxi*, Leduc not only steps away from the narrator upon which she has relied for so long, but at the same time she turns her back on the characters who have inhabited her narrative universe up to that moment. In *Le Taxi*, for the first time, we cannot recognize the figure of Violette, or any of her former loves (Fidéline, Berthe, Isabelle, Hermine, Gabriel, Maurice, Simone de Beauvoir, Genet, Jacques, René). This is another equally radical move on Leduc's part, and one that in my opinion is best explained by the reader seduction that we are investigating. I propose that Leduc's choice to leave behind those characters that her reader knows so well[26] (because they are so often visited) was made in an effort to reach her reader more readily. By stripping away not only narrative levels but her narrative universe, Leduc demonstrates a remarkable tactical shift in seducing her reader. Instead of reaching through the text, and through her characters as we have seen her do in *La Bâtarde* and *Thérèse et Isabelle* particularly (with conflation and associative positioning), Leduc is reaching *beyond* her text, completely bypassing characters, to grab her reader and hold on to her.

Leduc does this in *Le Taxi* by locating the action, which consists of dialogue and lovemaking, on the level of histoire, where two actors converse and act with each other directly, without mediation. In the case of *Le Taxi*, Leduc asks of her reader that she cross the boundary of the text to join her in the taxi *as one of the actors*. Turning our attention to the text itself, we can see how Leduc produces this metaleptic effect. The novel opens idiosyncratically with a command to come in: "—Entre!" This is a startling opening for the first-time reader, whom we can assume knows very few things about the text: that it is a small volume, written by Leduc, and that it must somehow involve a taxi. This direct command to enter cannot help but be disturbing to the reader, who will be expecting an indication (generally from a narrator, especially in Leduc's case) about the story and the characters in it. Instead, the reader finds herself faced with a command, but a command that is directed at no one in particular, since no recipient of the command is indicated. In the absence of any indication for whom this order is intended, this directive to enter may be interpreted by the reader as being directed to herself. I believe that this was Leduc's intention. This reading is borne out by the lines of dialogue that follow, which are, again, the opening lines of the text:

> — Entre!
> — . . .
> — Entre, entre . . .
> — J'entre.
> — Entre au fond!
> —   Je n'ose pas.

> ["Come inside."
> " . . ."
> "Come in, come in . . ."
> "I'm coming in."
> "Come in all the way!"
> "I don't dare."] (*Le Taxi* 7)

In these lines of dialogue, one voice commands another to enter, but the second voice hesitates. This second voice eventually capitulates and agrees to enter, but only provisionally: it does not dare to enter all the way. Soon, the reader deduces that these are the voices of two people making love ("— Pénètre. Plus profond . . . /— . . . /— Oui! /— Ajustés. Emboîtés. /— Serrés l'un dans l'autre" ["Penetrate. Deeper . . ." / " . . ."/ "Yes!" / "Perfect fit. Interlocked." / "The one snug inside the other"] [*Le Taxi* 7–8]) and still later that they are related and making love in a taxi.[27] But before the reader has access to any of this information, she must deal with the commands at hand. The reader might easily read the second voice as her own, as she hesitates to enter this bizarre text where she is in unknown territory without any signposts. Thus, by the end of the first page of text, Leduc manages, through the power of direct discourse,[28] to get the reader to identify with this second voice, thereby crossing a narrative boundary to become one of the pair of actors in this story. When Leduc (the originator of the command to enter according to my interpretation) and her reader have both arrived on the "scene" of the action—that is, when they are both situated inside the *I* as actors—the love story can commence.

In this romance, the spoken word is very often the medium of transmitting pleasure. In *Le Taxi*, the brother and sister make love to each other with their bodies, but also with their words.[29] This is where the erotic voice manifests itself. As the bodies are making love to each other in the taxi, one voice suggests to the other that they speak; but this use of the voice is for erotic purposes. Often they will tell each other what they are doing, as if to heighten their pleasure with the erotic discourse:

> — Je te traverse.
> —Continue.
> —Je te pétris.
> —J'espérais. L'amour sauve l'amour.
> —Je te savoure, trou insatiable.

> ['I'm traversing you.'
> 'Continue.'
> 'I'm grinding you.'
> 'I had hoped so. Love saves love.'
> 'I savor you, insatiable hole.'] (*Le Taxi* 53)

Not surprisingly, this erotic discourse follows the rhythm of the lovemaking: "Tu le dis, tu suis notre rythme ['You follow our rhythm as you speak']" (*Le Taxi* 20). The effect on the reader is the same as with Leduc's erotic touch and look: the reader finds herself implicated in—even inside—the text, taking on one of the voices as her own. In this case, however, the effect is amplified owing to the proximity of reader and writer.

At other times their lovemaking voices are not so much erotic as they are narrative, telling the story of how they prepared for their "big day." It seems that the figure of the brother is especially bent on the retelling: often he asks his sister to tell of their preparations ("Raconte nos leçons" [*Le Taxi* 20]). Especially pleasurable for him are thoughts of "tante Marie" missing her jewels. On two occasions, he asks her to "Imite tante Marie" (*Le Taxi* 12, 16), desiring a verbal performance that would stage the old woman's distress over losing her precious gems. Still later, he wants to speak of her again: "Parlons d'elle. / Encore tante Marie! / Nous sommes gais lorsque nous en parlons ['Let's talk about her.' / 'Aunt Marie again!' / 'We're happy when talk about her']" (*Le Taxi* 26). In general, it is the voice of the sister that cuts short the nostalgic wanderings of her brother. She often prefers to stay in the present of their lovemaking, as in this example: "Parle-moi de l'abat-jour. / C'est de la douceur sur de l'ardeur. / Tu as eu une patience avec les échantillons ['Talk to me about the shade.' / 'It's harsh-

ness overlaid with gentleness.' / 'You had such patience with the swatches']"
(*Le Taxi* 34). Here, she wants to savor the long-awaited moment—the quality of
light as it filters through their custom-made shade—while he prefers to dwell on
their preparations. However, the sister is occasionally prone to want to hear their
love story, as when she says "Parlons tout bas de nous deux dans le temps
['Let's speak in low voices of the two of us long ago']" (*Le Taxi* 47).

Although I have been differentiating between the voice of the brother and
that of the sister, this is perhaps misleading. In addition to there being no narrator to tell us who is speaking, there are very few places in the text which mark
who it is who speaks. Sometimes, readers of *Le Taxi* can tell which voice is active according to the gender role even if there are no grammatical gender markers given. For example, it is the brother who always looks out the window.[30]
Often, however, the voices are confusing: the reader does not always know who
is speaking. Most times, the voice with violent tendencies belongs to the
brother, but occasionally the sister borrows his more violent discourse. This
conflation of the two voices is followed by the conflation of the characters in the
fifth chapter of the text: the brother takes on decidedly feminine characteristics,
and the sister becomes more masculine. It is this conflation of voices and genders which allows for a shifting of roles and voices between the reader and
writer. Moreover, the gender confusion facilitates Leduc's reading in identifying
with either voice.

In this fifth, gender-bending chapter, the two protagonists verbally relive a
key event from their past. The girl was on the beach, digging a hole in the sand
as her brother watched ("Je te mangeais des yeux ['I was devouring you with
my eyes']" [*Le Taxi* 47], an obviously desiring look, marking this event as sexually charged from the beginning) when she hurt her knee with the shovel. The
girl bleeding in her hole[31] from a wound is a transparent reference to a loss of
virginity, and thus this scene prefigures their first and only love scene that occurs in the taxi.[32] In fact, it is suggested by an abrupt change in verb tense from
past to present that they are literally reenacting the scene:

> — Je te mangeais des yeux.
> — Je creusais, je me blesse avec ma pelle.
> — Je pousse un cri de terreur, je tombe dans ton trou.

> ["I was devouring you with my eyes."
> "I was digging, I wound myself with the shovel."
> "I cry out in terror, I fall into your hole."] (*Le Taxi* 47)

In an equally abrupt shift, their retelling of the story changes back to the past,
when the sister tells of her brother running over to lick her wound and having to
be forcibly removed from her: "Tu trépignais, tu griffais, tu te débattais ['You
were stamping your feet, you were clawing, you were flailing about']" (*Le Taxi*
48). His reaction to his sister's wound was so violent and dramatic, that adults
arriving on the scene thought that he was the one who had been hurt. This mis-
understanding sets up the confusion of gender roles for the rest of the chapter, as

he gets mistaken for "la blessée [the wounded one]."[33] The sister recounts that later that evening, as she was sitting on his bed in the hotel, "Tu es sorti du paravent dans une nouvelle chemise de nuit, une longue chemise de nuit ['You came out from behind the partition in a new nightdress,[34] a long nightdress']" (*Le Taxi* 50). In this way, the brother resembles a virgin bride on her wedding night, taking the role that was rightfully the sister's. Indeed, the brother insists on the performative aspect of this scene, having called it a "représentation [performance]" twice.[35] Thus the sister's sexually identified wound inspires a "pre"-enactment of their lovemaking fantasy that is realized in the taxi.

This reversal of roles even exists in their speech patterns. The brother's voice, very aggressive in the past, saying things such as "Je t'aurais massacrée ['I would've massacred you,']" (*Le Taxi* 26) and "Étrangle-moi ['Strangle me']" (*Le Taxi* 25), in this chapter (chapter five) becomes much more passive and caring, traits traditionally associated with the feminine. Conversely, the violent tone of the sister's voice, which had generally been quite subdued, escalates in this chapter:

> —Prends cette enfant. Prends-la dans les ronces, dans les orties. Dans la chaleur infecte.
> —La prendre? Je ne l'imaginais pas et j'en étais obsédée.
> —Supplicie cette enfant comme jamais enfant ne fut suppliciée.
> —Je prenais soin d'elle pendant qu'elle dormait.
> —Divise en quartiers pour tes aises.
> —Je soufflais sur ses joues dans la haie.

> ["Take this girl-child. Take her in the brambles and the stinging nettles. In the foul heat."
> "Take her? I couldn't imagine it and yet was obsessed by the idea."
> "Torture this girl as a girl has never been tortured before."
> "I would take care of her while she slept."
> "Cut her into quarters for your pleasure."
> "I blew on her cheeks in the hedge."] (*Le Taxi* 51)

In this notable passage, the sister begins by referring to herself in the third person, although in this case the gesture does not indicate alienation, but an offering: she is offering herself in the violent terms that she has seen her lover prefer. Remarkably, as her discourse becomes more and more violent, his becomes more protective. Her use of the imperative is also in sharp contrast to his use of the imperfect. She is demanding to be "taken" sexually in the nettles and even to be cut into pieces for his pleasure, yet he cannot stay in the present, but only reminisce about the ways in which he took loving care of her in the past. In this instant, the sister's speech is very close to her brother's—right down to the imagery. Only two pages later it is his voice that speaks: "Je vais te jeter dans les ravins à la pointe de mon épée ['I'm going to throw you in the ravine on the point of my sword']" (*Le Taxi* 53). This reversal of roles is also manifested in the call for silence at the end of the chapter. Previously, it had always been the brother's voice which had insisted "Ne parle pas! ['Don't speak!']" (*Le Taxi* 14) and "Tais-toi, tais-toi ['Be quiet!']" (*Le Taxi* 23), but this time it is the sister who says "Chut ['Shush']" (*Le Taxi* 52).

The fact that the brother and sister abruptly take on each other's speech patterns and traditional gender roles indicates that Leduc was not interested in insisting on the couple in the taxi as a heterosexual one. This is confirmed by the fact that the reader is given few grammatical and almost no discursive marks indicating gender. The conflation of the brother with the sister and vice-versa in this chapter suggests a certain textual freedom. As the brother and sister, speaking and lovemaking co-mingle, so can the reader and the writer, as well as the acts of reading and writing, in the Barthesian sense.

I propose that this short, long-neglected text is in fact one of those rare examples of the "writerly text," owing to its unique narrative mode. The reader's singular position in relation to the text, as well as the consistent use of the image-sensation metaphors, creates an atmosphere in which the reader is not only capable of writing herself into the text and thus creating its meaning: in *Le Taxi* she is *obliged* to.

Because the voices are not identified with a single speaker each time, the reader can choose to identify with one or the other. It no longer matters if Leduc identifies with the sister's voice and the reader with the hesitant brother's: the key is that they are engaging in an erotic discourse. Biological gender does not seem to matter much either, as the sister confuses her own body with that of her brother: "Je crois entrer en toi et c'est toi qui entres ['I feel that I am entering you but you are entering me']" (*Le Taxi* 18). All of this confusion and conflation leads to a sort of polymorphous perversity in the taxi wherein it matters not if it is the sister, the brother, Leduc, or her reader who is speaking or acting. Most liberating of all is that this fantasy moment[36] is one in which every participant's dream can be realized. For the brother and sister it represents the single moment of freedom in their "dix ans d'emprisonnement [ten years of imprisonment]" (*Le Taxi* 78), for Leduc it represents the fulfillment of her Dream of Love—the possibility of union with that absent presence, the reader—and for the reader it can represent whatever she wants: she is free to stage any desiring scenario that she desires in this well-equipped taxi. Thus, this fantastic taxi ride is seductive to all parties involved.

This text can, indeed must, be read on two levels. On one level, we must read this as a story of incest consummated in a taxi: this is a fascinating story, and one that keeps our interest as readers. The most fruitful reading, however, occurs when *Le Taxi* is read *at the same time* as a metaphor for Leduc's radical and illicit relationship with her reader. Only when it is read in this context does *Le Taxi*—a text that has consistently confounded critics of Leduc—appear as an integral part of Leduc's œuvre. When read both as a representation of and as a metaphor for an outlaw relationship, *Le Taxi* takes its rightful place next to Leduc's autobiographies, *Thérèse et Isabelle*, *L'Affamée*, and *Ravages*. Moreover, *Le Taxi* can also be read, not as one of a series of texts in which she explores different ways to engage her reader in the Dream of Love, but as *the* definitive text in that genre.

Le Taxi is a text that has been almost universally ignored by Leducian critics: thus far, only René de Ceccatty and Isabelle de Courtivron have given it any real attention. Even so, the attention they do give to *Le Taxi* is lackluster. Courtivron is the more generous of the two, writing that stylistically, "The hypnotic quality of the language and the richness of the silences, sighs, moans, pauses are often evocative of Marguerite Duras's work" (*Violette Leduc* 39). On an even more positive note, she hails—rightly, in my opinion—*Le Taxi* as a breakthrough text for Leduc:

> This short, subversive piece suggests that, toward the end of her life, Leduc has finally begun to free herself from external judgment as well as from negative self-perceptions. In *Le Taxi*, the erotic element is no longer mutilating or frustrated. It represents the revenge of emotions that have been systematically denied in other texts. . . . In putting behind her the "monstrous" years, painfully re-created in her autobiographical texts, an exorcised Leduc very possibly had begun to acquire the freedom and confidence to create new forms in which to cast more positive fantasies. (*Violette Leduc* 40)

Here Courtivron shows obvious admiration for this text. I certainly agree with her assessment of *Le Taxi*'s poetic style and singularly optimistic tone. Remarkably, in spite of the importance that she attributes to this slim volume, she does not give it the attention that I feel is its due. The comments cited here are taken from her chapter entitled "The Text: A Sum of Its Parts," in which she briefly summarizes and comments upon every one of Leduc's book-length texts. Because she mentions *Le Taxi* only one other time (and here she merely repeats what she had already said), this represents the absolute minimum of critical attention to this text on her part.

If Courtivron is laudatory of but inattentive to this text, Ceccatty, on the other hand, is frankly dismissive. Clearly, he has not been seduced. In his *Éloge*, he claims that "*Le Taxi* est moins frappant que ses autres livres [*Le Taxi* is less striking than her other texts]" (*Éloge de la bâtarde* 123), and goes on to say that it is because we know nothing about the two young lovers that their story fails to interest the reader: "Leur dialogue enflammé, leurs gestes ne reposent pas sur des personnages auxquelles nous nous intéressions. Ils manquent de poids, de crédibilité. C'est la limite des textes érotiques [Neither their enflamed dialogue nor their gestures spring from characters that interest us. They lack weight, credibility. It pushes the limit of what can be called an erotic text]" (*Éloge de la bâtarde* 123).[37] If Leduc's critics were to reread *Le Taxi* in light of the reading that I propose, I believe that they would find a richer meaning to *Le Taxi* than just a simple piece of erotic writing. According to my schema, the burning dialogue and the gestures are not uninteresting to the reader, because in effect, Leduc is staging a love scene for the reader, and the reader gets to participate. By the same token, if we read *Le Taxi* as a metaphor for Leduc's desired relationship with the reader, the characters are not empty or lacking in credibility at all: they represent the reader and the writer, speaking to each other, making love to each other, within the pages of the text. In this way, when the informed reader goes back to reread the text (Barthes' lesson that every reading is always a re-reading is particularly poignant here), the sister's command to enter (her body—so that she can be made love to) is also read as Leduc's directive to the reader to enter not just the text but also, figuratively, her body (again, so that she can be made love to). In this way, *Le Taxi* is the text in which Leduc comes the closest to achieving the Dream of Love with her reader. For what better way is there to represent an absent presence or a present absence than as the incestuous brother and sister—two figures constantly in each other's presence yet unable to express their true feelings? With their trip in the taxi, the brother and sister were finally able to reconcile this problematic presence and absence. With *Le Taxi*—a loving union that lasts exactly the time of the reading—Violette Leduc was finally able to "accomplish the impossible synthesis of presence and absence" with—and within—her reader.

CONCLUSION

In the conclusion to her book on contemporary French autobiography,[1] Hélène Jaccomard writes that "[Violette] abandonne d'avance la tentative de séduction du public et ne fait aucun effort pour être plus lisible ou plus persuasive [she abandons at the outset any attempt to seduce the public and makes absolutely no effort to be more easily read or more persuasive]" (*Lecteur et lecture* 435). As this book has shown, I do not agree with Jaccomard on this point, and in fact believe that, quite to the contrary, Violette does everything in her power to persuade her reader to fall under the charm of seduction. Indeed, instead of abandoning all attempts at reader seduction from the beginning, as Jaccomard suggests, Leduc hails her reader from the very first page of *La Bâtarde*. It is unclear how Jaccomard reached this conclusion—or even why she would want to untie the knot between Leduc and her audience at the end of this study of readers and reading. She goes on to say that it was liberating for Leduc to believe that no one was reading her work and that "même Simone de Beauvoir est plus un éditeur qu'une pure lectrice [even Simone de Beauvoir is more an editor than a pure reader]" (*Lecteur et lecture* 436). While it is true that Beauvoir read Leduc's work with a more critical eye than the average reader, it is hard to reconcile what Jaccomard suggests is indifference toward this particular reader with Violette's exclamation in *La Folie en tête* that "sa lecture m'exhaltait [her reading exalted me]." I hope that this book has served to reassert the primacy of that bond between Leduc and her reader upon which Beauvoir insisted in her preface.

If Jaccomard was not seduced by Leduc, she is in the minority of readers. This is clear from the volume of criticism—now growing at an impressive rate—that surrounds this little-known writer. Many of the critics discussed here have written on Leduc repeatedly: Courtivron, Ceccatty, Trout Hall, Hughes, Sheringham, Marks, and Evans are but a few examples. It is easy to establish that Leduc seduces with her writings, yet until now no one has exclusively addressed the issue of reader seduction in Leduc's texts. It is this critical lacuna that I have attempted to begin to fill with this volume.

✲
✲✲

This text has addressed both the "what" and the "how" of seduction in Leduc's writing: section one examined narrative and/or textual seduction in certain readers including Violette, and section two illustrated some ways in which Leduc attempted to achieve that seduction in her own readers via her use of the erotic touch, look, and voice. Because it was clear to me that Leduc seduced her readers (my own seduction having been powerful), I set out to establish the relationship between Violette Leduc and seduction. I have shown both how Violette herself was seduced by literature and the seductive effects of her writings on others, critics and non-critics alike. In order to explain Leduc's diverse (if still small) readership, as well as to entice future generations of Leduc readers, I established a continuum of reading pleasures with "Emma Bovary" and Roland Barthes as extreme examples. By showing that Leduc's writings could appeal to a reader who is bored by poetry but whose pulse races at intrigue, as well as to one whose pleasure—equally visceral—is textual rather than narrative, and derived from linguistic slippage, I hoped to impart that there is much in Violette Leduc's texts to seduce readers located between those extremes. I chose Violette, Leduc's narrator-protagonist, and her seduction by literature across *La Bâtarde* and *La Folie en tête* to illustrate this continuum: she read differently— and took different pleasures from the text—at different times. More important than illustrating the continuum, however, was showing the primacy of literature and literary seduction in Violette's life, even before she became a writer. This sheds a good deal of light on why she was so intent on seducing readers of her own. From early on she devoured autobiographically-inspired texts—starting with Chateaubriand, but continuing through Gide, Proust, Sachs, Beauvoir, Genet, Sarraute, and Duras, among others. As a writer of the same kind of text, it is likely that she hoped to inspire the same dream of love which she had experienced as a reader herself. Her legacy is evident in the writings of Ceccatty and Zackheim: the cycle of seduction continues with them.

Simone de Beauvoir wrote in her preface to *La Bâtarde* that the reader saves Violette from the anguish of all of her other relationships because "le lecteur accomplit l'impossible synthèse de l'absence et de la présence [The reader achieves the impossible synthesis of absence and presence]" (*La Bâtarde* 15). That the reader is absent is clear: even Beauvoir's picture over Violette's writing desk is more a marker of absence than of presence. Beauvoir further wrote that for Leduc, "La présence, c'est le corps; la communication s'opère de corps à corps [Presence is the body; communication is carried out from body to body]" (*La Bâtarde* 19). In order for Leduc to make her reader present, she must inscribe that reader—and, more specifically, the reader's *body*—into the text. In the second section of this volume, I have shown how Leduc operates this body-to-body communication: through the erotic touch, look, and voice.

✲✲

While there is more work to be done on other narrative scenarios, I chose to begin my study—the first of its kind—by examining three narratives of sexual initiation. This seemed an obvious place to start, as these texts are seductive on the levels of both content and style. A sexual initiation is the seduction scene par excellence, and when combined with Leduc's use of image-sensation metaphors, pacing, and conflation of the reader with the sexual seducee, the seduction becomes all the more transparent. Moreover, in the case of sexual initiation, the seduction operates both inside the text—within the couple—and through the text—between writer and reader. It was this two-pronged seduction that I hoped to show.

Leduc's special talent in writing sexual initiations lies not only in her ability to seduce the reader at the same time as the protagonist is seduced, however. Whether it was intentional or not (and I believe that it was), by bringing the reader inside the loving couple, Leduc manages to deflect any presence in the text of a damaging reader. Instead of the voyeuristic pleasure of a more traditional erotic text—one that invites a distant, dominating gaze—Leduc's texts offer the reader a place in bed between the lovers.

I have maintained that *Le Taxi* is the culmination of Leduc's attempts to fulfill her dream of love with the reader. While this is arguably her least autobiographical text, its structure enables reader and writer to communicate in a remarkably direct manner. By offering nothing but voices narrating sexual activity, Leduc comes closer to making love to her reader in *Le Taxi* than in any other text. Reading this story of adolescent incest as both a representation of and a metaphor for the outlaw relationship that Leduc wished to establish with her reader marks this slim volume, which has failed to interest critics in the past, as one of Leduc's richest texts.

✲✲

Jaccomard may have been one of those rare readers who has escaped Leduc's seduction attempt. I was not. Like Ceccatty, I was struck, on my first reading of *La Bâtarde*, with an "immediate need for identification." This feeling was so strong, in fact, that it pushed me to want to investigate the phenomenon of seduction in Leduc's works further; when Ceccatty's book was published, I knew that I was not alone in my seduction and have been lucky enough in the meantime to have met many more Leduc readers and critics who have happily succumbed to the same "need."

I am not so naïve as to assume that every reader of Leduc will undergo the same type of literary seduction, or even that the seduction strategies that I have mapped out in this text will be consistently effective for a single given reader. The nature of the plaisir du texte is that it is fleeting and arrives only when it is least expected. Instead, it has been my intention to point to different methods that Leduc employed in the hope of seducing her reader. This work is far from over; by examining narratives of sexual initiation, I have only begun to tickle the most obvious surface of Leduc's seductive strategies. I look forward to future treatises examining Violette Leduc, reader seduction, and the pleasures of the text.

APPENDIX

Violette Leduc Archive Holdings List: Institut Mémoires de l'Edition Contemporaine (January 2001)

Works by Violette Leduc

L'Affamée (handwritten)
1 notebook, 210 handwritten recto–verso pages, including 156 detached leaves
October 1947
Note: with a dedication to Jacques Guérin; irregular numbering
Reference: LDC2.A1–01

L'Affamée (handwritten)
200 handwritten leaves (photocopy)
October 1947
Note: this is the photocopy of LCD2.A1–01
Reference: LDC2.A1–02

L'Affamée (handwritten)
184 handwritten leaves (photocopy)
October 1947
Note: this is the photocopy of LCD2.A1–01
Reference: LDC2.A1–02

Ravages (handwritten) **first notebook**
1 notebook of handwritten pages numbered 1–162
Reference: LDC2.A1–03.01

La Vieille fille et le mort (handwritten fragment)
1 notebook of handwritten pages numbered 1–9, of which one is recto–verso
Reference: LDC2.A1–03.02

127

Trésors à prendre (handwritten) **first notebook**
1 notebook of handwritten pages numbered 1–48
Note: the notebook cover features the following remarks: "Violette Leduc 20 rue Paul–Bert Paris XIème, 1, à Simone de Beauvoir"
Reference: LDC2.A2–01

Trésors à prendre (handwritten) **second notebook**
1 notebook of handwritten pages numbered 49–80
Reference: LDC2.A2–01

Trésors à prendre (handwritten) **third notebook**
1 notebook of handwritten pages numbered 81–126
Reference: LDC2.A2–01

Trésors à prendre (handwritten) **fourth notebook**
1 notebook of handwritten pages numbered 127–74
Reference: LDC2.A2–01

Trésors à prendre (handwritten) **fifth notebook**
1 notebook of handwritten pages numbered 175–222
Reference: LDC2.A2–02

Trésors à prendre (handwritten) **sixth notebook**
1 notebook of handwritten pages numbered 223–70
Reference: LDC2.A2–02

Trésors à prendre (handwritten) **seventh notebook**
1 notebook of handwritten pages numbered 271–318
Added: 6 inserted handwritten leaves numbered 281–91
Reference: LDC2.A2–02

Trésors à prendre (handwritten) **seventh notebook**
1 notebook of handwritten pages numbered 319–66
Reference: LDC2.A2–03

Trésors à prendre (handwritten) **ninth notebook**
1 notebook of handwritten pages numbered 367–412
Added: 1 inserted handwritten leaf numbered 379
Reference: LDC2.A2–03

Trésors à prendre (handwritten) **tenth notebook**
1 notebook of handwritten pages numbered 413–60
Added: 10 leaves: 5 handwritten 5 typed with handwritten corrections numbered 425, 426 (the 5 typed leaves are numbered 429, 432, & 32–35), 458
Reference: LDC2.A2–03

Trésors à prendre (handwritten) **eleventh notebook**
1 notebook of handwritten pages numbered 461–87
Reference: LDC2.A2–03

Trésors à prendre (typed)
52 typed leaves with handwritten corrections numbered 1 and 157–210
Note: there are 2 pages numbered 1, the first entitled *le Causse noir*, the other *ma cathédrale albigeoise*
Reference: LDC2.A2–03

Trésors à prendre (typed)
49 typed leaves with handwritten corrections numbered 2–50
Note: page 1 is missing
Reference: LDC2.A2–04.02

Trésors à prendre (typed)
39 typed leaves with handwritten corrections numbered 2–41
Note: pages 1 and 35 are missing
Reference: LDC2.A2–04.03

Trésors à prendre (fragment)
8 typed leaves with handwritten corrections numbered 1–8
Reference: LDC2.A2–04.04

Trésors à prendre (fragment)
20 leaves: 7 handwritten and 13 typed leaves with handwritten corrections
Note: the handwritten leaves are numbered 291–300. The typed leaves have two different paginations, the first 301–04 and 308–16 (in the middle) and the second 13–25 (on the right)
Reference: LDC2.A2–04.05

Trésors à prendre (fragment)
6 leaves: 5 handwritten and 1 typed leaves
Note: pages numbered 1, 5, 31–32, 32 continued, 34, 35, and 36, and one leaf has no number
Reference: LDC2.A2–04.06

La Bâtarde (handwritten) second notebook
1 notebook of handwritten pages [no numbers listed]
Note: notebook with blue cover
Reference: LDC2.A2–05

La Bâtarde (handwritten) second notebook
1 notebook of handwritten pages [no numbers listed]
Note: notebook with black and pink checks
Reference: LDC2.A2–05

La Bâtarde (handwritten) third notebook
1 notebook of handwritten pages [no numbers listed]
Note: notebook with blue cover
Reference: LDC2.A2–05

La Bâtarde (handwritten) second notebook
1 notebook of handwritten pages [no numbers listed]
Note: notebook with black and pink checks
Reference: LDC2.A2–06

La Bâtarde (handwritten) fourth notebook
1 notebook of handwritten pages [no numbers listed]
Note: notebook with blue cover
Reference: LDC2.A2–06

La Bâtarde (handwritten) fourth notebook
1 notebook of handwritten pages [no numbers listed]
Note: notebook with black and pink checks
Reference: LDC2.A2–07

La Bâtarde (handwritten) fifth notebook
1 notebook of handwritten pages, including 4 detached leaves
Note: notebook with blue cover
Reference: LDC2.A2–07

La Bâtarde (handwritten) fifth notebook
1 notebook of handwritten pages [no numbers listed]
Note: notebook with black and pink checks; the title page carries the handwritten
remark: "photocopied"
Reference: LDC2.A3–01

La Bâtarde (handwritten) sixth notebook
1 notebook of handwritten pages [no numbers listed]
Note: notebook with black and yellow checks
Reference: LDC2.A3–01

La Bâtarde (handwritten) seventh notebook
1 notebook of handwritten pages + 12 detached leaves
Note: blue Joseph Gibert notebook
Reference: LDC2.A3–02

La Bâtarde (handwritten) seventh notebook, continued
1 notebook of handwritten pages [no numbers listed]
Note: notebook with blue cover
Reference: LDC2.A3–02

La Bâtarde (handwritten) seventh notebook
1 notebook of handwritten pages [no numbers listed]
Note: notebook with beige cover (torn)
Reference: LDC2.A13–01

La Bâtarde (handwritten) eighth notebook
1 notebook of handwritten pages [no numbers listed]
Note: notebook with black and green checks
Reference: LDC2.A13–01

La Bâtarde (handwritten) eighth notebook
1 notebook of handwritten pages [no numbers listed] + 23 detached leaves
Note: notebook with gray cover
Reference: LDC2.A3–02

La Bâtarde (handwritten) eighth notebook
1 notebook of handwritten pages [no numbers listed]
Note: notebook with beige cover; carries the handwritten remark: "Hermine (the end) (Denise Hertgès)"
Reference: LDC2.A3–03

La Bâtarde (handwritten) ninth notebook
1 notebook of handwritten pages [no numbers listed]
Note: notebook with blue cover
Reference: LDC2.A3–04

La Bâtarde (handwritten) ninth notebook
1 notebook of handwritten pages [no numbers listed]
Note: notebook with hard blue cover
Reference: LDC2.A3–05

La Bâtarde (handwritten) ninth notebook
1 notebook of handwritten pages [no numbers listed]
Note: notebook with blue cover
Reference: LDC2.A13–02

La Bâtarde (handwritten) tenth notebook
1 notebook of handwritten pages [no numbers listed]
Note: notebook with turquoise cover
Reference: LDC2.A13–02

La Bâtarde (handwritten) tenth notebook
1 notebook of handwritten pages [no numbers listed]
Note: notebook with turquoise cover
Reference: LDC2.A3–06

La Bâtarde (handwritten) tenth notebook
1 notebook of handwritten pages [no numbers listed]
Note: notebook with blue cover
Reference: LDC2.A3–06

La Bâtarde (handwritten) eleventh notebook
1 notebook of handwritten pages [no numbers listed]
Note: notebook with cream cover; caries the handwritten remarks: "The war, mariage, Sachs, her beginnings in [illegible], Faucon"
Reference: LDC2.A3–06

La Bâtarde (handwritten) eleventh notebook
1 notebook of handwritten pages [no numbers listed]
Note: notebook with green cover
Reference: LDC2.A3–07

La Bâtarde (handwritten) twelfth notebook
1 notebook of handwritten pages + 1 detached handwritten leaf
Note: notebook with red cover
Reference: LDC2.A3–08

La Bâtarde (handwritten) thirteenth notebook
1 notebook of handwritten pages [no numbers listed]
Note: notebook with green cover
Reference: LDC2.A3–08

La Bâtarde (handwritten) thirteenth notebook
1 notebook of handwritten pages [no numbers listed]
Note: notebook with black, blue, and white cover
Reference: LDC2.A13–03

La Bâtarde (handwritten) fourteenth notebook
1 notebook of handwritten pages [no numbers listed] + 4 detached leaves
Note: notebook with blue cover
Reference: LDC2.A4–01

La Bâtarde (handwritten) fourteenth notebook
1 notebook of handwritten pages [no numbers listed] + 2 detached leaves
Note: notebook with green cover
Reference: LDC2.A4–01

La Bâtarde (handwritten) fourteenth notebook
1 notebook of handwritten pages [no numbers listed]
Note: notebook with turquoise cover
Reference: LDC2.A4–02

La Bâtarde (handwritten) fifteenth notebook
1 notebook of handwritten pages [no numbers listed]
Note: notebook with blue cover
Reference: LDC2.A4–02

La Bâtarde (handwritten) fifteenth notebook
1 notebook of handwritten pages [no numbers listed] + 1 detached leaf
Note: notebook with gray cover
Reference: LDC2.A4–02

La Bâtarde (handwritten) fifteenth notebook
1 notebook of handwritten pages + 7 detached leaves numbered 1–7
Note: notebook with green cover
Reference: LDC2.A4–03

La Bâtarde (handwritten) sixteenth notebook
1 notebook of handwritten pages [no numbers listed]
Note: notebook with cream cover
Reference: LDC2.A4–03

La Bâtarde (handwritten) sixteenth notebook
1 notebook of handwritten pages [no numbers listed]
Note: notebook with blue cover
Reference: LDC2.A4–03

La Bâtarde (handwritten) seventeenth notebook
1 notebook of handwritten pages [no numbers listed]
Note: notebook with blue cover
Reference: LDC2.A4–04

La Bâtarde (handwritten) seventeenth notebook
1 notebook of handwritten pages [no numbers listed]
Note: notebook with green cover
Reference: LDC2.A13–03

La Bâtarde (handwritten) eighteenth notebook
1 notebook of handwritten pages + 18 inserted handwritten leaves
Note: notebook with blue cover
Reference: LDC2.A4–04

La Bâtarde (handwritten) eighteenth notebook
1 notebook of handwritten pages [no numbers listed]
Note: notebook with blue cover
Reference: LDC2.A4–05

La Bâtarde (handwritten) nineteenth notebook
1 notebook of handwritten pages [no numbers listed]
Note: notebook with yellow cover
Reference: LDC2.A4–05

La Bâtarde (handwritten) twentieth notebook
1 notebook of handwritten pages [no numbers listed]
Note: notebook with turquoise cover
Reference: LDC2.A4–05

La Bâtarde (handwritten) twenty-first notebook
1 notebook of handwritten pages [no numbers listed]
Note: notebook with hard turquoise cover
Reference: LDC2.A4–06

La Bâtarde (handwritten) twenty-second notebook
1 notebook of handwritten pages [no numbers listed]
Note: notebook with beige cover
Reference: LDC2.A4–06

La Bâtarde (handwritten) twenty-third notebook
1 notebook of handwritten pages [no numbers listed]
Note: notebook with beige cover
Reference: LDC2.A13–04

La Bâtarde (handwritten) twenty-fourth notebook
1 notebook of handwritten pages [no numbers listed]
Note: notebook with beige cover
Reference: LDC2.A4–07

La Bâtarde (handwritten) twenty-fifth notebook
1 notebook of handwritten pages [no numbers listed]
Note: notebook with beige cover
Reference: LDC2.A4–07

La Bâtarde (handwritten) twenty-sixth notebook
1 notebook of handwritten pages [no numbers listed]
Note: notebook with beige cover
Reference: LDC2.A13–04

La Bâtarde (handwritten) unnumbered notebook
1 notebook of handwritten pages [no numbers listed]
Note: the title page carries the handwritten remark: "(Th et I) (Seen, not photocopied)"
Reference: LDC2.A4–08

La Femme au petit renard (handwritten) first notebook
1 notebook of handwritten pages + 16 detached handwritten leaves
Note: notebook with cream cover
Reference: LDC2.A5–01

La Femme au petit renard (handwritten) first notebook
1 notebook of handwritten pages [no numbers listed]
Note: notebook with blue and black checks
Reference: LDC2.A5–01

La Femme au petit renard (handwritten) first notebook
1 notebook of handwritten pages [no numbers listed]
Note: notebook with black and white checks
Reference: LDC2.A5–02

La Femme au petit renard (handwritten) unnumbered notebook
Leduc, Violette
1 notebook of handwritten pages [no numbers listed]
Note: notebook with blue cover
Reference: LDC2.A5–02

La Femme au petit renard 3 (handwritten)
155 handwritten leaves numbered to 163
Note: the leaves numbered 41–42, 65–66, 134–36, 142–43, 145–46, 147–48, and 152–
54 are on the same leaves
Reference: LDC2.A5–03.01

La Femme au petit renard (handwritten fragment)
78 handwritten leaves with discontinuous pagination
Reference: LDC2.A5–03.02

Thérèse et Isabelle (First part of Ravages), (corrected typescript)
171 handwritten + 170 typed leaves with handwritten corrections numbered 1–190
Note: the pages numbered 47–48, 54–61, 66–67, 74, 75, 112–13, 133–34, 166–68, 175–
80 are on the same leaves; the first page of the text carries a dedication from Violette
Leduc to Monique and Daniel.
Reference: LDC2.A5–04

Thérèse et Isabelle (corrected typescript)
114 carbon copy leaves with handwritten corrections numbered 32–144
Added: one folder with the handwritten remark: "Thérèse et Isabelle"
Note: pages numbered 43–45 are missing; there are two paginations, one typed from 32–
114, the other stamped from 007–121
Reference: LDC2.A5–05.01

Thérèse et Isabelle (typed fragment)
3 typed leaves with handwritten corrections numbered 43–45
Note: ; there are two paginations, one typed from 43–45, the second stamped from 018–
020
Reference: LDC2.A5–05.02

Thérèse et Isabelle (corrected page proofs)
112 typed leaves with handwritten corrections numbered 1–112
Note: The first page features Violette Leduc's handwritten remark: "Good for new
emergency proofs in [illegible]"
Reference: LDC2.A5–05.03

Thérèse et Isabelle (mimeographed manuscript facsimile)
1 bound notebook
205 mimeographed pages
Note: Dedicated by V. Leduc to Jacques Guérin; rededicated by J. Guérin to Albert
Dichy; limited edition of 25 copies; copy number 23
Reference: LDC2.A12–03.01

La Folie en tête (handwritten)
1 notebook of handwritten pages [no numbers listed]
Reference: LDC2.A5–06

La Folie en tête (handwritten) first notebook (continued)
1 notebook of handwritten pages [no numbers listed]
1968 (29 May)
Note: notebook with blue cover
Reference: LDC2.A13–05

La Folie en tête (handwritten) first notebook (continued)
1 notebook of handwritten pages [no numbers listed]
Note: notebook with blue cover
Reference: LDC2.A13–05

La Folie en tête (handwritten) second notebook
1 notebook of handwritten pages [no numbers listed]
Note: notebook with beige cover; features Leduc's handwritten remark: "continuation of la bâtarde"
Reference: LDC2.A13–06

La Folie en tête (handwritten) second notebook (continued)
1 notebook of handwritten pages [no numbers listed]
Note: notebook with black and green checks
Reference: LDC2.A13–06

La Folie en tête (handwritten) second notebook (continued)
1 notebook of handwritten pages [no numbers listed]
Reference: LDC2.A5–06

La Folie en tête (handwritten) third notebook
1 notebook of handwritten pages [no numbers listed]
Note: notebook with red cover; features Leduc's handwritten remark: "continuation of la Bâtarde"
Reference: LDC2.A13–07

La Folie en tête (handwritten) third notebook (continued)
1 notebook of handwritten pages [no numbers listed]
Added: 7 inserted handwritten leaves
Note: notebook with red checked cover
Reference: LDC2.A13–08

La Folie en tête (handwritten) fourth notebook (continued)
1 notebook of handwritten pages [no numbers listed]
Note: notebook with green checked cover
Reference: LDC2.A13–08

La Folie en tête (handwritten) fifth notebook (continued)
1 notebook of handwritten pages [no numbers listed]
Note: notebook with blue checked cover
Reference: LDC2.A14–01

La Folie en tête (handwritten) sixth notebook (continued)
1 notebook of handwritten pages [no numbers listed]
Note: notebook with blue checked cover
Reference: LDC2.A14–01

La Folie en tête (handwritten) seventh notebook (continued)
1 notebook of handwritten pages [no numbers listed]
Note: notebook with blue checked cover
Reference: LDC2.A5–07

La Folie en tête (handwritten) eighth notebook (continued)
1 notebook of handwritten pages [no numbers listed]
Added: 2 handwritten leaves inserted
Note: notebook with checked cover
Reference: LDC2.A14–02

La Folie en tête (handwritten) ninth notebook (continued)
1 notebook of handwritten pages [no numbers listed]
Added: 2 handwritten leaves inserted
Note: notebook with green cover
Reference: LDC2.A14–02

La Folie en tête (handwritten)
50 handwritten leaves numbered 1–47
Note: there are double copies of pages 1–3
Reference: LDC2.A6–01 (1)

La Folie en tête (handwritten)
50 handwritten leaves numbered 48–97
Reference: LDC2.A6–01 (1)

La Folie en tête (handwritten)
50 handwritten leaves numbered 98–147
Note: there are two copies each of pages 98, 102, 113–19; pages 132–33 and 136–40 are
on the same leaves
Reference: LDC2.A6–01 (1)

La Folie en tête (handwritten)
50 handwritten leaves numbered 148–260
Note: pages 178–81 are on the same leaves; pages 207–36, 238–49, and 255 are missing
Reference: LDC2.A6–01 (1)

La Folie en tête (handwritten)
50 handwritten leaves numbered 261–346
Note: pages 267–69, 320–23, 331–34 are on the same leaves; pages 277–302, 313–14,
and 341 are missing
Reference: LDC2.A6–01 (1)

La Folie en tête (handwritten)
50 handwritten leaves numbered 347–86
Note: there are two copies or three of pages 356–58, 361, 372, 382, 384–85, and sometimes several variants
Reference: LDC2.A6–01 (1)

La Folie en tête (handwritten)
51 handwritten leaves numbered 387–420
Note: there are two copies or three of pages 389–91, 394, 396, 403–04, 412–20
Reference: LDC2.A6–01 (1)

La Folie en tête (handwritten)
49 handwritten leaves numbered 421–61
Note: there are two copies or three of pages 421–29, 434 , and sometimes several variants; pages 430–34 and 435–37 are on the same leaves
Reference: LDC2.A6–01 (1)

La Folie en tête (handwritten)
50 handwritten leaves numbered 462–510
Note: there are two copies of page 490
Reference: LDC2.A6–01 (1)

La Folie en tête (handwritten)
50 handwritten leaves numbered 511–63
Note: pages 522–25 are missing; page 562 exists in several variants
Reference: LDC2.A6–01 (1)

La Folie en tête (handwritten)
50 handwritten leaves numbered 564–609
Note: there are two copies of pages 568, 576–77, 595, 598, 599–602, 604–7; pages 577–85, 586–88, 593–94, 597–98, and 599–600 are on the same leaves
Reference: LDC2.A6–01 (1)

La Folie en tête (handwritten)
50 handwritten leaves numbered 610–65
Note: there are two or three copies each of pages 617, 659, 660–65; pages 627– 42 and 652–56 are missing
Reference: LDC2.A6–01 (1)

La Folie en tête (handwritten)
50 handwritten leaves numbered 666–94
Note: there are two or three copies each of pages 666–74, 682–83, and 691–93, sometimes several variants; 676–79 are missing
Reference: LDC2.A6–01 (1)

La Folie en tête (handwritten)
50 handwritten leaves numbered 695–714
Note: there are two or three copies each of pages 696, 700–702–714 [sic], and sometimes several variants
Reference: LDC2.A6–01 (1)

La Folie en tête (handwritten)
50 handwritten leaves numbered 715–28
Note: there are two or three copies each of pages 715–28 and sometimes several variants
Reference: LDC2.A6–01 (1)

La Folie en tête (handwritten)
50 handwritten leaves numbered 729–43
Note: there are two or three copies each and sometimes several variants
Reference: LDC2.A6–01 (1)

La Folie en tête (hardwritten)
51 handwritten leaves numbered 744–62
Note: there are two or three copies each and sometimes several variants
Reference: LDC2.A6–01 (1)

La Folie en tête (handwritten)
50 handwritten leaves numbered 763–86
Note: there are two or three copies each of pages 763–67, 771, 774–86
Reference: LDC2.A6–01 (1)

La Folie en tête (handwritten)
49 handwritten leaves numbered 787–804
Note: there are two or three copies each and sometimes several variants
Reference: LDC2.A6–01 (1)

La Folie en tête (handwritten)
50 handwritten leaves numbered 805–27
Note: there are two or three copies each and sometimes several variants
Reference: LDC2.A6–01 (1)

La Folie en tête (handwritten)
48 handwritten leaves numbered 828–51
Note: there are two or three copies each of pages 828–39 and 843–51
Reference: LDC2.A6–01 (1)

La Folie en tête (handwritten)
50 handwritten leaves numbered 852–78
Note: there are two or three copies each and sometimes several variants
Reference: LDC2.A6–01 (1)

La Folie en tête (handwritten)
52 handwritten leaves numbered 879–901
Note: there are two or three copies each and sometimes several variants
Reference: LDC2.A6–01 (1)

La Folie en tête (handwritten)
51 handwritten leaves numbered 902–23
Note: there are two or three copies each of pages 902–16 and 919–23 and sometimes several variants
Reference: LDC2.A6–01 (1)

La Folie en tête (handwritten)
50 handwritten leaves numbered 924–43
Note: there are two or three copies each and sometimes several variants
Reference: LDC2.A6–01 (2)

La Folie en tête (handwritten)
49 handwritten leaves numbered 944–61
Note: there are two or three copies each and sometimes several variants
Reference: LDC2.A6–01 (2)

La Folie en tête (handwritten)
50 handwritten leaves numbered 962–83
Note: there are two or three copies each and sometimes several variants
Reference: LDC2.A6–01 (2)

La Folie en tête (handwritten)
50 handwritten leaves numbered 984–1003
Note: there are two or three copies each and sometimes several variants
Reference: LDC2.A6–01 (2)

La Folie en tête (handwritten)
50 handwritten leaves numbered 1004–25
Note: there are two or three copies each and sometimes several variants
Reference: LDC2.A6–01 (2)

La Folie en tête (handwritten)
50 handwritten leaves numbered 1026–50
Note: there are two or three copies each and sometimes several variants
Reference: LDC2.A6–01 (2)

La Folie en tête (handwritten)
49 handwritten leaves numbered 1051–74
Note: there are two copies of pages 1052–74, three copies of page 1051
Reference: LDC2.A6–01 (2)

La Folie en tête (handwritten)
52 handwritten leaves numbered 1075–1105
Note: there are two copies of pages 1075–1104, three copies of page 1105
Reference: LDC2.A6–01 (2)

La Folie en tête (handwritten)
49 handwritten leaves numbered 1106–30
Note: there are two copies of pages 1106–30
Reference: LDC2.A6–01 (2)

La Folie en tête (handwritten)
50 handwritten leaves numbered 1131–56
Note: there are two copies of pages 1131–56
Reference: LDC2.A6–01 (2)

La Folie en tête (handwritten)
50 handwritten leaves numbered 1157–85
Note: there are two copies of pages 1157–84, three copies of page 1171
Reference: LDC2.A6–01 (2)

La Folie en tête (handwritten)
50 handwritten leaves numbered 1186–1224
Note: there are two copies of pages 1200–08, and 1210–23, three copies of page 1209; pages 1187–88, 1190–93, 1194–95, 1197–98, and 1199–1200 are on the same leaves; 1189 is missing
Reference: LDC2.A6–01 (2)

La Folie en tête (handwritten)
50 handwritten leaves numbered 1224–1257
Note: there are two copies of pages 1224, 1236–37, 1238–41, 1243–53, 1255–57; three copies of pages 1242, 1254; pages 1228–29 are missing
Reference: LDC2.A6–01 (2)

La Folie en tête (handwritten)
50 handwritten leaves numbered 1258–1308
Note: there are two copies of pages 1258–63, 1273; pages 1293–1300 are missing
Reference: LDC2.A6–01 (2)

La Folie en tête (handwritten)
50 handwritten leaves numbered 1311–81
Note: pages 1349–52, 1354–55, and 1358–72 are missing
Reference: LDC2.A6–01 (2)

La Folie en tête (handwritten)
50 handwritten leaves numbered 1382–1445
Note: pages 1421–26 are missing
Reference: LDC2.A6–01 (2)

La Folie en tête (handwritten)
50 handwritten leaves numbered 1446–99
Note: pages 1481–85 [are missing]
Reference: LDC2.A6–01 (2)

La Folie en tête (handwritten)
50 handwritten leaves numbered 1500–1614
Note: pages 1504–57, 1566–76 are missing
Reference: LDC2.A6–01 (2)

La Folie en tête (handwritten)
50 handwritten leaves numbered 1615–1690
Note: pages 1630–47, 1657, and 1680–86 are missing
Reference: LDC2.A6–01 (2)

La Folie en tête (handwritten)
50 handwritten leaves numbered 1691–1745
Added: 1 photograph
Note: pages 1709–32 are missing
Reference: LDC2.A6–01 (2)

La Folie en tête (typed, first version)
92 typed leaves with handwritten annotations numbered 1–95
Note: pages 61–62, 87–88 are missing; there are two copies of page 63
Reference: LDC2.A7–01

La Folie en tête (typed, first version)
76 typed leaves with handwritten annotations numbered 96–173
Note: pages 142–43, and 172–73 are on the same leaves
Reference: LDC2.A7–01

La Folie en tête (typed) [3]
119 carbon copy leaves with handwritten annotations numbered 174–289
Note: there are two copies of pages 174–81; pages 226–28, and 284 are missing
Reference: LDC2.A7–01

La Folie en tête (typed) [4]
73 carbon copy leaves with handwritten annotations numbered 290–368
Note: pages 336–41 are missing
Reference: LDC2.A7–01

La Folie en tête (typed) [5]
77 carbon copy leaves with handwritten annotations numbered 369–445
Reference: LDC2.A7–01

La Folie en tête (typed) [6]
100 carbon copy leaves with handwritten annotations numbered 500–99
Reference: LDC2.A7–01

La Folie en tête (typed) [7]
92 carbon copy leaves with handwritten annotations numbered 446–537
Note: pages 336–41 are missing
Reference: LDC2.A7–01

La Folie en tête (typed) [8]
64 carbon copy leaves with handwritten annotations numbered 538–601
Reference: LDC2.A7–01

La Folie en tête (typed) [9]
75 carbon copy leaves with handwritten annotations numbered 602–76
Reference: LDC2.A7–01

La Folie en tête (typed) [10]
78 carbon copy leaves with handwritten annotations numbered 677–774 [sic]
Reference: LDC2.A7–01

La Folie en tête (typed) [11]
26 carbon copy leaves with handwritten annotations numbered 755–79
Reference: LDC2.A7–01

La Folie en tête (typed) [I]
75 carbon copy leaves with handwritten annotations numbered 1–95
Note: pages 31–39, 54–55, 60–63, 69–70, 80, and 88 are missing
Reference: LDC2.A8–01

La Folie en tête (typed) [II]
61 carbon copy leaves with handwritten annotations numbered 96–173
Note: pages 102, 115, 122, 133–36, 156–57, 159–60, 166–67, and 169–70 are missing;
pages 142–43 and 172–73 are on the same leaves
Reference: LDC2.A8–01

La Folie en tête (typed) [IV]
50 carbon copy leaves with handwritten annotations numbered 290–368
Note: pages 292, 301–2, 307–10, 312–14, 316–19, 321, 323, 326–27, and 331–41 are
missing
Reference: LDC2.A8–01

La Folie en tête (typed) [V]
77 carbon copy leaves with handwritten annotations numbered 369–445
Reference: LDC2.A8–01

La Folie en tête (typed) [VI]
92 carbon copy leaves with handwritten annotations numbered 446–537
Reference: LDC2.A8–01

La Folie en tête (typed) [VII]
64 carbon copy leaves with handwritten annotations numbered 538–601
Reference: LDC2.A8–01

La Folie en tête (typed) [VIII]
24 carbon copy leaves with handwritten annotations numbered 602–77
Note: pages 615–17, 619, 624, and 633–76 are missing
Reference: LDC2.A8–01

La Folie en tête (typed) [IX]
73 carbon copy leaves with handwritten annotations numbered 677–754
Note: pages 710–13 are missing
Reference: LDC2.A8–01

La Folie en tête (typed) [X]
25 carbon copy leaves with handwritten annotations numbered 755–79
Reference: LDC2.A8–01

La Folie en tête (typed) [A]
70 carbon copy leaves with handwritten annotations numbered 1–70
Reference: LDC2.A9–01

La Folie en tête (typed) [B]
50 carbon copy leaves with handwritten annotations numbered 71–120
Reference: LDC2.A9–01

La Folie en tête (typed) [C]
68 carbon copy leaves with handwritten annotations numbered 121–88
Reference: LDC2.A9–01

La Folie en tête (typed) [D]
38 carbon copy leaves with handwritten annotations numbered 189–226
Reference: LDC2.A9–01

La Folie en tête (typed) [E]
34 carbon copy leaves with handwritten annotations numbered 227–60
Reference: LDC2.A9–01

La Folie en tête (typed) [G]
38 carbon copy leaves with handwritten annotations numbered 305–39
Note: there are two copies of pages 336–39
Reference: LDC2.A9–01

La Folie en tête (typed) [H]
81 carbon copy leaves with handwritten annotations numbered 339–420
Note: there are two copies of pages 340–44; pages 353–59 are on the same leaves
Reference: LDC2.A9–01

La Folie en tête (typed) [I]
87 carbon copy leaves with handwritten annotations numbered 421–503
Note: there are two copies of pages 484–86, and 489
Reference: LDC2.A9–01

La Folie en tête (typed) [J]
64 carbon copy leaves with handwritten annotations numbered 504–65
Note: there are two copies of pages 506
Reference: LDC2.A9–01

La Folie en tête (typed) [K]
178 carbon copy leaves with handwritten annotations numbered 566–740
Note: there are two copies of pages 570–72
Reference: LDC2.A9–01

La Folie en tête (typed) [L]
109 carbon copy leaves with handwritten annotations numbered 741–850
Note: page 766 is missing
Reference: LDC2.A9–01

Le Taxi (handwritten, first version I)
1 notebook of handwritten pages, 48 handwritten leaves
Note: the multicolored flowered paper covering the notebook features the handwritten remark: "1"; 4 pages of the notebook are collages/montages
Reference: LDC2.A10–01

Le Taxi (handwritten, first version II)
1 notebook of 22 handwritten leaves
Note: notebook with green cover
Reference: LDC2.A10–01

Le Taxi (handwritten, second version I)
1 notebook of handwritten leaves
Added: 1 fragment of 11 handwritten detached leaves
Note: notebook with blue cover
Reference: LDC2.A10–01

Le Taxi (handwritten, second version II)
1 notebook of handwritten leaves
Note: notebook with blue cover; 2 leaves are collages/montages
Reference: LDC2.A10–02

Le Taxi (corrected proofs)
81 handwritten leaves, 76 typed leaves with handwritten corrections, 3 printed leaves with handwritten corrections, of which one is a photocopy
Added: 1 fragment of 11 detached handwritten leaves
Note: 1 leaf is a collage/montage
Reference: LDC2.A10–03

La Chasse à l'amour (handwritten) **first notebook**
1 notebook of handwritten pages [no numbers listed]
Note: notebook with green cover
Reference: LDC2.A14–03

La Chasse à l'amour (handwritten) **third notebook**
1 notebook of handwritten pages [no numbers listed]
Note: notebook with red cover
Reference: LDC2.A14–03

La Chasse à l'amour (handwritten) **fourth notebook**
1 notebook of handwritten pages [no numbers listed]
Note: notebook with light blue cover
Reference: LDC2.A14–04

La Chasse à l'amour (handwritten) **fifth notebook**
1 notebook of handwritten pages [no numbers listed]
Note: notebook with blue cover
Reference: LDC2.A14–04

La Chasse à l'amour (handwritten) sixth notebook
1 notebook of handwritten pages [no numbers listed]
Note: notebook with red cover
Reference: LDC2.A14–05

La Chasse à l'amour (handwritten) seventh notebook
1 notebook of handwritten pages [no numbers listed]
Note: notebook with turquoise cover
Reference: LDC2.A14–05

La Chasse à l'amour (handwritten) twelfth notebook
1 notebook of handwritten pages [no numbers listed]
Note: notebook with beige cover
Reference: LDC2.A14–06

La Chasse à l'amour (handwritten) thirteenth and fourteenth notebooks
1 notebook [sic] of handwritten pages
Note: notebook with green cover
Reference: LDC2.A14–06

La Chasse à l'amour (handwritten) fifteenth and sixteenth notebooks
1 notebook [sic] of handwritten pages
Note: notebook with yellow cover
Reference: LDC2.A14–07

La Chasse à l'amour (handwritten) seventeenth and eighteenth notebooks
1 notebook [sic] of handwritten pages
Note: notebook with green cover
Reference: LDC2.A14–08

La Chasse à l'amour (handwritten) nineteenth notebook
1 notebook of handwritten pages [no numbers listed]
Added: 1 inserted handwritten leaf
Note: notebook with yellow cover
Reference: LDC2.A14–08

La Chasse à l'amour (handwritten) Chapter I
156 handwritten leaves numbered 1–156
Reference: LDC2.A11–01

La Chasse à l'amour (handwritten) Chapter II
123 handwritten leaves numbered 157–280
Reference: LDC2.A11–01

La Chasse à l'amour (handwritten) Chapter III
156 handwritten leaves numbered 281–452
Reference: LDC2.A11–01

La Chasse à l'amour (handwritten) **Chapter IV**
111 handwritten leaves numbered 322–432 [sic]
Reference: LDC2.A11–01

La Chasse à l'amour (handwritten) **Chapter V**
219 handwritten leaves numbered 433–650
Reference: LDC2.A11–01

La Chasse à l'amour (handwritten) **Chapter VI**
96 handwritten leaves numbered 651–736
Reference: LDC2.A11–01

La Chasse à l'amour (handwritten) **Chapter VII**
49 handwritten leaves numbered 737–85
Reference: LDC2.A11–01

La Chasse à l'amour (handwritten, second version) **Chapter I**
90 handwritten leaves numbered 1–90
Reference: LDC2.A12–01

La Chasse à l'amour (handwritten, second version) **Chapter II**
53 handwritten leaves numbered 91–144
Reference: LDC2.A12–01

La Chasse à l'amour (handwritten, second version) **Chapter III**
140 handwritten leaves numbered 145–285
Reference: LDC2.A12–01

La Chasse à l'amour (handwritten fragment, second version) **Chapter IV**
25 handwritten leaves numbered 286–330, of which 18 are recto-verso copies
Reference: LDC2.A12–01

Les Boutons dorés **(handwritten)**
83 handwritten leaves numbered 1–87, of which 47 are recto-verso copies
Note: pages 1, 10–13 are missing; [incomplete pagination]
Reference: LDC2.A12–02

Les Boutons dorés **(handwritten)**
81 handwritten leaves numbered 88–183, of which 54 are recto-verso copies
Reference: LDC2.A12–02

Notes and Criticism

Three notebooks
Violette Leduc
No date + 1968
Reference: LDC2.A12–03.02

Eloge de Violette Leduc
Jean Cocteau
1 handwritten leaf (photocopy)
[No date]
Reference: LDC2.D1–01.01

Violette Leduc c'est l'ordre, la frappe . . .
10 handwritten leaves
[No date]
Reference: LDC2.D1–01.02

Various Personal Effects

1 passport
Reference: LDC2.B1–01

1 datebook
Note: unmarked datebook from 1970
Reference: LDC2.B1–01

4 voter registration cards
1961–1968
Reference: LDC2.B1–01

1 Carte Vermeil (SNCF)
24–mai–71
Reference: LDC2.B1–01

1 Vaccination certificate
1967
Reference: LDC2.B1–01

1 livret de famille
Reference: LDC2.B1–02

1 tax notice
Reference: LDC2.B1–02

3 Checkbooks
Note: 3 partially used checkbooks, two from the Banque Nationale de Paris, 1 from the Société Marseillaise de Crédit
Reference: LDC2.B1–02

2 portraits
Lange, Monique
Note: The portrait de M. Lange is under glass + one non–identified portrait
Reference: LDC2.B1–03

1 portrait
Genet, Jean
Note: portrait de J. Genet sous verre
Reference: LDC2.B1–04

6 reproductions of photographs
Reference: LDC2.B1–05.01

Documents relating to construction work V. Leduc's house
Note: estimates, bills, etc.
Reference: LDC2.B1–05.02

Polonaises (score)
Chopin
1 book
Reference: LDC2.B1–05.03

Official documents concerning V. Leduc's divorce
15 leaves
1946–1950
Reference: LDC2.B1–05.04

Personal Correspondence

Amar, A. to Violette Leduc
1 handwritten letter
1 leaf + 1 envelope
1963
Reference: LDC2.C1–01

Audry, Colette to Violette Leduc
1 handwritten letter
1 leaf
[No date]
Reference: LDC2.C1–01

Belaval, Yvon to Violette Leduc
26 handwritten letters + 1 handwritten card
27 leaves
April 1947–August 1960
Included: 1 handwritten letter from Violette Leduc to Yvon Belaval (1 leaf, no date)
Note: 20 letters without date.
Reference: LDC2.C1–01

Appendix

Besnault, Claude to Violette Leduc
1 handwritten letter
1 leaf
[No date]
Reference: LDC2.C1–01

Bouché, André de to Violette Leduc
1 handwritten letter
1 leaf
[No date]
Reference: LDC2.C1–01

Camus, Albert to Violette Leduc
6 handwritten letters (plus copies)
12 leaves + 1 envelope
1945–1946
See also: from Violette Leduc to Albert Camus, 4 handwritten letters (photocopies), 4
leaves, 1945–1947 [in the IMEC fonds Albert CAMUS]
Reference: LDC2.C1–01

Castaing, Madeleine to Violette Leduc
3 handwritten letters
3 leaves + 2 envelopes
1970, 1972
Reference: LDC2.C1–01

Chapsal, Madeleine to Violette Leduc
1 handwritten letter
2 leaves
1964
Reference: LDC2.C1–01

Dr. Douillon to Violette Leduc
1 handwritten letter
1 leaf
1963
Reference: LDC2.C1–01

Estivales, Thérèse to Violette Leduc
60 handwritten letters + 1 handwritten card
90 leaves + 39 envelopes
1957–1969
Reference: LDC2.C1–01

Genet, Jean to Violette Leduc
6 handwritten letters
6 leaves
[No date]
Reference: LDC2.C1–02

Guiness, Alec to Violette Leduc
1 handwritten letter
1 leaf + 1 envelope
1965
Reference: LDC2.C1–02

J., Lucienne to Violette Leduc
1 post card
1954
Reference: LDC2.C1–02

Lange, Monique to Violette Leduc
4 handwritten letters
4 leaves + 1 envelope
1961–1963
Reference: LDC2.C1–02

Lem, André to Violette Leduc
1 handwritten card
1958
Reference: LDC2.C1–02

Lorent, Albert to Violette Leduc
1 typed letter + 1 post card
2 leaves. + 2 envelopes
1958, 1966
Reference: LDC2.C1–02

Malraux, Clara to Violette Leduc
1 handwritten letter
1 leaf
18 Dec. 19??
Reference: LDC2.C1–02

Maris–Banier, François to Violette Leduc
1 handwritten letter
1 leaf
1972
Reference: LDC2.C1–02

Mercier, Jacques ["Gabriel"] to Violette Leduc
1 handwritten letter
1 leaf
1944
Reference: LDC2.C1–02

Noel, Philippe to Violette Leduc
1 handwritten letter
2 leaves
1971
Reference: LDC2.C1–02

Petrier, François to Violette Leduc
1 handwritten letter
8 leaves + 1 envelope
1972
Reference: LDC2.C1–02

Reichenbach, François to Violette Leduc
1 handwritten letter + 1 card
2 leaves + 1 envelope
1954
Reference: LDC2.C1–02

Saraute, Nathalie to Violette Leduc
2 handwritten letters
2 leaves
1945
Reference: LDC2.C1–02

Sully–Dumas, Jean to Violette Leduc
1 handwritten card
1 leaf
[No date]
Reference: LDC2.C1–02

Tamagnot, Serge to Violette Leduc
4 handwritten post cards
4 leaves + 1 envelope
[No date]
Reference: LDC2.C1–02

Vallorz, Paolo to Violette Leduc
18 handwritten letters + 1 post card + 1 invitation
21 leaves + 14 envelopes
1963–1965
Reference: LDC2.C1–02

Warren, Michel to Violette Leduc
1 invitation
2 leaves + 1 envelope
[No date]
Reference: LDC2.C1–02

Unidentified Correspondence to Violette Leduc
5 handwritten letters + 1 post card + 1 card
12 leaves
1970–73 and [No date]
Reference: LDC2.C1–02

Letters to Berthe Dehous and Mme Maisonneuve regarding Violette Leduc
13 letters : 12 handwritten + 1 typed + 1 card
20 leaves + 12 envelopes
1972
Reference: LDC2.C1–02

Professional Correspondence

FILMSONOR to Violette Leduc
3 typed letters
3 leaves
1971
Included: 3 leaves from Madame Smolett, 3 typed leaves
Reference: LDC2.C1–03

Gallimard, Gaston to Violette Leduc
9 typed letters
10 leaves
1945–1966
Included: 3 book contracts: *l'Asphyxie* (Sept. 1945), *l'Affamée* (April 1948), *la Plaie et le Referenceau* [early title of *Ravages*] (Oct. 1954), + 1 typed leaf (torn) regarding the contract for *la Folie en tête*.
Reference: LDC2.C1–03

Leduc, Violette to Jean–Jacques Pauvert
1 typed letter
31 leaves
1966
Reference: LDC2.C1–03

NRF (Editions Gallimard) to Violette Leduc
18 typed letters + 3 handwritten cards
22 leaves + 7 envelopes
1948–1972
Included: 7 letters from the Caisse Nationale des Lettres to Violette Leduc regarding rights (payment stubs)
Reference: LDC2.C1–03

Rossignol, Jean to Violette Leduc
1 typed letter
1 leaf
1969
Included: 1 letter authorizing the film *Thérèse et Isabelle* par Radley Metzger
1 typed leaf
Reference: LDC2.C1–03

Les Temps Modernes **to Violette Leduc**
1 handwritten letter
1 leaf
[No date]
Reference: LDC2.C1–03

Wright, Ellen to Violette Leduc
1 typed letter
1 leaf
1964
Reference: LDC2.C1–03

NOTES

Notes to Introduction

1. Violette Leduc, *La Bâtarde* (Paris: Gallimard–Folio, 1964).
2. This is beginning to change, however, with the recent publication of Carlo Jansiti's biography *Violette Leduc* (Paris: Grasset, 1999), which got quite a bit of attention in the press, both Parisian and provincial.
3. Violette Leduc, *La Folie en tête* (Paris: Gallimard, 1970).
4. The beginning of Leduc's career as a serious writer coincides with the beginning of the famous review *Les Temps modernes*. She published an extract of *L'Asphyxie* as "Une mère, un parapluie, des gants" in *Les Temps modernes*'s second issue, November, 1945. Other extracts of works in progress published over the years in *Les Temps Modernes* were "L'Affamée" (n° 25, October, 1947), "L'Affamée, suite et fin" (n° 26, November, 1947), "Le Tailleur anguille" from *La Bâtarde* (n° 186, November, 1961), and "La Bâtarde" in the double issue n° 207–208, August–September, 1963. (Extracts from *Ravages*, *La Vieille Fille et le mort*, *Thérèse et Isabelle*, and *Trésors à prendre* were published in other literary magazines, including *La Nouvelle Revue Française*, *Cahiers du Sud*, *Parler*, and *L'Arbalète*. Please see the bibliography for more information.) Leduc also published a number of relatively obscure short stories in *Les Temps modernes*: "Le Dézingage," (n° 3, December, 1945), "Train noir," (n° 6, March, 1946), "Les Mains sales," (n° 15, December, 1946), "Au village," (n° 65, March, 1951), and "Désirée Hellé," (n° 80, June, 1952). Carlo Jansiti's biography is an invaluable resource for information regarding Leduc's publication history. His bibliography lists not only these and other important postwar publications, but also publication information regarding the work she did for the women's magazine *Pour Elle* in 1940–41 (twenty-three pieces in all) that she describes in *La Bâtarde*.
5. Simone de Beauvoir, Preface, *La Bâtarde*, by Violette Leduc (Paris: Gallimard–Folio, 1964) 7–23.
6. Violette Leduc, *L'Asphyxie* (Paris: Gallimard–Imaginaire, 1946).
7. Violette Leduc, *L'Affamée* (Paris: Gallimard–Folio, 1948).
8. Violette Leduc, *Ravages* (Paris: Gallimard, 1955). This text was heavily censored of its more erotic passages by the editor. The bulk of the censored material was the 100-page prologue. Leduc's friend Jacques Guérin arranged to have it published *hors commerce* in a deluxe limited edition under the title *Thérèse et Isabelle*. After the success

of *La Bâtarde*—which included some of the material that was censored from *Ravages*—Gallimard agreed to publish a revised version of *Thérèse et Isabelle* in 1966. The publishing history of these texts is important; readers should not make the mistake of thinking that *Thérèse et Isabelle* was written after the similar passages in *La Bâtarde*: they were both originally composed over fifteen years before they saw wide distribution. In *La Chasse à l'amour* Leduc writes of the emotional impact of having parts of her book excised, which she considered the ultimate rejection of her worth as a writer.

9. Violette Leduc, *La Chasse à l'amour* (Paris: Gallimard, 1973).

10. Simone de Beauvoir, *Tout compte fait* (Paris: Gallimard, 1972); *All Said and Done*, trans. Patrick O'Brian (New York: Putnam, 1974).

11. Carlo Jansiti's new biography proves this again and again. In fact, he notes that based on his research into the minutia of her life, Leduc was more often close to the "actual" events of her life in her earlier novels than in her later so-called autobiographies. Colette Trout Hall, in her excellent and very complete *Violette Leduc, la mal-aimée* (Amsterdam:Rodopi, 1999) also examines the "artifice" of Leduc's autobiographical writings (76).

12. See Mireille Brioude's book entitled *Violette Leduc: La mise en scène du "je"* for a complete discussion of this phenomenon.

13. As we shall see in chapter five, the scene in the brothel that does not exist in *La Bâtarde* is of primary importance.

14. Leduc has even changed the names of some of her characters when they move from real life to the text. The woman known as Hermine in Leduc's autobiographies was named Denise in real life; likewise Gabriel's real name was Jacques. In Leduc's case it behooves the reader not to blur the lines between real and imaginary life, as Michele Zackheim does, for example, when she writes of Gabriel and Hermine in her "biography" of Leduc.

15. See Margaret Ann Robe, "Conceiving a Self in Autobiography," diss., University of California–Los Angeles, 1988; Isabelle de Courtivron, *Violette Leduc* (Boston: Twayne, 1985); Michael Sheringham, *French Autobiography: Devices and Desires* (Oxford: Clarendon Press, 1994); Monika Kaup, *Mad Intertextuality: Madness in Twentieth-Century Women's Writing* (Trier: Wissenschaftlicher Verlag Trier, 1993): 167–206. In her chapter entitled "Moments of Disruption: Violette Leduc" Robe treats Leduc's relationship with the reader at some length, faintly echoing Beauvoir's assessment of the reader as "l'impossible synthèse" when she notes that "This bond with her readers, however tenuous and theoretical it may be, is the least troubled of her relationships, even if it is distorted by her neediness" (102). Readers, according to Robe, "occupy the position of her absent father" (102) but also represent the "good" prepartum mother lost forever when mother and daughter were separated at birth. Courtivron agrees, but instead of the readers being surrogates only for the lost mother and father, she argues that Leduc "conceiv[es] of her readers as the most unattainable love objects" (*Violette Leduc* 64). In chapters 4, 5, and 6, I will demonstrate the ways in which Leduc tries to attain that impossible synthesis. Insofar as Leduc has made a dramatic impact on the lives of a number of her readers (Cf. chapter 3 on Ceccatty and Zackheim as Leduc's seducees), I would argue that against all odds, Leduc is sometimes successful. Where Robe sees the reader standing in for the lost father, Kaup argues that Leduc casts the reader as analyst in her text: the listening other. Kaup's theory of the reader-as-therapist is supported by *La Chasse à l'amour*, wherein even when Violette does have an analyst, she rejects him, preferring to write texts to readers over writing letters to Lacan. In this light, Colette Trout Hall's comment in "*L'Ecriture Feminine* and the Search for the Mother in the Works of Violette Leduc and Marie Cardinal" (in Women and French Literature [Sara-

toga, CA: Anma Libri, 1988]: 231–38) that Leduc was "*Couching* on paper her rages, her despairs, and her thirst for love" (234) takes on new meaning: the paper upon which she writes takes the place of the analyst's couch. The fact that she writes 'from the couch' does not mean, however, that Leduc is respectful of psychoanalytic precepts. Kaup argues that *La Bâtarde* "represents a heresy in relation to analytical theories. Here there is an abundance of psychoanalytical concepts, such as fixation on the mother, ambivalence, repetition-compulsion, paranoia, and castration complex, but their use, allusively, is paradoxical, 'bastardized': the autobiographer born a bastard, flaunts her illegitimate descent in refusing to construct a superior origin and rebirth through the canonized discourse. Instead, she constructs a therapist in the figure of 'her reader' who is fashioned after the demands of her disorder. It is to this persona screen that she makes the psychoanalytic transference enabling her to redraft her existence" (169). (For more on writing as a cure for Leduc, see Jean Snitzer Schoenfeld's "*La Bâtarde*, or Why the Writer Writes," as well as Martha Noel Evans, "Writing as Difference in Violette Leduc's Autobiography *La Bâtarde*," in *The (M)other Tongue*.) In the end, the child who does not carry the *Nom du Père* subverts the laws of psychoanalytic discourse. From her position outside the Law, she flaunts her improper use of psychoanalytic concepts like she flaunts her big nose. Taking only what she needs from psychoanalysis—the notion of transference onto the "listening other"—she leaves the rest behind, turned on its ear. Kaup's argument that Leduc tailors her reader as a "persona screen" to her own needs is particularly germane in this study, for what is transference but a seduction? Even in the normal analytical situation, transference operates in both directions, with the analysand seducing the analyst as well as vice-versa. In this light, Kaup's theory can be seen as an excellent illustration of Elaine Marks' notion of the dream of love (see below), as well as an interesting reading of Beauvoir's suggestion that Leduc's reader represents the impossible synthesis of presence and absence: in all cases there is redemption to be found in the figure of the reader. This explains why she is to be so fervently courted. Michael Sheringham dedicates an entire section of his chapter "Dealing with the Reader" to *La Bâtarde*, and in this excellent study identifies three distinct phases of the writer's relation to the reader: ignoring her in favor of other addressees like Fidéline and Berthe, drawing the reader in to her dealings with other characters, and finally, using "the relationship with the reader as a channel through which she can demonstrate (or struggle towards) a new-found commitment to the extratextual world (the world outside her obsessions)" (*French Autobiography* 148). This final phase occurs near the end of *La Bâtarde*, when Violette invites the reader to join her in the present of the writing, both by announcing the date and time of that writing and by describing her surroundings as she writes: "21 août, 1963. Vite, lecteur, vite, que je te donne encore ce que tu connais: ce mol océan des campagnes, le foin coupé [August 21, 1963. Quickly reader, quickly, so that I can give you more of what you know: this limp ocean of countryside, the cut hay]" (*La Bâtarde* 631). By this time—the last pages of the book—Violette's relationship with the reader has changed from taker to giver. This gift—of the provençal landscape, and indeed the novel itself—is reciprocal, says Sheringham, for we as readers have enabled the writer's transformation: "Without lifting a finger, we have helped Leduc transform herself: our ministry as autobiographer's reader is truly a sinecure" (*French Autobiography* 156).

16. Many have wondered at Beauvoir's dedication to our writer, but Jansiti suggests in his biography that Beauvoir was equally indebted to Leduc as the reverse. Indeed, he claims that Sartre, and Beauvoir—his "petite conscience morale"—used Leduc and her black market connections to feed themselves well during the post-Occupation food shortages in Paris (*Violette Leduc* 155). In *L'Affamée* (described below), Leduc herself describes her attempts to get bread for "celle qui lit dans un café" (18-20).

17. See, among others, Jacob Stockinger "Legitimations of *la Bâtarde,*" diss., University of Wisconsin-Madison, 1979; René de Ceccatty, *Violette Leduc: Éloge de la Bâtarde* (Paris, Stock, 1994); Camille Lanparra. "Femme bâtarde/femme écrivain légitime: Dichotomie figurale de La Bâtarde de Violette Leduc," *From Dante to Garcia-Márquez: Studies in Romance Literatures and Linguistics,* ed. Bell-Villada et al. (Williamstown, MA: Williams College Press, 1987) 360–72; Colette Trout Hall, *Violette Leduc, la mal-aimée*; and Jansiti's biography.

18. This portion of *Ravages* (also published as "Je hais les dormeurs" in *L'Arbalète*) and the two mentions of *L'Asphyxie* appear in Simone de Beauvoir, *Le Deuxième sexe,* 2 vols. (1949; Paris: Gallimard–Folio essais, 1976) 2: 48, 79, 565–66; *The Second Sex*, trans. H. M. Parshley (New York: Vintage, 1989) 294, 391, 657.

19. This obsession with the gaze runs through Leduc's entire œuvre, beginning with the first chapter of her first book, in which the narrator often refers to her mother and "son regard dur et bleu [her hard blue look]" (*L'Asphyxie* 12, 13). It should be noted that Beauvoir's eyes were also blue. Simone de Beauvoir is a mother-figure for Violette and Leduc's other narrators not only in terms of her position as critic and judge, but also as the narrator's love object. Whereas Berthe was the object of Violette's childhood desire, Beauvoir becomes the adult Violette's equally inaccessible love object.

20. Deirdre Bair, *Simone de Beauvoir: A Biography* (New York: Simon and Schuster, 1990). Simone de Beauvoir, *A Transatlantic Love Affair: Letters to Nelson Algren* (New York: The New Press, 1998).

21. "Simone de Beauvoir et son ombre: Violette Leduc," *Simone de Beauvoir Studies* 13 (1996): 114–25.

22. Courtivron, "From Bastard to Pilgrim: Rites and Writings for Madame," *Yale French Studies* 72 (1986): 133–48.

23. Louise Gagnon, "L'Autobiographie de Violette Leduc: Pour une lecture féministe," diss., University of California-Berkeley, 1986.

24. Elaine Marks, "The Dream of Love: A Study of Three Autobiographies," *Twentieth-Century French Fiction: Essays for Germaine Brée,* ed. George Stambolian (New Brunswick, NJ: Rutgers UP, 1975): 72–88. Leduc is not treated here but very well could have been.

25. Isabelle de Courtivron, in *Violette Leduc,* agrees: "This attempt to seduce the reader is particularly applicable to Leduc and indeed essential to her writer's enterprise" (63).

26. We have already seen her beg the reader to come with her: "Lecteur, suis moi. Lecteur, je tombe à tes pieds pour que tu me suives [Reader, follow me. Reader, I fall at your feet so that you will follow me]" (*La Bâtarde* 294), which Louise Gagnon refers to as "une sorte d'appel au secours [a kind of cry for help]" (155).

27. Later, Hermine was too absent in her life when she would "betray" Violette (an insomniac) by sleeping, yet too present when she smothered her with attention, made her quit her job, and encouraged her to become the little housewife—a role which Violette did not enjoy.

Notes to Chapter One

1. Leduc was often referred to as a "female Genet;" perhaps one day people will speak of Genet as a "male Leduc."

2.   Cited in Valérie Marin la Meslée, "Genet, Violette Leduc: admiration et jalousie," *Magazine littéraire* 313 (Sept. 1993): 37–38.

3.   Ross Chambers, *Story and Situation: Narrative Seduction and the Power of Fiction* (Minnneapolis: U of Minnesota P, 1984).

4.   As Chambers formulates it, "the problem is not so much, perhaps, to recognize the seductive power of fiction as it is to understand it" (*Story and Situation* 216).

5.   This is not to suggest that there are not other, equally valid types of reading; certainly not. All readers bring with them different tastes, reading histories and desires when they open a book. I am rather developing this continuum of the pleasures of reading and narrative seduction in order to better explain this phenomenon.

6.   Whenever the character Emma Bovary is juxtaposed with the writer Roland Barthes, I will put her name in quotation marks to remind the reader that while both are products of writing, the one is a purely textual artifact and the other is not.

7.   Gustave Flaubert, *Madame Bovary* (Paris: GF-Flammarion, 1986); *The Collected Works of Gustave Flaubert: One Volume Edition* (New York: Walter J. Black, 1904). All subsequent references will be to these editions. In the parenthetical citations the first number refers to the French edition, and the second to the English-language edition.

8.   See Harry Levin "The Female Quixote," in *The Gates of Horn: A Study of Five French Realists* (New York: Oxford UP, 1963), 246–69.

9.   J. LaPlanche and J-B. Pontalis, eds., *Vocabulaire de la psychanalyse* (Paris: Presses Universitaires de France, 1967), 200; *The Language of Psycho-Anaysis*, trans. Donald Nicholson-Smith (New York: W. W. Norton, 1973), 211.

10.   Flaubert uses the verb *dévorer* ("devoured") to describe Emma's reading style on page 118/36.

11.   We will soon see that Violette Leduc suffers from the same problem, and finds her solution in literature, as Emma does.

12.   Roland Barthes, *Le Plaisir du texte* (Paris: Éditions du Seuil—Collection "Points," 1973); *The Pleasure of the Text*, trans. Richard Howard (New York: Hill and Wang, 1975). All subsequent references will be to these editions. In the parenthetical citations the first number refers to the French edition, and the second to the English-language edition.

13.   Roland Barthes, *S/Z* (Paris: Éditions du Seuil—Collection "Points," 1970); *S/Z: An Essay*, trans. Richard Howard (New York: Hill and Wang, 1974). All subsequent references will be to these editions. In the parenthetical citations the first number refers to the French edition, and the second to the English-language edition.

14.   John Sturrock, "Roland Barthes," in *Structuralism and Since: From Lévi-Strauss to Derrida* (Oxford: Oxford UP, 1979), 52–80.

15.   Tony Tanner, *Adultery in the Novel: Contract and Transgression* (Baltimore: Johns Hopkins UP, 1979).

16.   "Elle frémissait, en soulevant de son haleine le papier de soie des gravures, qui se levait à demi plié et retombait doucement contre la page [She trembled as she blew back the tissue paper over the engraving and saw it folded in two and fall gently against the page]" (*Madame Bovary* 97/23).

17.   "This sensuous rising and falling of the soft white paper seems like a morphological prefiguration of the more overtly erotic risings and fallings of clothes, sheets, bodies implied or described in Emma's later sexual life. . . . One could see that one triggering instance in her later life might be traced back to a fetishistic attachment to the childhood excitement of blowing back the tissue paper over pictures" (*Adultery in the Novel* 285–86).

18. Barthes, *Le Plaisir du texte*, 35/20.
19. Barthes, again in *Le Plaisir du texte*, says of the text: "il produit en moi le meilleur plaisir s'il parvient à se faire écouter indirectement; si, le lisant, je suis entraîné à souvent lever la tête, à entendre autre chose [it produces, in me, the best pleasure if it manages to make itself heard indirectly; if reading it, I am led to look up often, to listen to something else]" (41/24).
20. Sigmund Freud, *The Interpretation of Dreams*, ed., trans. James Strachey (New York: Avon Books, 1965). At the beginning of his chapter "The Dreamwork," Freud states that "the dream-content . . . is expressed as it were in a pictographic script" and likens dreams to rebuses (312).

Notes to Chapter Two

1. "La ville palpite quand la fille épouse un enfant trouvé dans un taillis, dans un panier [The entire town is aflutter when the daughter marries an orphan discovered in a basket in the bushes]" (*La Bâtarde* 31). André's sister married a bastard child, in spite of the public reaction. This piece of information, buried in the text, serves to further underscore André's cowardice in not accepting responsibility for his actions. If the family could welcome a bastard son-in-law, certainly they could have accepted a bastard grandchild, especially one whose mother was so well-liked by the family in the first place.
2. "D'origine noble, André Debaralle descendait d'une branche illégitime: son grand-père Felix ne fut reconnu par sa propre mère, Marie Fébronique Debaralle, qu'à l'âge de dix-huit ans. Le père de Félix serait le baron Alexandre Pujol de Mortry, ancien prévôt de Valenciennes et chevalier de Saint-Louis [Of noble origins, André Debaralle descended from an illegitimate branch: his grandfather Félix was not recognized by his own mother, Marie Fébronique Debaralle, until he reached the age of eighteen. Félix's father was supposedly the Baron Alexandre Pujol de Mortry, former provost marshal of Valenciennes and a Knight of Saint Louis.]" (*Violette Leduc* 19).
3. Significantly, this was the same orchard where the seventeen-year-old neighbor Aimé Patureau went to sing love songs to Violette's mother: "J'entrai dans le verger saccagé à côté de notre maison: le verger où Aimé Patureau, à la cime d'un arbre, sifflait et chantait pour ma mère les chansons d'amour des cahiers [I entered the neglected orchard next to our house: the orchard where Aimé Patureau used to whistle and sing love songs from the notebooks for my mother at the top of a tree]" (*La Bâtarde* 49).
4. Violette's first taste of literature in the tall weeds of the orchard and read from a cahier is replicated each day when the narrator of *La Bâtarde* goes out into the woods with her own cahier to write. Also of note regarding this citation is that the other connection with "anguille" in *La Bâtarde* is also a scene of seduction. In a passage remarkable for its drum rolls, Violette describes putting on her expensive "tailleur anguille [eel-colored suit]" designed by Schiaparelli to seduce men in the streets of Paris (*La Bâtarde* 272–82).
5. In *L'Asphyxie*, Leduc's first novel, the narrator-protagonist recounts losing her gold medallion—the one item of value she had ever received from her father—in one vignette, and losing an umbrella in another. The value of the gold medallion, presumably with the family crest, was not merely financial, but lay primarily in the fact that it was the single piece of evidence (besides the child's large nose) that she was André's daugh-

ter. Significantly, she discovers that the necklace is lost upon returning home from her first and only meeting with her father, to whom she is not introduced. Berthe's devastation following this meeting, both for herself (she calls her daughter a "boulot"—ball and chain) and for her daughter (Berthe takes her to André's house, holds her up to the lighted window, and tells her that everything in the house belongs to the girl) is raw and palpable. Near the end of the volume, the loss of a new umbrella unleashes a storm of violence onto the girl at the hands of Berthe, who in this text is consistently described in atmospheric terms. The girl, beaten to a pulp, ultimately finds love and redemption with her grandmother Fidéline and roses from their garden. These two stories are to my mind examples of some of Leduc's most powerful writing. The relationship between the unnamed narrator-protagonist and her mother Berthe is more intense and violent in *L'Asphyxie* than in *La Bâtarde*, when the same period of her life is narrated. Recently, Carlo Jansiti has shown that Leduc was often more faithful to real-life events in her novels than in her so-called autobiographies. We have just seen Violette professing a desire to heal her mother's wounds in *La Bâtarde*, but twenty years earlier, as she wrote *L'Asphyxie*, anger and hurt had not yet given place to a spirit of reconciliation.

6. Chapter 4 is dedicated to exploring Leduc's seduction through the use of a narrative erotic "touch," of which this is a preview. In it, we will see that quivering is a verb that is associated with jouissance. Moreover, in *La Bâtarde*, Leduc uses the expression "La pieuvre dans mes entrailles frémissait [The octopus in my entrails quivered]" (*La Bâtarde* 125) to indicate sexual pleasure.

7. This is not to suggest that Violette stops reading in *La Folie en tête*. Quite the contrary. Scenes of reading take a backseat to scenes involving writers and writing, but when Violette does mention reading, it is clear that she has been reading all along.

8. "Je sortais, je rencontrai [sic] la crépuscule, je me regardais dans les premières vitrines éclairées, je tournais la tête du côté de la pénombre, je toussais plusieurs fois pour un passant sur l'autre trottoir, je me rengorgeais parce que je ressemblais au tuberculeux, parce que je toussais comme lui. Je m'en allais dans sa rue, je courtisais les portes et les fenêtres de sa maison apparentant à d'autres. Je ne me disais pas: Ta mère s'est fatiguée pour eux et pour lui dans le jardin, ta mère s'en est sortie, ta mère a eu de l'énergie. Non. Je faisais les cent pas pour avoir l'illusion d'être l'héritière de cette grande maison, de cette rue toujours endormie [I would go out, I met with twilight, I looked at myself in the first lighted shop windows, I would turn my head toward the half-light and cough several times for a passer-by on the other side of the street, I puffed my chest out because I resembled the one with tuberculosis, because I coughed like him. I would go off down his street, I would pay court to the doors and windows of his house that belonged to others. I didn't say to myself: Your mother wore herself out for them and for him in the garden, your mother came out all right, your mother had energy. No. I paced up and down to have the illusion of being the heiress of this grand house, of this sleepy street]" (*La Bâtarde* 85). This particular scene is interesting as it represents a seduction attempt on Violette's part: she's wooing her father's house. Also, it plainly shows which side she has taken between her mother and her father. As in the carriage scene in which she spits blood, she goes to lengths to demonstrate her resemblance to her father by coughing as she imagines he has done. Moreover, by refusing to remember the exploitation that the house represents, she is turning her back on her mother and choosing to side with her father. Also of interest is her desire to watch her reflection in the lighted windows. Chapter five of the present volume explores Leduc's use of reflections as objects of desire and seduction in *Thérèse et Isabelle*.

9.   Elsewhere, in *La Folie en tête*, literature is associated with seduction insofar as it is employed as a vehicle through which to seduce others or as the backdrop to seduction, as we shall see.

10.   "Je l'écoutais avec, en plus, la présence de la merveilleuse couturière pour l'ourlet de ses lèvres, le sculpteur pour le modelé de la fossette au milieu du menton, le drapier pour le coup de ciseaux des yeux allongés, le ciseleur pour les cheveux bouclés dépassant la coiffe du chapeau à larges bords [I listened to him with, on top of everything, the attentiveness of the marvelous seamstress for the hem of his lips, the sculptor for the contours of the cleft of his chin, the tailor for the cut of his long eyes, the engraver for the hair curling out from under the lining of his wide-brimmed hat]" (*La Bâtarde* 166).

11.   Some instances in which she emphasizes her "adolescent" (Bovaryan) enthusiasm for literature—generally as opposed to her present (more Barthesian) one—occur on the following pages of *La Folie en tête*: 113, 118–19, 168, 216, 233, 253. It should be noted however, that Violette sometimes claims to read *as an adolescent* in the present of this novel.

12.   At their bi-weekly meetings, Simone de Beauvoir's traditional opening question was "are you writing?" This represents an interesting twist—one that demonstrated Beauvoir's belief that to be a good writer one must also be an avid reader—and something for Violette to ruminate.

13.   In addition to the passage we have just examined, several times in her œuvre we see Leduc using Beckett's characterization of writing as "noircir les pages [blackening pages]."

14.   Violette does not show us this first reading, which is from a deluxe edition lent to her by Beauvoir, outside her attachment to the physical aspect of the page containing publishing information. This was a much-anticipated reading; Beauvoir had promised to lend her the book three times before she finally left it for Violette at the register of the *Deux-Magots*. (Cf. *La Folie en tête* 55, 59, 70, 111.) Its heavy bindings invite biblical comparisons. In fact, Violette will treat the writings of Genet as holy objects throughout *La Folie en tête*, with the exception of his play, *Les Bonnes*. Ironically, this play had been dedicated to Leduc (Genet later withdrew the dedication), and her dispassionate reaction to the *mise en scène* was one of the causes of their eventual rupture (*La Folie en tête* 155–56, 162–64).

15.   Violette is very clear that it is a seduction in which she is participating: "Mais le jour où Antonin Artaud mourut . . . je ne cherchai pas à séduire [But the day that Antonin Artaud died . . . I didn't try to be seductive]" (*La Folie en tête* 234).

16.   We can attribute this need to Violette's feelings of loneliness at the time. Her assertions that "A vingt-cinq ans, je n'aurais pas répondu à sa lettre. A cinquante, j'aurais répondu avec deux lignes définitives [At twenty-five, I wouldn't have answered his letter. At fifty, I would've answered with two decisive lines]" (*La Folie en tête* 214) suggest this interpretation, as at the younger age she was in relationships with Hermine and Gabriel, and later she had realized that she was better off without the heartache that amorous relationships inevitably produced.

17.   This represents another, obviously sexual and no longer literary, seduction attempt: "Bouclettes, frisettes, filet, casque, séchoir, pinces, épingles, . . . usine à séduction, pour séduire une verge, il faut être séduisante. Bouclettes, frisettes, filet, casque, coup de peigne, mise en plis, combien vous dois-je, pourboire pour la verge de Patrice [Tiny curls, ringlets, hairnet, drier, clips, bobby pins, . . . seduction factory, to seduce a penis, one has to be seductive. Tiny curls, ringlets, hairnet, drier, brush out, set, how much do I owe you, a tip for Patrice's dick]" (*La Folie en tête* 254).

18. The scene takes the form of a debate with herself over how she will go about seducing Patrice "Où couchera-t-il? A l'hôtel? Dans mon lit. Un gosse n'a pas d'argent. J'éteindrai, nous parlerons de Michaux, de Breton. Tu es prévoyante, dévergondée sur le qui-vive. Michaux, Breton dans l'obscurité de ta chambre, après? . . . Après, après? Un enfant, c'est maladroit, c'est indécis. Nous le forcerons. Jeune homme, vous étiez vieux dans vos lettres [Where will he sleep? In a hotel? In my bed. A kid doesn't have money. I'll turn out the light, we'll discuss Michaux, Breton. You're foresightful, you shameless hussy on the prowl. Michaux, Breton in the darkness of your room, and then what? . . . What about afterward? A kid is clumsy, unsure. We'll force him. Young man, you were old in your letters]" (*La Folie en tête* 253).

19. "Lire au lit jusqu'au départ n'est pas une mauvaise idée [Reading in bed until my departure is not such a bad idea]" (*La Folie en tête* 269). Ironically, this was one of the poses she had been considering taking the night before, trying to look nonchalant for his arrival: "Une idée . . . Si je me tenais tout près du livre de Steinbeck sur la table, devant les volets fermés. Je me jetterai sur le roman américain après qu'il aura frappé [An idea . . . what if I stayed near the Steinbeck book on the table, in front of the closed shutters. I'll throw myself on the American novel when he knocks]" (*La Folie en tête* 266). In these two instances we revisit two of the uses Violette had for literature in *La Bâtarde*: literature as a substitute for love, as with Aline, and as a pretext for it, as when Isabelle came to find Violette reading in bed and invited her to come across the hall with her book.

20. Beauvoir is particularly sensitive on this point, as the substance of *L'Affamée* turns on her own presence or absence in the narrator's life as depicted in this novel.

Notes to Chapter Three

1. Zackheim insists that what she has written is a fictional *biography*. In this manuscript, however, one senses that she uses Leduc as a vehicle to her own autobiography, itself distorted and embellished.

2. Going up to her old apartment on the rue Paul-Bert, he noticed that the name on the door was Mignere—his great-grandmother's name—with the first name of René.

3. "j'y mêlais des éléments, plus ou moins voilés, de ma vie personnelle [I mixed in elements, more or less veiled, of my personal life]" (*Éloge de la bâtarde* 52).

4. "Me suis-je identifié à elle ou ai-je forcé les ressemblances? Les deux, c'est probable [Did I identify with her, or did I push the similarities? Both, probably]" (*Éloge de la bâtarde* 256).

5. He writes that "je découpais mes analyses en fragments dont chacun portait un titre plutôt poétique, à la manière des essais de Barthes qui était mon modèle inavoué [I broke my analyses into fragments, each of which carried a more or less poetic name, after the manner of the essays of Barthes who was my unavowed model]" (*Éloge de la bâtarde* 52).

6. "L'une et l'autre savaient transfigurer une réalité terne et quotidienne, sans s'en détacher: en y apportant la profondeur, l'authenticité de leur regard, la qualité de l'observation, leur générosité de romancières [Each one had the gift of transfiguring a dull and humdrum reality, without getting away from it: bringing to it the depth, the

authenticity of their gaze, the quality of observation and their novelists' generosity]" (*Éloge de la bâtarde* 142) is another example.

7. This is not to suggest that artists have not made excellent critics in the past; in Violette Leduc's own life, Cocteau is a perfect example of this. I only mean to suggest that Zackheim's purpose in writing is not critical but artistic in nature.

8. Nowhere in the novel does the narrator get named, but with the exception of her husband's name, she claims the life experiences of Michele Zackheim.

9. "'It seems to me, and correct me if I'm wrong,' she continued, 'that you are searching for the part of Violette that is not newsworthy. People have been attracted to her eccentricity, but they have overlooked her seriousness, her beautiful use of language, her commitment to art. I like the idea that you are trying to understand her from an instinctive point of view'" (*Violette's Embrace* 23). Is this Zackheim's own pre-emptive strike against the scholars certain to critique her work?

10. "Des cris, des hurlements, des rugissements m'ont réveillée à cinq heures du matin. Je me suis rendormie pour me séparer du cauchemar d'une femme qui souffre. J'apprends dans la matinée qui l'ennemi est venu à cinq heures du matin, qu'il a emmené Esther. Les voisins ont dû arracher le tuyau à gaz des mains de sa mère. Mme Lita, Mme Keller partaient comme d'habitude aux commissions avec l'étoile jaune cousue sur leur corsage. Elles n'osaient pas parler de l'enlèvement d'Esther [Cries, wails, howls woke me up at five o'clock in the morning. I went back to sleep to distance myself from the nightmare of a suffering woman. I learn the next morning that the enemy came at five a.m., that they took Esther. The neighbors had to tear the gas pipe out of her mother's hands. Mme Lita, Mme Keller went out shopping as usual wearing the yellow star sewn on their bodices. They didn't dare speak of Esther's capture]" (*La Bâtarde* 479).

11. "La demoiselle qui tenait l'harmonium m'apprit que Gérard avait été emmené avec son frère et sa mère. Gérard se plaignait souvent de son frère, un zazou. Pris dans un bar à la mode pendant une rafle, le zazou fut forcé de donner son adresse. L'ennemi les arrêta tous les trois [The woman who played the harmonium told me that Gérard had been taken away with his brother and his mother. Gérard had often complained about his brother, a hipster. Taken in a fashionable bar during a sweep, the hipster was forced to give up his address. The enemy arrested all three]" (*La Bâtarde* 623).

12. "Near the arroyo a short distance from our house in New Mexico is a mulberry tree, similar to Violette's in Faucon. It has the same shiny leaves the silkworm loves—but without the silkworms. It is said that there is no silkworm industry in the United States because there is no cheap labor to hand-harvest the leaves. In the Vaucluse, if it gets too cold, the women keep the silkworm eggs warm between their breasts. When it becomes warmer, they carefully place them in a special silkworm room. Then the silkworms begin to eat, so noisily that you can hear them. Our mulberry tree looks like a stage prop . . ."

13. Both tactics are evident in the following passage: "How do I express the extent to which Violette's suffering and *jouissance* resonates with me, within me? Do I just hope that if I keep on writing, stroking these keys, some day soon my perseverance will pay offandtypingfasterandfasterthescreenwillbegintoundulateterespondtomytouchasIdoand thenexplodeinwavesofcolorsoundandlightpiercingmyfacewithshardsofglassandplasticlike sharpfingernailsorteethwhiletherestofmybodyisenveopedfireandvelvetandsofullofsensatio nthatifanythingweretotouchitmyskinwoulddripopentoomuchsurfacetension?"

Notes to Chapter Four

1.   Most recently Leduc was anthologized in *Erotica III: An Illustrated Anthology of Sexual Art and Literature*, ed. Charlotte Hill and William Wallace (New York: Carroll and Graf, 1996). Before that, an excerpt from *La Bâtarde* (the *"scène du voyeur"* between Violette and Hermine, uncommented) appeared in a volume arranged by Fiona Pitt-Kethly: *The Literary Companion to Sex: An anthology of prose and poetry,* (London: Sinclair-Stevenson Limited, 1992). The anthology of Claudine Brécourt-Villars, *Écrire d'amour: Anthologie de textes érotiques féminins (1799-1984),* (Paris: Ramsey, 1985) contains excerpts from *L'Affamée* and *La Bâtarde*. Brécourt-Villars's efforts in putting this volume together are stunning.

2.   Robe has also suggested the bodily link between autobiographer and reader: "Readers' attention to her poetic writing assures Leduc of intersubjectivity with them while their reading continues. It is an intimacy as imaginary as that which she imagines having shared with her mother while in her womb. Mother and daughter were 'communicating vessels' (*LB* 6) through the medium of maternal flesh; the autobiographer and her readers are as intimately (and as imaginarily) linked through the body of the text" (106).

3.   In French, see Hélène Cixous' "Rire de la méduse," ("The Laugh of the Medusa," in *New French Feminisms*) Verena Andermatt Conley's volume on Cixous is an excellent source of information on this author. For a more complete survey of this style in English, see E. Marks and I. de Courtivron, eds, *New French Feminisms: An Anthology,* (New York: Schocken, 1981). Colette Trout Hall marvels at the fact that Leduc has not been assimilated to the school of "écriture féminine," (24) and that feminists—both in France and abroad—have failed to take up the cause of Violette Leduc (*Violette Leduc, la mal-aimée* 14–16).

4.   Some examples of image-sensations in this passage are the "Drugs in my feet," "my sky [that] is opening up," "My hell [that] is rarefying," and feeling dizzy and hyper-electrified.

5.   Anny Brackx has also noted Leduc's considerable talents for translation: "I picked up a book which apparently had made the French catholic establishment blush because of its explicit sex. I skimmed through the pages in search of Violette's 'extravagant loves' and was not disappointed. The description of her first affair at boarding school with Isabelle and their nights together, is one of the finest evocations of awakening sexuality, loss of innocence and lesbian love-making I have ever come across. I remember being dazzled, even then, by her eloquence and the virtuosity with which she managed to translate into language the subtlest of emotions." (Anny Brackx, Introduction, *La Bâtarde*, by Violette Leduc, trans. Derek Coltman [1965; London: Virago Press Limited, 1985] v–x: vi.)

6.   If the sensuality seems very overt in this passage, perhaps Leduc no longer felt the need to be as discreet as she had been when writing for *Ravages*, as *La Folie en tête* was written during the period of *La Bâtarde's* stunning success.

7.   In note 15 to the introduction, we have seen Michael Sheringham mention the gift of writing. The very final paragraph of *La Bâtarde* begins with the gift to the reader of the Provençal sun on that day: "22 août 1963. Le mois d'août aujourd'hui, lecteur, est une rosace de chaleur. Je te l'offre, je te la donne [August 22, 1963. The month of August today, reader, is a rose window of heat. I'm offering it to you, it's yours]" (*La Bâtarde* 634). This is another example, though not sexual this time, of the image-sensation: the dazzling stained-glass sunburst for the experience of baking in the sun.

Finally, Violette's gift consists not just of the startling metaphors and the natural phenomena that inspire them, but also of a glimpse of the writer as a whole, healthy, legitimate person. This gift is the reward for those readers who stayed with the often desperate, much maligned "bâtarde" through six hundred pages. It is a gift that Leduc's seducees rejoice at receiving.

8. T. S. Eliot once wrote that "Genuine poetry can communicate before it is understood" ("Dante," 1929).

9. Alexandrian, *Histoire de la littérature érotique* (Paris: Éditions Seghers, 1989).

10. He takes his definition from the Greek: *porno-* (prostitute) *graphy* (writing). In this strictest sense, any writing having to do with the sex act is to be considered pornographic. He writes: "La pornographie est la description pure et simple des plaisirs charnels, l'érotisme est cette même description revalorisée en fonction d'une idée de l'amour ou de la vie sociale. Tout ce qui est érotique est nécessairement pornographique, avec quelque chose en sus [Pornography is the pure and straightforward description of carnal pleasures, eroticism is this same description enhanced according to a certain notion of love or social behavior. Everything that is erotic is necessarily pornographic, with something else added]" (*Histoire de la littérature érotique* 8)

11. Margaret Reynolds, ed., *Erotica: Women's Writing from Sappho to Margaret Atwood* (New York: Fawcett Columbine, 1990). Two excerpts of Winterson's writings appear in this volume. Leduc is conspicuously absent, considering her place in the writing of erotic literature by French women. She is understandably left out of volumes anthologizing only anglophone writers, but the history of French women writers is well-represented here, with this exception, as Reynolds includes pieces by Marie de France, Christine de Pizan, George Sand, Colette, Marguerite Duras, Monique Wittig, Hélène Cixous, Luce Irigaray, and Annie Leclerc.

12. Because their respective definitions of obscenity and pornography are so similar—and because Winterson's choice of words corresponds more closely to other critics' usage—I will employ her terminology, using the terms pornography and pornographic where Alexandrian would use the terms obscenity and obscene.

13. Audre Lorde, *Uses of the Erotic: The Erotic as Power* (Trumansburg, NY: Out & Out Books, 1978). This pamphlet consists of eight pages of unnumbered text.

14. It is curious that the women writers consistently identify the erotic with the nurturing, empowering feminine, and the pornographic with the exploitative, misogynistic masculine while the male theorist claims that "there is no difference between the two" (*Histoire de la littérature érotique* 8).

15. Pauline Réage, *Histoire d'O* (Paris: Jean-Jacques Pauvert, 1954); *Story of O*, trans. Sabine d'Estrée (New York: Ballantine Books, 1993). This is a complex, fascinating, and compelling, if somewhat horrifying, novel. In it, the protagonist loses her identity and is referred to only as the cipher O, despite the fact that she has had, in the past, another name. She is taken by her lover René to a château in Roissy where he "gives" her to a secret society of men to which he belongs. There she is repeatedly flogged, raped, and humiliated as well as branded and mutilated to teach her that she belongs not to herself but to the society, and that she must be available for their sexual use at all times. The most offensive aspect, however, to a feminist reader of today is not that O endures these tortures—we know of politically oppressed women in the real world who are forced into sexual servitude and survive—but that she accepts and even desires them, out of love for René. Although feminist ideology does not necessarily direct the writing of non-feminists, it does inform the post-modern reader's sensibility. Ultimately it is its attitude toward women that makes *Histoire d'O* a much more dated text than *Ravages*.

16. The book was published under the pen name of Pauline Réage, and it was in this article that the author's real name was revealed for the first time, forty years after the book's original publication. All information on *Histoire d'O* comes from the following article by John de St. Jorre: "The Unmasking of O" *The New Yorker* LXX, 23 (August 1, 1994): 42–50.

17. Although she is called O from the very beginning of the text, the reader learns on page 18/18 that she once had a different one when René calls her by her name.

18. "Vos mains ne sont pas à vous, ni vos seins, ni tout particulièrement aucun des orifices de votre corps, que nous pouvons fouiller et dans lequel nous pouvons nous enfoncer à notre gré [Your hands are not your own, nor are your breasts, nor, most especially, any of your body orifices, which we may explore or penetrate at will]" (*Histoire d'O* 15/15–16).

19. Violette Leduc's case is just the opposite: she does not refrain from explicitly naming the body parts in question (cf. her trip to the salon to seduce "Patrice's dick" treated in chapter 2).

20. It is clear from the text that this is to be understood as abuse: the men are described as "ceux qui la violeraient et la tourmenteraient [those who would violate and torment her]" (*Histoire d'O* 10/11) and she is told that "on ne vous bandera les yeux que pour vous maltraiter [You will be blindfolded only to be maltreated]" (*Histoire d'O* 16/17).

21. Aury, St. Jorre writes, feared that Paulhan "was going to abandon her. 'I wasn't young, I wasn't pretty, it was necessary to find other weapons. The physical side wasn't enough. The weapons, alas, were in the head.'" Aury reports that Paulhan practically dared her to do it, saying that he didn't think she was capable of that kind of writing ("The Unmasking of O" 43).

22. This preface (entitled "Happiness in Slavery") realizes all of the dangers that Winterson and Lorde ascribe to pornographic texts. In it, Paulhan clearly advocates abusive behavior toward women. At the same time, however, he claims that it was never he, but instead Pauline Réage who shows that "il faudrait sans cesse nourrir [les femmes], sans cesse les laver et farder, sans cesse les battre. Qu'elles ont simplement besoin d'un bon maître [(women) have constantly to be nourished, constantly washed and made up, constantly beaten. That all they need is a good master]" (*Histoire d'O* v/xxv).

23. Paulhan claims that René and Sir Stephen (the man with whom he shares O after she leaves the Roissy château training camp) are not sadistic at all, and do not enjoy whipping her, but that they are obliged to because she deserves to be punished for having sexual thoughts of other men.

Notes to Chapter Five

1. I have chosen to use the term "look" rather than "gaze" to indicate that in Leduc's text, there are two distinct kinds of looking in question: the loving versus the dominating. The term "gaze" has been used to represent the masculine, dominating variety of looking, which is precisely the look that Leduc defies in this short novel.

2. René de Ceccatty writes that this was a "roman qui avait été lu avec enthousiasme par Violette Leduc, selon le témoignage de Daniel Depland [novel which had been

read with enthusiasm by Violette Leduc, according to (her Faucon neighbor and young protégé) Daniel Depland]" (*Éloge de la bâtarde* 125).

3.   *Thérèse et Isabelle* is not an autobiography in the strictest sense—the name of the narrator-protagonist is not the same as that of the author—but this story is clearly inspired by elements from the author's life. It follows almost exactly the story of Violette's love affair with Isabelle recounted in the explicitly autobiographical text, *La Bâtarde*.

4.   Cf. chapter 3. This citation comes from his book jacket blurb.

5.   According to Ceccatty, Lemarchand confused Marc, Thérèse's companion and then husband, with his friend, Paul, a minor character, which suggests that he did not take the time to read the manuscript with much care before declaring it obscene. Futhermore, the report itself appears to have been written in haste if we are to judge by the mismatched punctuation.

6.   The reader will recall having read excerpts from *La Folie en tete* detailing the writing of this novella in the last chapter.

7.   Cf. Alex Hughes's chapter "*Thérèse et Isabelle*: An Idyll Abandoned" in *Violette Leduc: Mothers, Lovers and Language* (London: Maney and Son for MHRA, 1994): 81–113 for the exception.

8.   In the film version of this text, the choice of actresses reinforces the idea that Isabelle serves as a double or replacement for Thérèse's mother: both are tall, blond, coquettish women with strikingly similar faces and characters. This represents a departure from Leduc's text, however, which does not represent Isabelle as an identical character type to the figure of the mother.

9.   As we will show in this chapter, Leduc positions the reader as an audience for the young couple. This positioning is established from the very beginning of the novella.

10.   She uses the following citations to support her argument:

Nous nous serrions jusqu'à l'étouffement. (p. 9)
—Plus fort, plus fort . . . Serrez à m'étouffer, dit-elle. (p. 10)
J'ouvris la bouche, [son sein] entra. Je croquais dans les veines précieuses, je me souvenais du bleuté: il m'étouffait. (p. 95)

[We squeezed each other to the point of suffocation. . . . "Harder, harder. . . . Squeeze me until I can't breathe anymore," she said. . . . I opened my mouth, (her breast) entered. I was munching on precious veins, I remembered the blueness: it overpowered me] (*Mother, Lovers and Language* 91).

11.   Here, the use of the term *voyeuristic* is meant to highlight the sexual nature of the gaze and not to imply any secrecy.

12.   Luce Irigaray, *Le Corps-à-corps avec la mère* (Montreal: Editions de la pleine lune, 1981).

13.   Cf. for example Laura Mulvey's 1973 article "Visual Pleasure and Narrative Cinema," *Visual and Other Pleasures*, (Bloomington: Indiana UP, 1989) 14–26.

14.   "La main d'Isabelle dans les plis de mon tablier me caressa. C'était fou. Je pourrissais, mes chairs étaient blettes. . . . Je m'écroulai. . . . Je m'étais fait disparaître parce que je ne pouvais pas l'aimer en public: le scandale que je nous avais épargné retombait sur moi seule [Isabelle's hand in the folds of my pinafore caressed me. It was incredible. I was disintegrating, all my flesh was overripe. . . . I collapsed. . . . I had made

myself disappear because I could not love her in public: the scandal that I had spared us from fell entirely on me]" (39–40).
15. "Violette Leduc, ou le corps morcelé," diss., Université de Haute Bretagne II, 1988.

Notes to Chapter Six

1. I am referring only to her free-standing texts, and not the various articles for magazines or the short stories and excerpts that were published by *Les Temps modernes*.
2. In the English translations, these last three are published in a single volume entitled *The Woman with the Little Fox*.
3. "Elle effleure soixante années [She is coming up on sixty]" (*La Femme au petit renard* 31). In fact, at the time of the writing (1964–65), Leduc herself was approaching sixty. As I consider this to be a highly autobiographical piece, *La Femme au petit renard* represents one of the few texts in which Leduc writes of herself without considerable chronological distance. *L'Affamée* and *Trésors à prendre* are the other two exceptions to this rule.
4. "Est-ce que la concierge chuchotait contre elle avec les livreurs? [Was the concierge whispering against her to the deliverymen?]" (*La Femme au petit renard* 33).
5. "avec Bernadette je tentais de vendre tout . . .un assortiment de renards roux. Je courais Paris, je ne vendais rien [(...) with Bernadette I tried to sell everything: (...) an assortment of red foxes. I rushed all over Paris, I didn't sell a thing]" (*La Bâtarde*, 485).
6. "Elle récita la table des 8, elle insista sur 8 fois 8 = 64 [She recited the multiplication table for 8, she emphasized 8 times 8 = 64]" (*La Femme au petit renard* 50) and "c'est le moment de la table de multiplication si elle veut le revoir. Deux et deux quatre, deux et deux quatre, deux et deux quatre ... Non. Un et un deux, un et un deux, un et un deux jusqu'à ce que le préssentiment qu'il va venir se déclenche [it's time for the multiplication table if she wants to see him again. Two and two four, two and two four, two and two four . . . No. One and one two, one and one two, one and one two until the feeling that he's about to arrive is triggered]" (*La Femme au petit renard* 23).
7. Occasionally Violette will refer to herself as "elle" in a first-person narrative such as *La Bâtarde*, but this occurs infrequently, and only when she is at her most alienated.
8. This was *after* she had refused to make love to him before going to the town hall (*La Bâtarde* 401).
9. Leduc is clearly referring to "Amélie," the beloved sister in the autobiographical *René*. It is only in *Mémoires d'outre tombe* that she is called by her real name. Chateaubriand is less explicit about the erotic nature of his fraternal love in the later text, however.
10. "[La voiture] revint; et alors, sans parti pris ni direction, au hasard, elle vagabonda. On la vit à Saint-Pol, à Lescure, au mont Gargan, à la Rouge-Mare et place du Gaillardbois; rue Maladrerie, rue Dinanderie, devant Saint-Romain, Saint-Vivien, Saint-Maclou, Saint-Nicaise,—devant la Douane,—à la Basse-Vieille-Tour, aux Trois Pipes et au Cimetière Monumental. De temps à autre, le cocher, sur son siège, jetait aux cabarets des regards désespérés. Il ne comprenait pas quelle fureur de la locomotion poussait ces individus à ne point vouloir s'arrêter. Il essayait quelquefois, et aussitôt il entendit derrière lui partir des exclamations de colère [It came back; and then, without any fixed plan

or direction, wandered about at hazard. The cab was seen at Saint-Pol, as Lescure, at Mont Gargan, at La Rouge-Mare, and Place du Gaillardbois; in the Rue Maladrerie, Rue Dinanderie, before Saint-Romain, Saint-Vivien, Saint-Maclou, Saint-Nicaise,—in front of the Customs, at the 'Vieille Tour,' the 'Trois Pipes,' and the Monumental Cemetery. From time to time the coachman on his box cast despairing eyes at the public-houses. He could not understand what furious desire for locomotion urged these individuals never to wish to stop. He tried now and then, and at once exclamations of anger burst forth behind him] (*Madame Bovary* 317–18/153)."

11. This recalls the scene in *Madame Bovary* explicitly: "La voiture [...] entra au grand galop dans la gare du chemin de fer [The cab (...) entered the station at a gallop]" (*Madame Bovary* 317/153). In addition, *Le Taxi*'s "Rue Vivienne" suggests the "Saint-Vivien" of Flaubert's text.

12. "[L]es bourgeois ouvraient de grands yeux ébahis devant cette chose si extraordinaire en province, une voiture à stores tendus, et qui apparaissait ainsi continuellement, plus close qu'un tombeau et ballotté comme un navire [the good folk opened large, wonder-stricken eyes at this sight, so extraordinary in the provinces, a cab with blinds drawn, which appeared thus frequently, shut more closely than a tomb, and tossing about like a vessel]" (*Madame Bovary* 318/153).

13. "Une fois, au milieu du jour, [...] une main nue passa sous les petits rideaux de toile jaune et jeta des déchirures de papier, qui se dispersèrent au vent et s'abattirent plus loin, comme des papillons blancs, sur un champ de trèfles rouges tout en fleur.

"Puis, vers six heures, la voiture s'arrêta dans une ruelle du quartier Beauvoisine, et une femme en descendit qui marchait le voile baissé, sans détourner la tête.

[Once in the middle of the day, (...) a bared hand passed beneath the small blinds of yellow canvas, and threw out some scraps of paper that scattered in the wind and farther off alighted like white butterflies on a field of red clover all in bloom.

At six o'clock the carriage stopped in a back street of the Beauvoisine Quarter, and a woman got out, who walked with her veil down, and without turning her head]" (*Madame Bovary* 318/153–54).

14. "— Descends. L'autre taxi nous attend.
—Ne m'aide pas à descendre. Allume ta cigarette.

['Step out. The other taxi is waiting.'
'Don't help me to get out. Light your cigarette.'] (*Le Taxi* 100)"

15. Robyn Warhol, *Gendered Interventions: Narrative Discourse in the Victorian Novel*. (New Brunswick: Rutgers UP, 1989).

16. "Generally speaking, a distancing narrator discourages the actual reader from identifying with the narratee, while an engaging narrator encourages that identification" (*Gendered Interventions* 31). One way narrators discourage that identification is by providing too much specific information on the narratee, making readers feel they have little to do with that figure. I propose that another is by creating a metafictional text, thus exposing the fictional nature of the text. This is opposed to Warhol's idea that engaging narrators want to maintain the fiction that their story is "real."

17. Warhol writes that "many of the realist novelists were also interested in the world of lived experience and the impact their novels might have on it. Writers such as Elizabeth Gaskell, George Eliot, and Harriet Beecher Stowe thought of the novel as a vehicle for exerting influence on readers who would, in turn, work changes in the worlds of politics, society, and personal morality" (*Gendered Interventions* xi).

18. I believe Warhol would agree. In her book she looked exclusively at Victorian texts which featured narrators, and so did not consider the question posed by Leduc's text. However, based on the importance she places on making an impact on the reader, I am sure that she would consider *Le Taxi* to be an engaging text rather than a distancing one.

19. In Gérard Genette, *Figures III* (Paris: Éditions du Seuil, 1972), and in English: *Narrative Discourse: An Essay in Method*, trans. Jane E. Lewin (Ithaca, NY: Cornell UP, 1980).

20. I consider this to be the development or outgrowth of her use of direct address: here she creates a conversation in direct discourse with the reader, as I will show.

21. Mieke Bal, "Narration et focalisation: Pour une théorie des instances du récit," *Poétique* (1977) 29: 107–26. I have chosen to cite her work heavily because her argument is at the same time a useful discussion of Genette's theories and an elaboration on them, particularly as regards narration and focalization, which is our focus here.

22. Bal writes that there is always a spectator in the text, one who can see what is being narrated: "Ce spectateur ne peut pas être le lecteur: c'est dans la nature du récit que le contenu de l'information ne peut pas être perçu directement par le lecteur. Ce n'est pas le narrateur non plus: celui-là n'a droit qu'à la parole. Il doit être le focalisateur, celui qui voit «à la place du» lecteur [This spectator cannot be the reader: it is in the nature of the récit that the content of the information cannot be directly perceived by the reader. Neither is this the narrator, who has a right only to speech. It must be the focalizer, that one who sees 'in the place of' the reader]" ("Narration et focalisation" 121).

23. Let me emphasize that the choice to use theatrical vocabulary to describe *Le Taxi* is a conscious one. This piece, because it lacks a narrator, more closely resembles a dramatic than a novelistic composition. Even the term *mimesis*, referring to the *miming* of reality, is suggestive of dramatic performance.

24. *Discours rapporté* is Genette's term for *discours directe,* or direct discourse: material that comes directly out of the mouth of the actors and that is unmediated by a narrator or focalizer.

25. We even can see her employ some of the same ones: the sense of being drugged, being lit up and electrified make up a large part of Leduc's vocabulary of sexual pleasure. In chapter 4 we have seen them used as "mes jambes droguées [my drugged legs]," "rateau de lumière [rake of light]," and "je suis survoltée [I'm wired]." Floral imagery is often used to describe lesbian encounters in her works; here the tree can be seen as its more phallic counterpart.

26. This assumes that most readers start not with *Le Taxi*, one of Leduc's more obscure texts, but, as most often happens, with the text for which she is best known: *La Bâtarde*.

27. The first indication that the two are related comes on page 11 when one says that "Tante Marie pouvait lui payer ça [Aunt Marie could certainly afford to buy that for her]" referring to the quantities of beer used to ply Cytise for the brother's lessons. The confirmation that they are brother and sister comes only on page 19. The reader's first indication that the lovers are riding in a taxi occurs near the beginning of the second chapter when one (the sister) asks where they are and the brother responds: "— Place de l'Alma" (*Le Taxi* 15).

28. See Richard Sennett for dutiful obeisance that is inspired by direct discourse (*Authority*, chapter 5).

29. In fact, in the polymorphously perverse atmosphere of the taxi, it does not matter (and it is often impossible to tell) whose voice belongs to whom. Thus, Leduc's

voice is not always located in the sister's dialogue and the reader's in the brother's speech, as we shall see.

30. I have ascertained this by counting forwards and backwards from the grammatical gender markers. However, this method is not always reliable. Often, cuts have been made, and the voices do not match up: counting forward from one grammatical marker and back from another frequently results in two consecutive masculine or feminine voices. This phenomenon exists even in the notebook manuscripts of *Le Taxi* housed at the IMEC (there are two, an earlier and a later version). With Leduc, it is nearly always impossible to discern the "original" text, as she pastes rewritten page over rewritten page. The result is that the thin student notebooks that she writes in—the recto and verso of each sheet having several more sheets glued to it—become very fat. The most dramatic examples of this are the notebooks for *Ravages*, each of which is around five inches thick, or a good twenty times more voluminous than the original blank notebook.

31. Her vagina is referred to again as a "hole" soon after, on pages 53 ("trou insatiable [insatiable hole]") and 54 ("— Les évadés vont entrer dans ton trou./ — Toi, tu vas entrer. Tu entres. ['The escapees will go into your hole.'/ 'You, you will come in. You are coming in']").

32. This is confirmed elsewhere in the text. Here, in reference to the shovel wound, the sister says "— Je ne voulais pas saigner, je ne voulais pas crier ['I didn't want to bleed, I didn't want to cry out']" (*Le Taxi* 51). In chapter 7, however, when the brother speaks of their preparations ("— Il nous fallait du confort, des précautions, tout un apprentissage ['We needed comfort, precautions, a whole apprenticeship']") she responds by repeating "— Je ne voulais pas saigner, je ne voulais pas crier" (*Le Taxi* 60). As part of their preparations, their apprenticeship would include sex lessons. They did not want to spoil their one shot at consummating their relationship due to inexperience, pain, and blood.

33. "— Confusion. Ils te prenaient pour la blessée ['A mix-up. They mistook you for the wounded one']" (*Le Taxi* 48).

34. In French "chemise de nuit" is a unisex term, meaning "nightgown" for women, and "nightshirt" for men. Leduc plays on the polymorphous suggestivity of this ambiguity.

35. "—Tu chuchotais: «C'est pour une représentation.» Je suis entrée dans ta chambre ['You whispered: 'It's for a performance.'' I went into your room']" (49) and "—Je suis parti derrière le paravent, j'ai crié: «La représentation commence» ['I went behind the partition, I yelled: "The performance is beginning"']" (*Le Taxi* 49-50).

36. Paul Zweig refers to it as a "marvelous fairy tale" in "The Taxi," *New York Times Book Review*, 9 July 1972.

37. Ceccatty's comment here that *Le Taxi* "pushes the limit of the erotic text" seems to imply that he views the sexuality in it as nearly gratuitous, bordering on the pornographic. Certainly it is, according to Alexandrian: siblings "doing it" over and over again in the backseat of a cab is sex without the "something else" of a certain idea of love or society. As an aficionado of Leduc's erotic writings, Ceccatty's sensibilities seem offended by the characters whose outlines are barely sketched. He almost seems to wish that Leduc had tried a little harder in writing this novella, instead of resting on her erotic laurels. According to our reading of the story, however—that the brother and sister are mere roles to be played by Leduc and her reader—the flimsy nature of these characters is absolutely necessary: the costumes of these polymorphously perverse substitutes need to be cut to fit one-size-fits-all.

Note to Conclusion

1. Hélène Jaccomard, *Lecteur et lecture dans l'autobiographie française contemporaine: Violette Leduc, Françoise d'Eaubonne, Serge Dubrovsky, Marguerite Yourcenar* (Geneva: Droz, 1993).

BIBLIOGRAPHY OF WORKS
CITED AND CONSULTED

Texts by Violette Leduc:

L'Affamée. Paris: Gallimard-Folio, 1948.
L'Asphyxie. Paris: Gallimard-Imaginaire, 1946.
La Bâtarde. With a preface by Simone de Beauvoir. Paris: Gallimard-Folio, 1964.
La Chasse à l'amour. Paris: Gallimard, 1973.
La Femme au petit renard. Paris: Gallimard, 1965.
La Folie en tête. Paris: Gallimard, 1970.
Ravages. Paris: Gallimard, 1955.
Le Taxi. Paris: Gallimard-Rose, 1971.
Thérèse et Isabelle. Paris: Gallimard-Rose, 1966.
Thérèse et Isabelle, texte intégral. With a postface and notes by Carlo Jansiti. Paris: Gallimard, 2000.
Trésors à prendre. Paris: Gallimard, 1960.
La Vieille Fille et le mort. Paris: Gallimard, 1958.

English Translations of Texts by Violette Leduc:

La Bâtarde. Trans. Derek Coltman, with a forward by Simone de Beauvoir. New York: Farrar, Straus, and Giroux, 1965; New York: Riverhead Books, 1997.
In the Prison of Her Skin. Translation of *L'Asphyxie* by Derek Coltman. London: Rupert Hart-Davis, 1970.
Mad in Pursuit. Trans. Derek Coltman. New York: Farrar, Straus, and Giroux, 1971.
Ravages. Trans. Derek Coltman. Includes *Thérèse and Isabelle* as a prologue. London: Arthur Barker Limited, 1968.
The Taxi. Trans. Helen Weaver. New York: Farrar, Straus, and Giroux, 1972.
Thérèse and Isabelle. Trans. Derek Coltman. New York: Farrar, Straus, and Giroux, 1967.
The Woman in the Little Fox Fur: Three Novellas by Violette Leduc. Trans. Derek Coltman. New York: Farrar, Straus, and Giroux, 1966.

175

Short Pieces by Leduc:

"Une mère, un parapluie, des gants," extract from *L'Asphyxie*, *Les Temps modernes*, no. 2, November 1945.

"Le Dézingage," *Les Temps Modernes*, no. 3, December 1945.

"Train noir," *Les Temps Modernes*, no. 6, March 1946.

"Les Mains sales," *Les Temps Modernes*, no. 15, December 1946.

"L'Affamée," extract, *Les Temps Modernes*, no. 25, October 1947.

"L'Affamée, suite et fin," extract, *Les Temps Modernes*, no. 26, November 1947.

"Je hais les dormeurs," extract from the manuscript of *Ravages*, *L'Arbaète*, no. 13, summer 1948.

"Les Maisons de quatre heures du matin," *Contemporains*, no. 2, December 1950.

"Au village," *Les Temps Modernes*, no. 65, March 1951.

"Desirée Hellé," *Les Temps Modernes*, no. 80, June 1952.

"La Vieille Fille et le mort," extract, *Cahiers du Sud*, no. 345, 1957.

"Thérèse et Isabelle," extract, *Parler*, no. 5, winter 1958.

"Le Causse noir," extract from *Trésors à prendre*, *Cahiers du Sud*, no. 354, 1960.

"Trésors à prendre," extract, *La Nouvelle Revue Française*, no. 88, April 1960.

"Le Tailleur anguille," extract from *La Bâtarde*, *Les Temps Modernes*, no. 186, November 1961.

"La Bâtarde," extract, *Les Temps Modernes*, no. 207–08, August–September 1963.

"The Great Craftsmen of Paris," *Vogue* (U.S.), March 1965. Reprinted in *Vogue* (France) as "Une ville c'est une femme," March 1965.

"Balenciaga," *Vogue* (U.S.), April 1965. Reprinted in *Vogue* (France), April 1965.

"Courrèges: A Slaying in the Corrida of Fashion," *Vogue* (U.S.), May 1965.

"I Went on Location with Zhivago," *Vogue* (U.S.), September 1965.

"La Bâtarde," extract in English translation, *Vogue* (U.S.), October 1965.

"Présentation du peintre Michel Warren," brochure distributed for the preview of the exhibit organized by Knoll International (France), 23 November 1965.

"Steal-Scening with Hepburn & O'Tolle. Quick takes on a fake theft of fake art at the filming of *How to Steal a Million*," *Vogue* (U.S.), April 1966.

"Brigitte Bardot," *Adam*, June 1966.

"De Palerme à Trapani," *La Revue des Voyages*, no. 63, winter 1966. Reprinted in *Visitez l'Italie du Sud avec . . .* Plon, 1969.

"Lettres," *Masques*, no. 11, Fall 1981.

"Lettres à Simone de Beauvoir," *Les Temps Modernes*, no. 495, October 1987.

Secondary Sources on Leduc:

Acton, Harold. "Strange Bedfellows." *New York Review of Books* 6 Jan. 1966: 12–13.

Athill, Diana. "*La Bâtarde*: An Autobiography by Violette Leduc." Translated by Derek Coltman." *The Listener* 25 Nov. 1965: 868–69.

Aubaud, Camille. "Le XXe siècle: Aspects de l'érotisme féminin." *Lire les femmes des lettres*. Paris: Dunod, 1993.

Aury, Dominique. "Violette Leduc." *Nouvelle Revue Française* 255 (mars 1974): 114–16.

Bair, Deirdre. *Simone de Beauvoir: A Biography*. New York: Simon and Schuster, 1990.

Beauvoir, Simone de. *Le Deuxième sexe*. 1949; Paris: Gallimard-Folio essais, 1976. 2 vols. Translated and edited by H. M. Parshley, *The Second Sex*. New York: Vintage Books, 1989.

———. Preface. Leduc, *La Bâtarde* 7–23. Trans. Derek Coltman, "Foreword," *La Bâtarde*.

———. *Tout compte fait*. Paris: Gallimard, 1972. Trans. Patrick O'Brian, *All Said and Done*. New York: Putnam, 1974.

———. *A Transatlantic Love Affair: Letters to Nelson Algren*. New York: New Press, 1998.

———. "Violette Leduc: La passion de vivre." *Nouvel Observateur* 5–11 juin 1972: 68.

Brackx, Anny. Introduction. *La Bâtarde*. By Violette Leduc. Trans. Derek Coltman. 1965. London: Virago Press Limited, 1985. v–x.

Bréchet-Anaheim, Didier. "Violette Leduc, Pour Qui?" *Le Démocrate* 3 sept. 1973.

Brécourt-Villars, Claudine. *Écrire d'amour: Anthologie de textes érotiques féminins (1799-1984)*. Paris: Ramsey, 1985.

Brioude, Mireille. *Violette Leduc: La Mise en scène du "je."* Amsterdam: Rodopi, 2000.

———. "Simone de Beauvoir et son ombre: Violette Leduc," *Simone de Beauvoir Studies* 13 (1996): 114–25.

Broc-Lapeyre, Monique. "Du trafic à la littérature." *Critique* nov. 1970: 935–43.

Ceccatty, René de. "Tirésias et le trio." *Nord'* 45–50.

———. *Violette Leduc: Éloge de la Bâtarde*. Paris: Stock, 1994.

Chapsal, Madeleine. "La folle solitude de Violette Leduc." *L'Express* 25–31 oct. 1965: 90–91.

———. "Violette Leduc. *La Bâtarde*. Profil." *L'Express* 19-25 oct. 1964: 70–71.

Charles-Merrien, Ghyslaine. "Le rôle des objets dans l'univers de Violette Leduc." *Nord'* 31–44.

———. "Violette Leduc, ou le corps morcelé." Diss. Université de Haute Bretagne II, 1988.

Conchon, Georges. "La Revanche de Violette Leduc." *Lire* 15 mai 1970: 50.

Courtivron, Isabelle de. "From Bastard to Pilgrim: Rites and Writings for Madame." *Yale French Studies* 72 (1986): 133–48.

———. *Violette Leduc*. Boston: Twayne Publishers, 1985.

———. "Violette Leduc (1907–1972)." Sartori 285–95.

———. "Violette Leduc's *L'Affamée*: The Courage to displease." *L'Esprit créateur* 19. 2: 95–106. (été 1979).

Crosland, Margaret. "The Search for Love," *Women of Iron and Velvet: French Women Writers after George Sand*. New York: Taplinger, 1976. 201–10.

Depland, Daniel. "Le Pouls régulier de *La Folie en tête*." *Nord'* 91–98.

d'Eaubonne, Françoise. "Violette Leduc et la condition féminine." *Nord'* 23–30.

Evans, Martha Noel. *Masks of Tradition: Women and the Politics of Writing in Twentieth-Century France*. Ithaca, New York: Cornell University Press, 1987.

———. "La mythologie de l'écriture dans *La Bâtarde* de Violette Leduc." *Littérature* (mai 1982): 82–92.

———. "Writing as Difference in Violette Leduc's Autobiography *La Bâtarde*." Garner, Kahane, and Sprengnether 306–17.

Gagnon, Louise. "L'Autobiographie de Violette Leduc: Pour une lecture féministe." Diss. U of California-Berkeley, 1986.

Galey, Mattieu. "Les cahiers de l'angoisse." *L'Express* 22–28 oct. 1973: 79.

———. "Extravagante Violette." *Réalités* nov. 1973: 120–21.

Girard, Pier. "«L'affammée» de Violette Leduc." *Topique: Revue freudienne* 34 (janv. 1985): 113–28.

———. *Œdipe masqué: Une lecture psychanalytique de* L'Affamée *de Violette Leduc.* Paris: des femmes, 1986.

Guérin, Jacques. "Violette vient dîner." *Nord'* 11–12.

Hall, Colette Trout. "*L'Ecriture féminine* and the Search for the Mother in the Works of Violette Leduc and Marie Cardinal." *Women and French Literature.* Ed. Michel Guggenheim. Saratoga, CA: Anma Libri, 1988. 231–38.

———. *Violette Leduc, la mal aimée.* Amsterdam: Rodopi, 1999.

Haynes, Muriel. "Self as Freak and Outcast." *Tribune* 17 Dec. 1965: 14.

Hill, Charlotte, and William Wallace. *Erotica III: An Illustrated Anthology of Sexual Art and Literature.* New York: Carroll and Graf, 1996.

Holland, Mary. "Weeping Ovaries." *The Observer* 7 Nov. 1965: 28.

Hughes, Alex. *Violette Leduc: Mothers, Lovers, and Language* . London: W.S. Maney and Son for the Modern Humanities Research Association, 1994.

——— and Kate Ince, eds. *French Erotic Fiction: Women's Desiring Writing, 1880–1990.* Oxford, UK: Berg, 1996.

Jaccomard, Hélène. *Lecteur et lecture dans l'autobiographie française contemporaine: Violette Leduc, Françoise d'Eaubonne, Serge Dubrovsky, Marguerite Yourcenar.* Geneva: Droz, 1993.

Jansiti, Carlo. "Chronologie." *Nord'* 5–9.

———. "«Ils ont refusé le début de Ravages. C'est un assassinat»." Extrait d'une biographie en cours." *Nord'* 77–89.

———. *Violette Leduc.* Paris: Grasset, 1999.

Kaup, Monika. "Autobiographies of Women's Madness: Hallucinations and Confessions," *Mad Intertextuality: Madness in Twentieth-Century Women's Writing.* Trier: Wissenschaftlicher Verlag Trier, 1993. 167–206.

Keefe, Terry, and Edmund Smith, eds. *Autobiography and the Existential Self: Studies in Modern French Writing.* New York: St. Martin's Press, 1995.

Klein, Marie-Eve. "Violette Leduc ou la revanche du quotidien." Diss. Université de Strasbourg, 1983.

Lange, Monique. "Les passions de la bâtarde." *Le Nouvel Observateur* 23–29 mars 1970: 35–36.

Laparra, Camille. "Femme bâtarde/femme écrivain légitime: la dichotomie figurale de *La Bâtarde* de Violette Leduc." *From Dante to García-Márquez: Studies in Romance Literatures and Linguistics,.* Ed. Gene H. Bell-Villada et al. Williamstown, MA: Williams College Press, 1987. 360–72.

Maclean, Mary. *The Name of the Mother: Writing Illegitimacy.* London: Routeledge, 1994.

Mantello, Elisabeth Lucette Roberte. "L'Autobiographie dérangée: *Mémoires d'une jeune fille rangée* de Simone de Beauvoir, *La Bâtarde* de Violette Leduc." Diss. University of Wisconsin-Madison, 1986.

Marin la Meslée, Valérie. "Genet, Violette Leduc: admiration et jalousie." *Magazine littéraire* 313 (Sept. 1993): 37–38.

Marks, Elaine. "Lesbian Intertextuality." *Homosexualities and French Literature.* Ed. Elaine Marks and George Stambolian. Ithaca: Cornell UP, 1979.

———. "I Am My Own Heroine: Some Thoughts About Women and Autobiography in France." *Female Studies IX: Teaching About Women in the Foreign Languages.* Ed. Sidonie Cassirer. Old Westbury, New York: Feminine Press, 1975.

Marson, Susan. *Le Temps de l'autobiographie: Violette Leduc ou la mort devant la lettre.* Saint-Denis: Presses Universitaires de Vincennes, 1998.

Nord'. "Violette Leduc." Special Issue 23 (juin 1994).

Nourissier, François. "La revanche de la bâtarde: Violette Leduc." *Nouvelles littéraires* 23 avril. 1970: 5.

Peyre, Henri. *French Novelists of Today.* New York: Oxford UP, 1967.

———. "Passions of a Gallic Sappho." *Saturday Review* 30 Oct. 1965: 46–47.

Piatier, Jacqueline. "Un grand livre: *La Bâtarde* de Violette Leduc. *Le Monde* 10 oct. 1964: 12.

———. "La suite de *La Bâtarde*: *La Folie en tête* de Violette Leduc." *Le Monde* 11 avril 1970, I–II.

Pitt-Kethly, Fiona. *The Literary Companion to Sex: An anthology of prose and poetry.* London: Sinclair-Stevenson Limited, 1992.

Poirot-Delpech, Bertrand. "Le Salut par l'écriture—*La Chasse à l'amour,* de Violette Leduc; *L'Ivre Livre,* de Marcel Moreau." *Le Monde* 18 oct. 1973: 19.

Renard, Paul. "*L'Asphyxie*: Les débuts d'une autobiographie." *Nord'* 69–76.

Respaut, Michele. "Femme/ange, femme/monstre: *L'Affamée* de Violette Leduc." *Stanford French Review* 7.3 (winter 1983): 365–74.

Rinaldi, Angelo. "Impérial Violette." *L'Express* 10 nov. 1994: 193.

Robe, Margaret Anne. "Conceiving a Self in Autobiography by Women." diss. U of California-Los Angeles, 1988.

Rule, Jane. "Violette Leduc." *Lesbian Images.* London: Peter Davies, 1975.

Saksens, Nita. "A Feeling of Inadequacy." *Thought* 9 July 1966: 18.

Sartori, Eve Marie, and Dorothy Winne Zimmerman. *French Women Writers: A Bio-Bibliographical Sourcebook.* New York: Greenwood Press, 1991.

Schoenfeld, Jean Snitzer. "*La Bâtarde,* or Why the Writer Writes." *French Forum* 7 (1982): 261–68.

Sheringham, Michael. *French Autobiography: Devices and Desires.* Oxford, UK: Clarendon Press, 1994.

———. "The Sovereignty of Solitude and the Gift of Writing in Violette Leduc's *La Folie en tête.*" Keefe and Smith 127–46.

Stockinger, Jacob. "The Legitimations of *la Bâtarde.*" Diss. U. of Wisconsin-Madison, 1979.

Tennant, Emma. "Insatiable Entrails." *New Statesman* 5 Nov. 1965: 706.

Viollet, Catherine. "Violette Leduc: écriture et sexualité." *Tangence* 47 (mars 1995): 69–83.

Weightman, John. "Blushing Violette." *The Observer* 11 July 1971: 28.

———. "Prizefighters and their Betters." *The Observer* 3 Jan. 1965: 24.

———. "The Stories Women Tell." *Harper's Magazine* Nov. 1965: 162–67.

Wilwerth, Evelyne. "Les Sensuelles." *Visages de la littérature féminine.* Bruxelles: Pierre Mardaga, 1987.

———. "A Woman's World." *The Observer* 24 Oct. 1965: 23.

Yalom, Marilyn. *Maternity, Mortality, and the Literature of Madness.* University Park: Pennsylvania State UP, 1985.

———. "They Remember *Maman*: Attachment and Separation in Leduc, de Beauvoir, Sand and Cardinal." *Essays in Literature* 8.1 (1981): 73–90.

Zackheim, Michèle. *Violette's Embrace.* New York: Riverhead Books, 1996.

———. *Words on Loan.* Manuscript for *Violette's Embrace.*

Zweig, Paul. "The Taxi." *New York Times Book Review* 9 July 1972.

Feminism and Literature:

Abel, Elizabeth, ed. Introduction. *Writing and Sexual Difference.* Spec. Issue *Critical Inquiry* 8 (1981): 173–78.
Brée, Germaine. Foreword. Brodzki and Schenck ix–xii.
———. *Women Writers in France.* New Brunswick, NJ: Rutgers UP, 1973.
Brodzki, Bella, and Celeste Schenck, eds. *Life/Lines: Theorizing Women's Autobiography.* Ithaca, NY: Cornell UP, 1988.
Burke, Carolyn Greenstein. "Report from Paris: Women's Writing and the Women's Movement." *Signs* 4 (1978): 843–54.
Butler, Judith. *Gender Trouble: Feminism and the Subversion of Identity.* New York: Routledge, 1990.
Chodorow, Nancy. *The Reproduction of Mothering: Psychoanalysis and the Sociology of Gender.* Berkeley: U of California P, 1978.
Cixous, Hélène. "Le rire de la méduse." *L'Arc* 61 (1975): 39–54.
———. *Vivre l'orange.* Trans. Ann Liddle and Sarah Cornell. Paris: des femmes, 1979.
———, and Catherine Clément. *The Newly Born Woman.* Trans. Betsy Wing. Minneapolis: U of Minnesota P, 1986.
Conley, Verena Andermatt. *Hélène Cixous: Writing the Feminine.* Lincoln: U of Nebraska P, 1984.
Duchen, Claire. *Feminism in France.* London: Routledge and Kegan Paul, 1986.
Felman, Shoshana. "Rereading Femininity." *Yale French Studies* 62 (1981): 19–44.
Flieger, Jerry Aline. *Colette and the Fantom Subject of Autobiography.* Ithaca, NY: Cornell UP, 1992.
Furman, Nelly. "Textual Feminism." McConnell-Ginet, *Women and Language in Literature and Society.*
Gallop, Jane. *Around 1981: Academic Feminist Literary Theory.* New York: Routeledge, 1992.
———. *The Daughter's Seduction: Feminism and Psychoanalysis.* Ithaca, NY: Cornell UP, 1982.
———. *Reading Lacan.* Ithaca, NY: Cornell UP, 1985.
Garner, Shirley Nelson,, Claire Kahane and Madelon Sprengnether, eds. *The (M)other Tongue: Essays in Feminist Psychoanalytic Interpretation.* Ithaca, NY: Cornell UP, 1985.
Heilbrun, Carolyn G. *Writing a Woman's Life.* New York: Ballantine Books, 1988.
Hirsch, Marrianne. "A Mother's Discourse. Incorporation and Repetition in La Princesse de Clèves." *Yale French Studies* 62 (1981): 67–87.
Irigaray, Luce. *Le Corps-à-corps avec la mère.* Montreal: Editions de la pleine lune, 1981.
———. *Speculum, de l'autre femme.* Paris: Editions de Minuit, 1974.
Jones, Anne Rosalind. "Writing the Body: Toward an Understanding of L'écriture féminine." *Feminist Studies* 7 (1981): 247–63.
McConnell-Ginet, Sally, ed. *Women and Language in Literature and Society.* New York: Praeger, 1980.
Marks, Elaine. "The Dream of Love: A Study of Three Autobiographies. *Twentieth-Century French Fiction: Essays for Germaine Brée.* Ed. George Stambolian. New Brunswick, NJ: Rutgers UP, 1975. 72–88.
———. "Review Essay: Women and Literature in France." *Signs* 3 (summer 1978): 832–42.

————, and Isabelle de Courtivron, eds. *New French Feminisms: An Anthology*. New York: Schocken Books, 1980.

Martin, Biddy. "Lesbian Identity and Autobiographical Difference[s]." Brodzki and Schenck 77–103.

Miller, Nancy K. "Changing the Subject: Authorship, Writing, and the Reader." In *Feminist Studues/Critical Studies*. Ed. Teresa de Lauretis. Bloomington: Indiana UP, 1986.

————. "Writing Fictions: Women's Autobiography in France." Brodzki and Schenck, 45–61.

Mitchell, Juliet. *Psychoanalysis and Femininsm: Freud, Reich, Laing, and Women*. New York: Vintage, 1974.

————, and Jacqueline Rose, eds. *Feminine Sexuality: Jacques Lacan and the école freudienne*. New York: Norton, 1982.

Nin, Anaïs. *Delta of Venus: Erotica by Anaïs Nin*. New York: Harcourt Brace Jovanovich, 1977.

Riley, Denise. *"Am I That Name?" Feminism and the Category of "Women" in History*. Minneapolis: U of Minnesota P, 1988.

Schor, Naomi. *Breaking the Chain: Women, Theory, and French Realist Fiction*. New York: Columbia UP, 1985.

————. *Reading in Detail: Aesthetics and the Feminine*. New York: Methuen, 1987.

Smith, Sidonie. *Subjectivity, Identity and the Body: Women's Autobiographical Practices in the Twentieth Century*. Bloomington: Indiana UP, 1993.

Spender, Dale. *Man Made Language*. London: Routledge and Kegan Paul, 1980.

Spivak, Gayatri Chakrovorty. "French Feminism in an International Frame." *Yale French Studies* 62 (1981): 154–84.

Warhol, Robyn. *Gendered Interventions: Narrative Discourse in the Victorian Novel*. New Brunswick, NJ: Rutgers UP, 1989.

Winterson, Jeanette. Introduction. *Erotica: Women's Writing from Sappho to Margaret Atwood*. Ed. Margaret Reynolds. New York: Fawcett Columbine, 1990.

Wittig, Monique. *Les Guérillères*. Paris: Éditions de Minuit, 1969.

Literature and Psychoanalysis:

Abraham, Nicolas, and Maria Torok. *The Shell and the Kernel*. Ed. and trans. Nicholas Rand. Chicago: U of Chicago P, 1994.

————. *The Wolf Man's Magic Word: A Cryptonomy*. Trans. Nicholas Rand. Minneapolis: U of Minnesota P, 1986.

Bowie, Malcolm. *Lacan*. Cambridge, MA: Harvard UP, 1991.

Brooks, Peter. *Psychoanalysis and Storytelling*. Cambridge, UK: Blackwell, 1994.

Felman, Shoshana. *Jacques Lacan and the Adventure of Insight: Psychoanalysis in Contemporary Culture*. Cambridge, MA: Harvard UP, 1987.

————. "La Méprise et sa chance." *L'Arc* 58 (1974): 40–48.

————. ed. *The Question of Reading: Otherwise*. Spec. Issue of *Yale French Studies* 55/56 (1977).

Freud, Sigmund. "Femininity." *New Introductory Lectures on Psychoanalysis*. 1933. Ed. and trans. James Strachey. New York: Norton, 1964. 112–39.

———. "From the History of an Infantile Neurosis." *Three Case Histories*. 1918. New York: Macmillan, 1963. 187–316.

———. *The Interpretation of Dreams*. 1900. Ed. and trans. James Strachey. New York: Avon, 1965.

———. *Jokes and their Relation to the Unconscious*. 1905, 1912. Ed. and trans. James Strachey. New York: Norton, 1960.

———. *An Outline of Psycho-Analysis*. 1940. Ed. and trans. James Strachey. New York: Norton, 1949.

———. *The Psychopathology of Everyday Life*. Ed. and trans. James Strachey. New York: Norton, 1966.

———. *Three Essays on the Theory of Sexuality*. 1905. Ed. and trans. James Strachey. New York: Basic Books, 1962.

———, and Josef Breuer. *Studies on Hysteria*. 1893-1895. Ed. and trans. James Strachey. New York: Basic Books, 1957.

Lacan, Jacques. "Dieu et la jouissance de la femme." *Le Séminaire livre XX: Encore*. Paris: Editions du Seuil, 1975. 61–71.

———. "L'instance de la lettre dans l'inconscient ou la raison depuis Freud." *Ecrits I*. Paris: Editions du Seuil, 1966. 249–89.

———. "De la jouissance." *Le Séminaire livre XX: Encore*. Paris: Editions du Seuil, 1975. 9–18.

———. "Position de l'inconscient." *Ecrits II*. Paris: Editions du Seuil, 1966. 193–217.

———. "La signification du phallus." *Ecrits II*. Paris: Editions du Seuil, 1966. 103–15.

———. "Le stade du miroir comme formateur de la fonction du *Je*." *Ecrits I*. Paris: Editions du Seuil, 1966. 89–97.

———. Subversion du sujet et dialectique du désir dans l'inconscient freudien." *Ecrits II*. Paris: Editions du Seuil, 1966. 151–91.

LaPlanche, J., and J-B Pontalis. *Vocabulaire de la psychanalyse*. Paris: Presses Universitaires de France, 1967. Trans. Donald Nicholson-Smith, *The Language of Psycho-Anaysis*. New York: W. W. Norton, 1973. 211.

Leclaire, Serge. *Psychanalyser*. Paris: Editions du Seuil, 1968.

Nancy, Jean-Luc and Philippe Lacoue-Labarthe. *The Title of the Letter: A Reading of Lacan*. Trans. François Raffoul and David Pettigrew. Albany: SUNY Press, 1992.

Torok, Maria. "The Meaning of 'Penis Envy' in Women." Abraham and Torok 41–48.

———. "A Remembrance of Things Deleted: Between Sigmund Freud and Emmy von N." Abraham and Torok 234–52.

Other sources:

Alexandrian. *Histoire de la littérature érotique*. Paris: Éditions Seghers, 1989.

Auerbach, Erich. *Mimesis: The Representation of Reality in Western Literature*. Trans. Willard Trask. Princeton, NJ: Princeton UP, 1953.

Bal, Mieke. "Narration et focalisation: Pour une théorie des instances du récit." *Poétique* (1977) 29: 107–26.

Barthes, Roland. "The Death of the Author." In *Image-Music-Text*. Trans. Stephen Heath. New York: Hill and Wang, 1977.

———. *Le Plaisir du texte*. Paris: Éditions du Seuil-Points, 1973. Trans. Richard Howard, *The Pleasure of the Text*. New York: Hill and Wang, 1975.

————. *Roland Barthes par Roland Barthes*. Paris: Seuil-Ecrivains de toujours, 1975.

————. *S/Z*. Paris: Éditions du Seuil-Points, 1970. Trans. Richard Howard, *S/Z: An Essay*. New York: Hill and Wang, 1975.

Bersani, J. *La Littérature en France depuis 1945*. Paris: Bordas, 1970.

Brooks, Peter. *Reading for the Plot: Design and Intention in Narrative*. New York: Knopf, 1984. 37–61.

Chambers, Ross. *Story and Situation: Narrative Seduction and the Power of Fiction*. Minneapolis: U of Minnesota P, 1984.

Culler, Jonathan. *On Deconstruction: Theory and Criticism After Structuralism*. Ithaca, NY: Cornell UP, 1982.

————. *The Pursuit of Signs: Semiotics, Literature, Deconstruction*. London: Routeledge and Kegan Paul, 1981.

Eagleton, Terry. *Literary Theory: An Introduction*. Minneapolis: U of Minnesota P, 1983.

Fish, Stanley. "Literature in the Reader: Affective Stylistics." Tompkins 70–100.

Flaubert, Gustave. *Madame Bovary*. Paris: GF-Flammarion, 1986. *The Collected Works of Gustave Flaubert: One Volume Edition*, New York: Walter J. Black, 1904.

Foucault, Michel. *The History of Sexuality, Volume 1: An Introduction*. New York: Vintage, 1980.

Genette, Gérard. *Figures III*. Paris: Éditions du Seuil, 1972.

Heath, Stephen. *Questions of Cinema*. Bloomington: Indiana UP, 1981.

Hunter, Dianne. *Seduction and Theory: Readings of Gender, Representation and Rhetoric*. Urbana, Ill: U of Chicago P, 1989.

Lanser, Susan Sniader. *Fictions of Authority: Women Writers and Narrative Voice*. Ithaca, NY: Cornell UP, 1992.

————. "Toward a Feminist Narratology." *Style* 20: 3 (1986): 341–63.

Lejeune, Philippe. *L'Autobiographie en France*. Paris: A. Colin, 1971.

————. *«Je est un autre»: L'Autobiographie, de la littérature aux médias*. Paris: Editions du Seuil-Poétique, 1980.

————. *Le Pacte Autobiographique*. Paris: Editions du Seuil-Poétique, 1975.

Levin, Harry. "The Female Quixote." *The Gates of Horn: A Study of Five French Realists*. New York: Oxford UP, 1963. 246–69.

Mulvey, Laura. "Visual Pleasure and Narrative Cinema." *Visual and Other Pleasures*. Bloomington: Indiana UP, 1989. 14–26.

Paulhan, Jean. "Le Bonheur dans l'esclavage." Réage i–xvii; "Happiness in Slavery." Réage xxi–xxxvi.

Prince, Gerald. "Introduction to the Study of the Narratee." Tompkins 7–25.

————. "Notes on the Reader as Text." Suleiman 225–40.

Réage, Pauline. *Histoire d'O*. Paris: Jean-Jacques Pauvert, 1954. Trans. Sabine d'Estrée, *Story of O*. New York: Ballantine Books, 1993.

St. Jorre, John de. "The Unmasking of O." *The New Yorker* LXX, 23 August 1994: 42–50.

Saussure, Ferdinand de. *Course in General Linguistics*. New York: McGraw-Hill, 1966.

Schleifer, Ronald. *A.J. Greimas and the Nature of Meaning: Linguistics, Semiotics, and Discourse Theory*. Lincoln: U of Nebraska P, 1987.

Sennett, Richard. *Authority*. New York: Vintage, 1981.

Sturrock, John, ed. *Structuralism and Since: From Lévi-Strauss to Derrida*. Oxford, UK: Oxford UP, 1979.

————. "Roland Barthes." Sturrock 52–80.

Suleiman, Susan Rubin. *Authoritarian Fictions: The Ideological Novel As a Literary Genre.* New York: Columbia UP, 1983.

————— and Inge Crosman, eds. *The Reader in the Text: Essays on Audience and Interpretation.* Princeton, NJ: Princeton UP, 1980.

Tanner, Tony. *Adultery in the Novel: Contract and Transgression.* Baltimore: Johns Hopkins UP, 1979.

Tompkins, Jane P. ed. *Reader-Response Criticism: From Formalism to Post-Structuralism.* Baltimore and London: Johns Hopkins UP, 1980.

—————. "An Introduction to Reader-Response Criticism." Tompkins ix–xxvi.

Index

L'Affamée, 2, 13, 47, 127, 157n16,
169n3; read by Ceccatty, 54, 55;
relationship with "Madame" in, 5–
6, 48–49, 163n20; in Les Temps
Modernes, 155n4
Alexandrian, 75–77, 80, 166n9,
166n12, 166n14, 173n37
Algren, Nelson, 5, 57, 158n20
Amar, A., 149
André, 8, 29, 156n15, 160n1; as "le
séducteur," 28–31, 35. See also
identification, modern literature
anti-Semitism, 58–59. See also Holocaust
L'Arbalète, 155n4, 158n18
Argentine, 37–39, 44, 45, 46, 59
Arras, 30
Artaud, Antonin, 162n15
L'Asphyxie, 2, 44, 158n18; Berthe's
"hard blue look," 158n19; Berthe's seduction in, 7; narrator-
protagonist in, 160n5; writing of,
27–28
associative positioning, 8, 65, 74, 101–
2, 111, 114, 125
Audry, Colette, 149
Aury, Dominique, 167n16, 167n21;
and Leduc, 78–79; Histoire d'O,
9, 68, 78–81, 167nn15–18,
167n20, 168n23
autobiography, 2, 65, 83, 101; as
dramatization or fiction, 2, 104,
106, 155n11, 155n14, 160n5; narrator-protagonist in, 2, 9, 170n7;
seduction by 34–35; writing inspired by Leduc, 52, 163n1,
163n3. See also La Bâtarde, La

Chasse à l'amour, "The Dream of
Love," La Folie en tête, narrator-
protagonist
autovoyeurism, 9, 81, 98–99; definition
of, 96–97

Bair, Deirdre, 5, 158n20
Bal, Mieke, 111–13, 171nn21–22
Barthes, Roland, 8, 15–16, 57, 120,
159n6, 164n5; emportement, 42–
44; Le Plaisir du texte, 11, 20–21,
22–23, 41, 42, 125; S/Z, 21–22;
readerly text, 22, 24, 27, 49;
writerly text, 22, 24–26, 27, 49,
73, 119
Barthesian reader, 8, 15–16, 118, 124;
appealing to, 24–26, 54; Barthes
as, 21–22; Violette as, 27–28, 39–
42, 49, 162n11; Zackhiem as, 57.
See also La Folie en tête
La Bâtarde, 10, 51, 53, 129–34, 155n8,
156n15; as autobiography, 2, 27–
39, 85, 160n5; Bovaryan reader in,
27, 32–39; eroticism in, 33–34,
65–68, 72–76, 78, 80–81, 160n4,
161n6, 165n5; in Les Temps Modernes, 155n4; reception of, 1, 86;
relation to reader in, 3, 7; as
writerly text, 23–26. See also
Beauvoir
Beauvoir, Simone de, 13, 124, 157n16;
book dedication to, 127; Le
Deuxième sexe, 1, 4, 158n18;
préface to La Bâtarde, 1–2, 7, 31,
48, 68–69, 77–78, 81, 121, 155n5,
156n15; as love object, 4, 41, 45,
54, 57, 85 158n19; as mentor, 85–

185

About the Author

Elizabeth Locey received her doctorate in French Studies from the University of Wisconsin-Madison in 1997 under the direction of Elaine Marks. She is currently director of the French program at Emporia State University in Kansas, where she also teaches courses in Gender Studies and Film. Her articles, reviews, and translations have appeared in *The French Review, Husserl Studies, Simone de Beauvoir Studies, Cincinnati Romance Review,* and *Women in French Studies,* and she penned the Leduc entry for Routledge's *Who's Who in Contemporary Women's Writing.* Future projects include a Leduc reader and a critical anthology of Francophone West African and Caribbean plays and playwrights. When not at the IMEC or visiting the family home in Amboise, she lives on the wide Kansas prairie with her philosopher and her westie.